DAD'S LETTERS

Wisdom for Sons *on* Faith,
Identity, *and* Becoming *the* Man
God Created You to Be

Aaron D. Davis

Copyright © 2026 Aaron D. Davis

No part of this book may be reproduced in any written, electronic, recording, or photocopying form without written permission of the publisher or author. The exception would be in the case of brief quotations embodied in the critical articles or reviews and pages where permission is specifically granted by the publisher or author.

Although every precaution has been taken to verify the accuracy of the information contained herein, the author and publisher assume no responsibility for any errors or omissions. No liability is assumed for damages that may result from the use of information contained within.

Scripture quotations marked NKJV are taken from the New King James Version®. Copyright © 1982 by Thomas Nelson. Used by permission.
All rights reserved.

Scripture quotations marked NLT are taken from the *Holy Bible*, New Living Translation, copyright © 1996, 2004, 2007 by Tyndale House Foundation. Used by permission of Tyndale House Publishers, Inc., Carol Stream, Illinois 60188.
All rights reserved.

Scripture quotations marked TPT are from The Passion Translation®. Copyright © 2017, 2018, 2020 by Passion & Fire Ministries, Inc. Used by permission. All rights reserved. ThePassionTranslation.com

Scripture quotations taken from the Amplified® Bible (AMPC), Copyright © 1954, 1958, 1962, 1964, 1965, 1987 by The Lockman Foundation Used by permission.
Printed in the United States of America.

For more information, or to book an event, contact:
Aaron@TattooPreacher.com
http://www.tattoopreacher.com

Book design by Aaron D. Davis

Cover design by Aaron D. Davis

All rights reserved.

Paperback ISBN-13: 978-1-947837-15-7
Hardcover ISBN-13: 978-1-947837-16-4
Ebook ISBN-13: 978-1-947837-17-1

Dedication

I would like to dedicate this book to my son, Rocky.

Happy 18th birthday, Son.

I Remember…

I remember your first laugh when I was getting your belly with the little red toy monkey—you always did, and still do, laugh with your whole heart.

I remember before you could talk you would grunt when we hit a bump in the road and I called you, "Grunt-Grunt." When you were two years old and would say, "Fight, Daddy, fight," run up behind me, and punch me in the back of the head. How you would laugh and scream when I would grab you and tickle you.

I remember pushing you on a swing or helping you climb the monkey bars at the park. Committing to never let you dance alone and breaking out into dance any time you did, whether it was in the frozen food aisle when you were three, walking down the sidewalk at the outlet mall in Florida when you were fifteen, or just in the living room doing the "Andrew from *The Chosen*" dance when you were seventeen.

I remember running the entire Halo campaign with you when you were four years old and getting on you for purposefully shooting your teammates as you laughed so hard when you did it. Lego Star Wars and Lord of the Rings. So many hours of fighting, racing, skateboarding, Wii Sports, and warfare video games.

I remember seeing you overcome fear as you learned to ride a bike— "Don't let go, Daddy"—compete in jiu-jitsu, ride a skateboard down a big hill, half pipe, or bowl at the skate park, climbing the rock wall, reaching the top, and saying, "I did it, Daddy, but you always knew I could, didn't you?" Teaching you to breathe to center your nerves before competing or daring something new— "In through the nose, out through the mouth."

I remember putting you on my shoulders and walking through the mall. Throwing you and making you do flips in the air in the pool. Walking you into school on your first day of kindergarten.

I remember you coming into my room asking me to pray for you before school and praying for you every night before bed. Picking you up out of your crib and carrying you around the room, praying for you and your future. Coming into your room at night while you slept, when you were too big to carry anymore, and just sitting on the edge of your bed, placing my hand on your head or back and praying blessings over you.

I remember teaching you to win and lose with class and honor. Celebrating your championships and coaching you through disappointment.

I remember snuba-diving in the Caribbean. Waterfalls and glaciers in Alaska. Surfing in Dana Point. Watching the sun set in La Jolla. Sitting on the edge of the Grand Canyon. Snowboarding in Edmonton. Seeing the Milky Way and cliff jumping in the desert of Sedona. Showing you Saturn and Jupiter through the telescope. Karaoke on cruise ships. Jet skis, wakeboards, fishing excursions, parasailing, and dolphin encounters. Disney trips, Gator Land, Dinosaur World, roller coasters, log cabins, white-water rafting, and bears in Gatlinburg. Beaches and sea kayaks in Florida, tree jumping and paddling to exhaustion in the crystal-clear waters of Weeki Wachee. Mud runs and God encounters at camp in Tampa. Rollerblading at the skate parties. Airsoft fights where I low-key also taught you tactical movement and situational awareness. Shooting guns and bows. Driving a car in the snow and ice. Sledding when it snowed in Nashville and pulling you behind the Jeep on the sled. Nerf sword and lightsaber duels. Late night ice-cream drives to Sonic. Dirt bikes when you were little, Z125's when you were fifteen, and Harleys when you were sixteen. Throwing the football, wrestling, playing with the dog, trampolines, and inflatables. Business and ministry conferences. Christmases and birthday parties. Milestones and difficult lessons.

I remember baptizing you and watching you grow in your faith and relationship with the Lord.

I remember all of it and so much more, and it has been my greatest joy and honor in life to have been blessed to be your father. My life has been so full because of you, and I am so thankful that God honored me with that opportunity.

I pray that this book is something that you can glean wisdom from for many years to come and that you will not only implement the principles within it but build upon them as you lay the foundation for your own legacy.

I cannot tell you how proud I am of you and how much I have loved being your dad.

I love you, son. I hope you always know it. —Dad

CONTENTS

Section/Chapter	Title	Page
Preface	Preface	ii
	Apology to the Sons	vii
Introduction	Introduction - A Father's Instruction	1
Chapter 1	God's Not Mad at You — Part 1	5
Chapter 2	God's Not Mad at You — Part 2	7
Chapter 3	God's Not Mad at You — Part 3	9
Chapter 4	Your Word Is Your Oath	11
Chapter 5	You Are Not Defined by Your Past	13
Chapter 6	Don't Quit: Faith Beyond Disappointment	15
Chapter 7	Faith Begins Where the Will of God Is Known	17
Chapter 8	Forge Your Own Path	19
Chapter 9	God Doesn't Abuse His Kids	21
Chapter 10	I Trust You Daddy	23
Chapter 11	You Are Worth the Fight	25
Chapter 12	Don't Let Fear Lead You - The Rockwall	26
Chapter 13	The Gold That Really Matters	28
Chapter 14	Guard Your Thoughts, Guard Your Future	30
Chapter 15	Don't Draw Back - Draw In	32
Chapter 16	Lead or Support—Know Your Moment	34
Chapter 17	Anchored in the Truth of God's Word	36
Chapter 18	When Your Experience Doesn't Meet Your Expectation	38
Chapter 19	When Your Experience Doesn't Meet Your Expectation Part 2	40
Chapter 20	"But Did You Die?" — The Perspective That Keeps You Going	42
Chapter 21	The Marks of a Leader of Leaders	44
Chapter 22	Seeing Like God Sees – The Comparison Deception	46
Chapter 23	Title And Leader Are Not Synonymous	48
Chapter 24	Honor the Gift, Honor the Giver	49
Chapter 25	They're Looking for What You Already Have	50

Chapter 26	The Lie of Sin Consciousness	52
Chapter 27	Don't Be That Guy	54
Chapter 28	Grace Is Stronger Than Your Shame	56
Chapter 29	Don't Assume—Be Intentional	58
Chapter 30	The God Who Fights Beside You	60
Chapter 31	Don't Live Your Labels	62
Chapter 32	The Power of a Surrendered Will	64
Chapter 33	Go Deep, Son	66
Chapter 34	The Heart of a Warrior	68
Chapter 35	The Father Who Dreams Over You	70
Chapter 36	You're Just the Ass	72
Chapter 37	Excellence is Your Standard	74
Chapter 38	Intentional Fatherhood	76
Chapter 39	People Before Process	78
Chapter 40	The Wisdom of Right Now	79
Chapter 41	"Who" You Ask? They.	80
Chapter 42	Choose To Sow Life	82
Chapter 43	Listen For the Lesson	84
Chapter 44	Training Them to Live Without You	86
Chapter 45	Famous To Me	87
Chapter 46	What's In Your Hand?	89
Chapter 47	God of the Watch	91
Chapter 48	God of the Watch — Part 2	93
Chapter 49	God Is Still Good	95
Chapter 50	Choose Your Counsel Wisely	97
Chapter 51	Include God in the Fight	99
Chapter 52	Relationships Will Make or Break You	100
Chapter 53	See Beyond What You See	102
Chapter 54	Don't Compare Your Way into Compromise	104
Chapter 55	The Leadership That Washes Feet	106
Chapter 56	It's So Much Harder to Keep Your Mouth Shut Than It Is to Fight	108
Chapter 57	Don't Let Pain Set the Ceiling of Your Faith	110

Chapter 58	Make Decisions in Faith, Not Fear	112
Chapter 59	Be A Man of Integrity	113
Chapter 60	Stewarding Your Talent	114
Chapter 61	Choose His Way First	116
Chapter 62	Listen for His Voice	118
Chapter 63	Praise Is a Weapon	120
Chapter 64	Keep Praying Anyway	122
Chapter 65	God's Will, Your Part	124
Chapter 66	Live, Move, And Have Your Being In Him	126
Chapter 67	Do It Well	128
Chapter 68	Guard Your Heart Without Hardening It	130
Chapter 69	The Power that Confirms the Message	132
Chapter 70	Don't Do It—Even If They Deserve It	134
Chapter 71	Forgiveness is a Choice	136
Chapter 72	The Elevation of Title Above Capacity	138
Chapter 73	Keep Your Eyes on the Right Battle	140
Chapter 74	Be Known for Love, Not Division	142
Chapter 75	Garbage In Garbage Out	144
Chapter 76	The Detail of Obedience	146
Chapter 77	Legacy Lives Through You	148
Chapter 78	The Reward of Putting God First	150
Chapter 79	Discerning God's Voice	152
Chapter 80	You Can't Lead the Unwilling	154
Chapter 81	Lead with Strength, Not Fear	156
Chapter 82	Stay in Your God-Given Lane	158
Chapter 83	Choose Thankfulness in Every Season	160
Chapter 84	Choose Grace Over Judgment	162
Chapter 85	How You Fill Your Lane Matters	164
Chapter 86	You Are Enough	166
Chapter 87	You Don't Know God	168
Chapter 88	Better Than Fear	170
Chapter 89	Humility Will Take You Further Than Pride Ever Will	172
Chapter 90	Call Out the King In Others	174

Chapter 91	Guard Your Heart from Entitlement	176
Chapter 92	Don't Let Your Gift Become Your God	178
Chapter 93	Leadership Without Entitlement	180
Chapter 94	Guard Your Imagination, Guard Your Life	182
Chapter 95	Don't Let Foolish Voices Shape Your Life	184
Chapter 96	The Last Word Belongs to God	185
Chapter 97	Love Big Anyway	186
Chapter 98	Dis-Appointment	188
Chapter 99	When It's All True	190
Chapter 100	The Lens You Choose	192
Chapter 101	The Purina Cantina - Don't Become Cat Food	194
Chapter 102	The Kingdom Has Arrived	196
Chapter 103	Choose Compassion	198
Chapter 104	When Grief Whispers, Speak the Word	200
Chapter 105	As He Is, So Are You	203
Chapter 106	Breaking the Cycle, Building a Legacy	205
Chapter 107	Small Choices, Strong Character	207
Chapter 108	What You Learn in the Climb	209
Chapter 109	You Carry Heaven with You	211
Chapter 110	Salvation Is Free—Blessing Is Cultivated	213
Chapter 111	The Power of Thankfulness	215
Chapter 112	The Power That Shapes You	217
Chapter 113	Becoming the Man God Made You to Be	220
Chapter 114	The Power of "Thank You, Daddy"	222
Chapter 115	Guard Your Peace with Fierce Intention	224
Chapter 116	The Power of Unity	226
Chapter 117	What Money Can't Buy	228
Chapter 118	The Quitter's Harvest	230
Chapter 119	When Fear Loses Its Grip	232
Chapter 120	Well-Fertilized Growth	234
Chapter 121	The ROI of a Life Well Invested	236
Chapter 122	Defined by God, Not by Wounds	238
Chapter 123	Legacy Doesn't Replace Relationship	240

Chapter 124	Your Lens Is Your Battlefield	242
Chapter 125	One Morning at a Time	244
Chapter 126	Be Slow to Judge What You Don't Yet Understand	246
Chapter 127	When You Fall, Come Home Quickly	248
Chapter 128	Don't Take the Bait	250
Chapter 129	Dream With God	252
Chapter 130	You Are Not What You Feel — You Are What You Decide	254
Chapter 131	Identity And the Enemy's Favorite Lie	256
Chapter 132	Living in The Tension Between Calling and Becoming	258
Chapter 133	You Are Enough—Because God Says You Are	260
Chapter 134	Nothing Means Nothing	262
Chapter 135	The Seeds You Sow Shape the Life You Live	264
Chapter 136	Understanding Grace The Right Way	266
Chapter 137	God's Kid First	268
Chapter 138	What Do You See?	270
Chapter 139	Faith Works When You Work It	272
Chapter 140	Be the Husband Who Loves Like Christ	274
Chapter 141	The Power of Relationship: The Weight of Choosing a Wife	276
Chapter 142	The Power of Relationship: Kids	278
Chapter 143	The Power of Relationship: Kids - Part 2 Train Up a Child	280
Chapter 144	The Power of Relationship: Friends	282
Chapter 145	Speak Life	284
Chapter 146	Part 1 - Jesus Came to Show You the Father	286
Chapter 147	Part 2 That Which Was Lost	288
Chapter 148	You Are Who God Says You Are	290
Chapter 149	Courage to Kill What Your Father Tolerated	292
Chapter 150	Your 100 Year Dot	294
Chapter 151	A Father's Instruction	297
Chapter 152	Last Letter: Lead Well — Your Legacy Begins Now	299
A Guide for Group Study	A Guide for Group Study	302
About the Author	About the Author	309

Preface

Several years ago, I began writing these letters for my son. Drawing from decades of life experience—as a pastor for over thirty years, a husband for over thirty years, an entrepreneur, a detective, a SWAT team member, a best-selling author, and a leader in various professional roles—I felt a responsibility to capture the lessons I have learned and the spiritual leadership perspective God has entrusted to me, in my own voice. My purpose was simple: that my son would always have the steady, familiar voice of his father to reference as he navigated life, faith, and relationships.

As an experiment, I began sharing some of these short, direct, and intentionally concise letters anonymously on social media under the name *Dad's Letters*, designed to be read in just a few minutes. From time to time, I would also repost them on my personal accounts without acknowledging that I had written them. Before long, my son began reposting them as well.

One day, one of his jiu-jitsu coaches—a young man in his mid-twenties—approached him during practice and asked, *"I see these Dad's Letters posts that you often repost. Do you happen to know who's writing them?"* My son replied, *"Actually, my dad writes them anonymously online."* The coach responded, *"Please tell your dad thank you. I didn't have a dad, and the spiritual wisdom in those letters has helped shape my life in ways I can't fully explain."*

That moment changed everything.

Over time, I began receiving texts, emails, and direct messages from others expressing gratitude for what they were reading. I realized these letters were meant to be more than private reflections for just my son—they were meant to become a book.

As I reflected on the responses, it became clear that while some readers, like my son's coach, had never had a present father, many others had fathers who were physically present but unable—or unprepared—to provide balanced instruction, godly example, or spiritual perspective. This book covered all of those bases.

Initially, I imagined this book as a meaningful graduation gift for high school or college students. But as I continued to write and shared the concept with friends, they challenged me to think broader. They suggested its value for men's ministries, small groups, and even prisons—where statistically, many men grew up without any consistent, positive male role model. These were audiences I hadn't originally considered, but the more I reflected, the more sense it made.

Throughout the book, you'll find the letters loosely categorized around the following 10 themes (and you'll see one of these wax seals at the beginning of each letter to identify the theme):

1. Your Identity in the Father's Heart

Ephesians 1:4–5 (NIV) "For he chose us in him before the creation of the world to be holy and blameless in his sight. In love he predestined us for adoption to sonship through Jesus Christ, in accordance with his pleasure and will."

2. Deepening Faith and Intimacy with God

Hebrews 11:6 (NIV) "And without faith it is impossible to please God, because anyone who comes to him must believe that he exists and that he rewards those who earnestly seek him."

3. Building Godly Character and Integrity

Proverbs 10:9 (NIV) "Whoever walks in integrity walks securely, but whoever takes crooked paths will be found out."

4. Healing Pain and Growing in Emotional Maturity

Psalm 34:18 (NIV) "The Lord is close to the brokenhearted and saves those who are crushed in spirit."

5. Discipline, Consistency, and Spiritual Growth

Hebrews 12:11 (NIV) "No discipline seems pleasant at the time, but painful. Later on, however, it produces a harvest of righteousness and peace for those who have been trained by it."

6. Leadership, Authority, and Kingdom Influence

1 Peter 5:2–3 (NIV) "Be shepherds of God's flock that is under your care, watching over them—not because you must, but because you are willing, as God wants you to be; not pursuing dishonest gain, but eager to serve; not lording it over those entrusted to you, but being examples to the flock."

7. Mastering Your Mind and Inner World

Romans 12:2 (NIV) "Do not conform to the pattern of this world, but be transformed by the renewing of your mind. Then you will be able to test and approve what God's will is—his good, pleasing and perfect will."

8. Wisdom, Discernment, and Godly Decisions

James 1:5 (NIV) "If any of you lacks wisdom, you should ask God, who gives generously to all without finding fault, and it will be given to you."

9. Resisting Comparison and Cultural Pressures

Galatians 1:10 (NIV) "Am I now trying to win the approval of human beings, or of God? Or am I trying to please people? If I were still trying to please people, I would not be a servant of Christ."

10. Building Legacy and Finishing Strong

2 Timothy 4:7–8 (NIV) "I have fought the good fight, I have finished the race, I have kept the faith. Now there is in store for me the crown of righteousness, which the Lord, the righteous Judge, will award to me on that day—and not only to me, but also to all who have longed for his appearing."

I intentionally wanted this book to feel devotional and conversational rather than rigidly structured. As a result, the letters follow a natural rhythm—encouragement followed by challenge, identity truths interwoven with practical growth, moments of pain balanced by hope. Heavy reordering or strict thematic grouping felt like it might make the book feel engineered rather than relational.

For readers reading one or two letters at a time, this organic flow provides variety and balance. Themes resurface naturally for reinforcement, tones shift gently, and emotional weight is evenly distributed.

However, with that said, for those who desire a more structured, step-by-step experience—whether for personal growth or group study—I've included a thematic reading guide in the back of the book. In that section, the chapters are organized by theme rather than sequence, and the order intentionally builds upon itself to create progression within each subject.

Finally, while these letters were written with my son in mind, I am convinced they were God-inspired for any Son looking for wisdom on faith, identity, and becoming the man God created you to be.

As you read, I want to challenge you not only to hear the voice of *a father*, but to listen for the voice of *The Father*—the One who calls you His son, loves you more than you can imagine, and desires for you to become everything He created you to be.

Apology to the Sons

Disclaimer: Initially, I did not intend to include this "apology to the sons" in this book. However, as I was nearing the final stages of editing, I felt a strong and unmistakable prompting that for some readers to fully receive what this book carries, this apology needed to be present. It will not be for everyone. But for those who have experienced abandonment, or emotional, physical, sexual, or spiritual abuse at the hands of a father or father figure, I urge you not to overlook this section. I believe the Holy Spirit has something personal and restorative that He wants to speak to you through it.

Many years ago, I was teaching a five-week Wednesday night discipleship class called *Battlefield of the Mind*. A couple attended the class once, then again, and when they showed up for the *third* time, curiosity got the better of me—I had to ask why.

Their answer opened my eyes to something deeper. The husband said, *"We understand what you're teaching. It all makes sense. But for some reason... we just can't seem to apply it. So we figured we must be missing something."*

Immediately, I recognized what was happening. Their struggle wasn't a lack of information—it was a stronghold. Something deeper was blocking their ability to walk in the truth they understood.

That moment became the catalyst for the book, curriculum, and breakthrough conference I eventually created: *Limitless: You Can Experience the Freedom, Power, and Potential You Were Created For.*

One of the most important topics in that curriculum deals with fatherly—or father-figure—abuse, neglect, and abandonment. We discovered something crucial: **Many people need to hear an apology they may never receive.**

Sometimes the person who hurt them is gone. Sometimes they are unreachable. Sometimes they are unwilling. Sometimes they are alive—but unsafe.

Still, the heart needs to hear the words it was owed and this is why I have included this apology to begin this book of letters.

So, for every spiritual son who has been hurt and reads the remainder of this letter, I encourage you to receive the words as if they were spoken *directly* from the man who wounded you **as the apology your heart should have been given by the man who hurt you, but may have never heard.**

A Proxy Apology for Physical Abuse

Today, I want to speak to you and ask for your forgiveness on behalf of any man who has ever caused you harm. I am truly sorry for every time I was physically abusive towards you.

First and foremost, I need you to know that none of this was your fault. I was a person consumed by my own pain and, regrettably, I took it out on you. For that, I am deeply sorry. I should have never hurt you.

I allowed my anger, frustration, and sadness to control my actions, using my physical strength to dominate you—there's no excuse for what I did.

I seek your forgiveness for all the times I raised my hand against you, caused pain and injury, and broke your spirit when I should have been showing you love, kindness, and affection.

It was my duty to set an example of what a good man is supposed to be, and I fell short of that. For this failure, I am deeply sorry. Please forgive me.

A Proxy Apology for Verbal and Emotional Abuse

I deeply regret the moments when I chose to use my words to bring you down instead of lifting you up. Rather than offering you support and encouragement, I unfairly took out my insecurities on you. Today, I'm asking your forgiveness for every instance where I criticized you and tried to intimidate you with my raised voice.

I apologize for using my words as weapons that hurt your heart and made you feel undeserving of my love and acceptance. I'm genuinely sorry for yelling at you when you were trying your best, even if it wasn't exactly the way I wanted things done. I sincerely apologize for neglecting your needs and making you feel inadequate or incapable of meeting my high expectations.

I'm so sorry for telling you that you were worthless and would never amount to anything, using my words to devalue you when it was my own inadequacies blinding me to your true worth. I was your dad but I was so wrapped up in myself that I failed to recognize the incredible gift that you are. Please forgive me.

A Proxy Apology for Abandonment and Neglect

I'm sorry for walking out on you when you were young and not being the father, you needed at a time when you couldn't possibly understand why. Forgive me for neglecting you and failing to provide the love and support you rightfully deserved.

When your mother and I divorced, please forgive me for making you feel isolated and alone, as if you were somehow the cause of our problems. I'm sorry for when I was manipulative and controlling, using fear and anger to get my way. Please forgive me for treating you poorly. I'm truly sorry that I wasn't able to connect with you emotionally when you were a child, or express my love for you in the ways you needed to hear and see.

For all the promises I made but didn't keep, assuring you I would be there and then not showing up, leaving you to handle family responsibilities by yourself. It was wrong to make you feel like it was your duty to support and protect me, when it should have been my job to protect you. I am sorry for being unfaithful, breaking our bond, and shattering your heart. I was selfish, and you never deserved to be treated that way.

I'm sorry for using threats and allowing my anger to control and intimidate you. For all of this, I sincerely repent and ask for your forgiveness.

A Proxy Apology for Sexual Violation

I apologize on behalf of any man who has ever exploited you, assaulted you, overpowered you, or violated you.

Please forgive me for the times I molested you as a child, your innocence was taken from you without regard for the pain it caused—please hear this: I am so sorry. What happened to you was never your fault.

For exposing you to sex through pornography and adding to your confusion about sex and your sexual identity before you were mature enough to understand it, I'm so sorry.

For violating you as a young man—through manipulation or luring you into sex and taking advantage of you, —you deserved better and I am sorry for what I did to you.

My own twisted actions and perversion were entirely to blame and had nothing to do with you.

I was wrong and I am so sorry for the pain, the fear, and the lasting impact I caused you. For all of these things, I repent.

A Proxy Apology for Spiritual Abuse

As your spiritual leader, I deeply regret the moments when I should have been there to serve and protect you but instead chose to manipulate situations for my own benefit.

I'm sincerely sorry for those actions. I ask for your forgiveness for the times I mishandled your private information to undermine you or tarnish your reputation.

I also apologize for being judgmental and harsh when what you needed was love and grace. In those moments, you were vulnerable and I failed to represent God's heart towards you as your leader, and for that, I am truly sorry.

When I, as a father, failed to take on the role of spiritual leader in our home and didn't adequately provide the feelings of safety, protection, and support you needed, I deeply regret it.

I was supposed to represent the heart of God to you, and instead, I misrepresented Him.

Please forgive me.

A Final Apology

I realize now that my failures became heavy weights you carried into adulthood. I should have been your example, but instead I became the source of wounds you had to overcome.

I was broken—and I modeled brokenness. For that, I am sorry.

But hear me, son… **What was done to you does not define you. You are not ruined. You are not forsaken. You are not disqualified.**

This is the apology your heart deserved. Let it loosen the grip of resentment, shame, and confusion so you can step into the freedom God intended for you.

Deepening Faith and Intimacy with God

Introduction - A Father's Instruction

Son,

In Proverbs 4, Solomon—renowned for his wisdom—writes a *"father's instruction"* to his sons. In that passage, he references the teachings handed down from his own father, King David.

PROVERBS 4

A Father's Instruction

1Listen to my correction, my sons, for I speak to you as your father. Let discernment enter your heart and you will grow wise with the understanding I impart.

2My revelation-truth is a gift to you, so remain faithful to my instruction.

3For I, too, was once the delight of my father and cherished by my mother— their beloved child.

4Then my father taught me, saying, "Never forget my words. If you do everything that I teach you, you will reign in life."

5So make wisdom your quest—search for the revelation of life's meaning. Don't let what I say go in one ear and out the other.

6Stick with wisdom and she will stick to you, protecting you throughout your days. She will rescue all those who passionately listen to her voice.

7Wisdom is the most valuable commodity—so buy it! Revelation-knowledge is what you need—so invest in it!

8Wisdom will exalt you when you exalt her truth. She will lead you to honor and favor when you live your life by her insights.

9You will be adorned with beauty and grace, and wisdom's glory will wrap itself around you,

making you victorious in the race.

Two Pathways

10 My son, if you will take the time to stop and listen to me and embrace what I say, you will live a long and happy life full of understanding in every way.

11 I have taken you by the hand in wisdom's ways, pointing you to the path of integrity.

12 Your progress will have no limits when you come along with me, and you will never stumble as you walk along the way.

13 So receive my correction no matter how hard it is to swallow, for wisdom will snap you back into place—her words will be invigorating life to you.

14 Do not detour into darkness or even set foot on that path.

15 Stay away from it; don't even go there!

16 For troublemakers are restless if they are not involved in evil. They are not satisfied until they have brought someone harm.

17 They feed on darkness and drink until they're drunk on the wine of wickedness.

18 But the lovers of God walk on the highway of light, and their way shines brighter and brighter

until the perfect day.

19 But the wicked walk in thick darkness, like those who travel in fog, and yet don't have a clue why they keep stumbling!

Healing Words

20 Listen carefully, my dear child, to everything that I teach you, and pay attention to all that I have to say.

21 Fill your thoughts with my words until they penetrate deep into your spirit.

22 Then, as you unwrap my words, they will impart true life and radiant health into the very core of your being.

23 So above all, guard the affections of your heart, for they affect all that you are. Pay attention to the welfare of your innermost being, for from there flows the wellspring of life.

24 Avoid dishonest speech and pretentious words. Be free from using perverse words no matter what!

Watch Where You're Going

25 Set your gaze on the path before you. With fixed purpose, looking straight ahead, ignore life's distractions.

26Watch where you're going! Stick to the path of truth, and the road will be safe and smooth before you.

27Don't allow yourself to be sidetracked for even a moment or take the detour that leads to darkness.

When I read this section in *The Passion Translation*, I'm moved by the heart of a loving father who genuinely desires good things for his children. Solomon wanted his sons to succeed. He saw the blessings that came from his father's pursuit of God's heart and instruction, and he also witnessed the failures of his father who loved the Lord deeply yet sometimes lost his way in his own humanity, pride, lust, and power.

Yet despite receiving profound godly instruction—and despite watching David's life unfold with both triumphs and painful lessons—Solomon did not follow the Lord with the same humility. And because he neglected the wisdom he had been given, he, his legacy, and the nation of Israel ultimately suffered for it.

Solomon's life, leadership, and most importantly, legacy could have been radically different had he been intentional with what he was taught. Wisdom without implementation is worthless. But wisdom that is embraced and lived out? The results are limitless. That is why I'm writing these letters—so that you don't merely *receive* wisdom, but so you learn to *apply* it.

I've written this book as a reference and a roadmap—something to equip you, your legacy, and anyone who reads these letters long after we are gone. My hope is that you will learn early in life the principles that took me a lifetime to understand and implement.

Son, much of this will sound familiar, because it is the same teaching, encouragement, and correction I've poured into you your whole life. For others reading this—many who may have never had the steady voice of a spiritual father speaking wisdom and truth into them—I'm inviting you into this family as a spiritual son or daughter of legacy. When you read these pages, hear the voice of a loving father speaking directly to you. Do not treat these letters as if they were written for someone else. Take them personally, apply them intentionally, and know that I wrote them with *you* in mind.

And then, beneath my voice, I want you to hear the voice of your heavenly Father—the One who gives wisdom, who loves you fiercely, and who wants you to know His heart so deeply that your life, your identity, and your future are shaped by His truth.

Finally, when you come to the closing line of each chapter— *"I love you, son. I hope you always know it."*—hear it from me as a spiritual father, but also hear it from the God who loves you more than you will ever fully comprehend.

I'm eager to hear the victories that will come from what you learn. I look forward to celebrating your accomplishments. And I cherish the knowledge that I will rejoice with your legacy—my legacy—from the grandstands of glory, as the wisdom imparted in these pages continues echoing into eternity.

I love you, son… and for my spiritual sons reading this—I love you too. I hope you always know it. — Dad

Your Identity in the Father's Heart

CHAPTER ONE
God's Not Mad at You — Part 1

Son,

As you step into adulthood, with its responsibilities and challenges, I want you to settle something deep in your heart—something that could shape the way you see God for the rest of your life. It's this: **God is not mad at you.** Most people walk around with the quiet fear that God is disappointed, frustrated, or tired of their mistakes. They hear "God hates sin" and assume that means God must hate *them*, because they still struggle. But that's not how the Father works.

When I read the Bible, I'm amazed at the men Jesus chose. They weren't polished or impressive. They were misfits, hotheads, doubters, and failures. Peter couldn't control his temper. Matthew was a tax collector despised by his own people. James and John nearly got into a fistfight over who was more important. Another time they wanted to call down fire on an entire town just for rejecting them. And yet, Jesus didn't reject them. He didn't fire them. He taught them, believed in them, corrected them, and loved them.

Even Paul—who literally hunted and killed Christians—wasn't written off by God. If anyone had a reason to believe God hated him, it was Paul. But instead, God interrupted his life, healed him, restored him, and turned him into a man who wrote much of the New Testament.

So why do people still assume God is angry? Because shame whispers lies. And if the enemy can convince you that God is mad at you, then he can convince you to run from the very One who wants to heal you, lead you, and restore you. When you believe God is disappointed in you, every mistake becomes a reason to hide. Every hardship becomes "God punishing me." And you begin to see God as a tyrant rather than a good and loving Father.

Son, I want to break that lie before it ever settles into your heart. You will fail at times. You will sin, struggle, and fall short. But your failures do not change the love of your father or the love of your God. You are not defined by your worst moment, your weakest habit, or the sin you haven't mastered yet. You are loved—and that love is patient, strong, and unwavering.

I love you, son. I hope you always know it. — Dad

Your Identity in the Father's Heart

CHAPTER TWO
God's Not Mad at You — Part 2

Son,

Now that we've covered God isn't angry with you, I want you to see *why* that matters so deeply. So many people live in cycles of guilt and defeat because they misunderstand God's heart. They think every bad thing in life is God punishing them—car troubles, sickness, a failed test, a broken friendship. They assume their problems prove God's disapproval. But that is a lie designed to keep them far from *the Father* who loves them.

Let me give you a picture. As a father myself, I can't imagine the grief I'd feel if someone kidnapped you, hurt you, and then convinced you that *I* approved of it. That the pain was part of *my will* for your life. That the suffering you endured was somehow a punishment I wanted you to experience. That thought breaks my heart—and yet that is exactly what the enemy convinces people about God. He traps them in sin, pain, and confusion, then whispers, "This is what God wants for you. He's mad. He's done with you."

Son, nothing could be further from the truth.

Yes, the Bible says God hates sin—but not because sin threatens Him. He hates sin because it destroys *you*. Sin steals peace, fractures purpose, and blinds you to who you were created to be. God hates sin for the same reason a father hates anything that harms his child. His anger is never against you—it's against what hurts you.

Romans says, "The wages of sin is death," but it also says the gift of God is eternal life. God is not trying to crush you; He's trying to rescue you. He gives life. He restores what is broken. He perfects what concerns you. He lifts your head instead of pushing it down.

When you finally grasp that God adores you, something inside you shifts. Shame loses its grip. Temptation loses its pull. And your walk with God becomes less about fear and more about freedom. That's when real change happens—from the inside out, not from striving or self-punishment.

This is the foundation for everything else you will learn in life. Who God is. Who you are. Where you come from. Where you're going. And the truth underneath it all remains the same: **God's not mad at you. He loves you more than you can understand.**

I love you, son. I hope you always know it. — Dad

Your Identity in the Father's Heart

CHAPTER THREE
God's Not Mad at You — Part 3

Son,

Now that you know God isn't angry with you, I want to show you what that truth is meant to produce in your life. It's one thing to *believe* God loves you—it's another to *live* like it. Many people know about God's grace but still walk around defeated because shame has trained them to expect disappointment from Him. But once you settle God's heart toward you, everything begins to change.

See, when you think God is mad at you, you hide from Him. You avoid prayer. You avoid church. You avoid anything that makes you feel exposed. But when you know you're loved—truly loved—you run *toward* Him, not from Him. You stop praying like someone begging for mercy and start praying like someone talking to their Father. You stop trying to earn His approval and realize you already have it.

And here's the part most people miss: **Knowing God's love empowers you to become the person He created you to be.**

Love doesn't excuse sin—but it breaks the power of it. When you're secure in *the Father's* affection, you stop chasing cheap substitutes that promise fulfillment but never deliver. Sin loses some of its appeal when your heart is already full.

This is why understanding God's heart is your first step into real growth. You won't change because you're afraid of God's anger. Fear might control your behavior for a moment, but it can't transform your heart. Only love can do that. Love gives you courage. Love gives you strength. Love gives you a reason to stand back up when you fall.

And you will fall sometimes. Everyone does. But God's love doesn't waver with your performance. He's not tallying your failures. He's not waiting to hit you with judgment. He's guiding you, shaping you, training you—just like I've tried to do as your dad.

So, when you mess up, don't run from God. Run to Him. Talk to Him. Bring Him your fears, your failures, your doubts. Let His love do the work in you that your willpower never could.

Son, the day you truly believe *God loves you, and He's not mad at you* is the day you step into the kind of freedom most people spend their whole lives searching for. And I want that for you—not just because you're my son, but because you're God's son too.

I love you, son. I hope you always know it. — Dad

Building Godly Character and Integrity

CHAPTER FOUR
Your Word Is Your Oath

Son,

I'm going to be very direct here: **people matter to God**, and because people matter to God, **your integrity must matter to you.**

James 5:12 tells us that our *word*—our integrity—is of supreme importance. One of the biggest issues I've seen in the church is a casual, almost flippant disregard for keeping one's word. People shrug it off as "forgetful," but most of the time, it's not forgetfulness—it's a **character issue**. It's the failure to steward your time, your commitments, and ultimately, the hearts of the people on the receiving end of your inconsistencies.

This becomes even more important when you're a leader. When you tell someone you will do something and you don't, whether it was intentional or not, the message they receive is: **"I am not important enough for you to remember."**

And Son, that cuts deeply—more deeply than most "forgetful" people realize.

Ask yourself this honest question: **"Would I be late, forgetful, or careless with my commitments if the meeting were with someone who could bless me, promote me, or advance my goals?"**

If the answer is *no*, but you regularly forget, cancel, or show up late to commitments with those who have nothing to offer you, then you are living out exactly what James 2 warns against—showing honor to the "rich" while dishonoring the "poor." That behavior exposes a type of quiet prejudice, a belief—whether admitted or not—that some people deserve your best while others can accept whatever scraps remain.

This is not the way of the Kingdom of God.

Your word is your oath.
Your calendar testifies to your integrity.
Your consistency reveals your character.
And your treatment of "the least of these" reveals who you really

are when no one influential is watching.

If you are going to lead, you MUST steward your commitments with honor—*every* commitment to *every* person. The Kingdom you represent is far bigger than your convenience, your schedule, or your mood.

To whom much is given, much is required.
So Son, act like you understand what is required of you.

Integrity matters. Do what you say—or do not say it at all.

I love you, son. I hope you always know it. —Dad

Healing Pain and Growing in Emotional Maturity

CHAPTER FIVE
You Are Not Defined by Your Past

Son,

Always remember this truth: **you are not defined by what you've done—you are defined by God alone.**

One of the enemy's greatest strategies is to attack your identity. He will remind you of every mistake you've made and try to convince you that you are less than who God declares you to be. If you ever start believing those lies, you will begin to live beneath the life God intended for you. That's why you must be determined—*absolutely resolved*—not to buy what the enemy is selling.

Scripture says, *"If any man is a believer in Christ, he is a new creature: old things are passed away; and all things have become new." (2 Corinthians 5:17)* That is who you are.

And the Bible also declares that *"the same Spirit that raised Christ from the dead lives in you." (Romans 8:11)*
That is what you carry.

Those two truths—among many others—reveal God's perspective of you.
And His perspective is the only one that matters.

The beauty of salvation through Christ is that He restored your authority and gave you power over ***all*** the works of the enemy. But if you don't remind yourself of that, life will try to steal that truth from your heart. Circumstances, emotions, and lies will attempt to convince you that you're powerless.

Don't buy the lie.
Because when you believe the lie, you empower the liar.

And in doing so, you begin to live far below the potential and authority God has given you.

When you face difficult moments, go back to the Word. Find out what

God says about your situation and place your faith in *that*. Proverbs tells us, *"Trust in the Lord with all your heart and do not lean on your own understanding; seek and acknowledge Him in all your ways, and He will make your paths straight."*

I'm not saying it's always easy—faith rarely is. But it *is* simple.

Don't let the enemy complicate what God made clear:
You have power.
You have authority.
And the One who lives in you is always greater than the enemy under your feet.

Walking in victory begins with believing you can.

I love you, son. I hope you always know it. —Dad

Deepening Faith and Intimacy with God

CHAPTER SIX
Don't Quit: Faith Beyond Disappointment

Son,

Over the years I've known many people who faced disappointment or failure, blamed God for the outcome, and walked away from Him. I understand the temptation. I've felt the deep sting of disappointment myself. I've been hurt by people who were supposed to represent God well. I've made mistakes that cost me influence. I've poured out everything I knew to give and still felt empty. I know the weight of those moments more than I wish I did.

And when you're hurting at that level, it's easy to feel entitled to more than you're experiencing. It's easy to assume God should have done something differently. But Son, don't act like a child who throws down his glove and walks off the field because he disagrees with the referee. Be a man! Get up. Dust yourself off. Take your frustration *to God*—even if you're frustrated *with* God. He can handle it.

We are human. We see through narrow lenses. We rarely understand in the moment what God may be protecting us from or preparing us for. Sometimes what feels like punishment is preparations and many times what feels like God's silence is actually our lack of capacity to comprehend the bigger picture until maturity gives us hindsight.

Your enemy knows very well that victory comes to those who stay the course. So he works overtime to get you to quit—because quitting is the only real way he can keep you from what God has promised. You have free will, and free will always gives you the option to walk away before the promise manifests. *The purpose of the distraction is destruction.*

This is why the Bible tells us to *walk by faith and not by sight*. Faith is what pulls the unseen into the seen. Sometimes the only thing that carries you through a storm is the vision God gave you when the skies were clear. **Never forget in the darkness what God taught you in the light.**

You can be tired. You can be confused. You can be frustrated. All of that is human. BUT YOU CANNOT QUIT!

Do not draw a line in the sand with God and tell Him you're done if He doesn't move by your deadline. That isn't faith—that's emotion masquerading as logic. Emotion-led decisions almost always lead to faithless spirals and unnecessary destruction.

Scripture says that *He who began a good work in you is faithful to complete it (Philippians 1:6)*. Acknowledge Him in all your ways—including the painful ones—and He will direct your path and straighten what feels crooked.

So, hear me, Son:

Don't quit. Not ever. Not on God. Not on your calling. Not on yourself.

I love you, son. I hope you always know it. —Dad

Deepening Faith and Intimacy with God

CHAPTER SEVEN
Faith Begins Where the Will of God is Known

Son,

The Bible is clear when it says that *without implementing faith, it is impossible to please God* (Hebrews 11:6). In other words, you will never fully accomplish what God has called you to do without operating in faith. Many times, walking in faith will require doing what you know you're supposed to do even when it doesn't make sense on paper. This is what it means to *"walk by faith and not by sight."*

One of the biggest hurdles to walking in faith is the question people wrestle with: *"But is this God's will?"*
That's what I want to make absolutely clear for you in this letter.

If you ever want to know with certainty whether something is God's will, remember this: **THE WORD OF GOD IS THE WILL OF GOD.**

Ask yourself:

- Is it a promise in God's Word?

- Did Jesus say it?

- Did Jesus model it?

- Did the disciples and early church walk in it or experience it?

If the answer to any of those questions is *yes*, then it IS the will of God. If Jesus did it, you can do it. Jesus Himself said, *"Greater things shall you do because I go to the Father."*

Once you know something is God's will, you can confidently exercise faith toward it. But as long as you're unsure, unbelief becomes the driving force—and your enemy will make sure of that. That's why I've always said, **"Faith begins where the will of God is known."** So anchor this truth deeply: **If it's in God's Word, it is God's will.**

When unbelief is removed, and you are certain you are acting in agreement with God's will, the Bible says even the smallest measure of faith can move mountains if you release it by *speaking* to the mountain standing between you and God's promise.

It *is* God's will that you be healed, whole, blessed, successful, strengthened, anointed, and empowered to carry heaven into every place you see hell manifesting on earth.

You will never walk in these things if you don't believe God wants them for you. But once you believe—and once you put your faith into action in the direction of His will—there is NOTHING you cannot accomplish.

I love you, son. I hope you always know it. —Dad

Building Godly Character and Integrity

CHAPTER EIGHT
Forge Your Own Path

Son,

One of my favorite poems has always been *The Road Not Taken* by Robert Frost. It's a poem worth memorizing, because its meaning deepens the longer you live. At its core, it speaks to the courage required to choose your own path—especially when others don't understand or approve. The closing lines have stayed with me for years, because they remind us that the choices we make in quiet, decisive moments often shape the entire course of our lives:

I shall be telling this with a sigh
Somewhere ages and ages hence:
Two roads diverged in a wood, and I—
I took the one less traveled by,
And that has made all the difference.

It's so important for you to realize that you were created to forge your own path. You are not defined by what you do for a living—you are defined by who you are on the inside, no matter what path you pursue. You don't live in anyone's shadow, and you don't exist to meet anyone's expectations but God's. Your responsibility is to follow His leading, develop your gifts, and walk confidently in the purpose He designed you for.

I heard a heartbreaking story recently about Elvis Presley's grandson. He took his own life in his late twenties because he felt crushed under the weight of people's expectations for him to be as famous as his grandfather. But the truth is this: those expectations only held power because *he adopted them*. He allowed the opinions of others to define him rather than forging his own path and finding security in his own calling.

Son, hear me—you must resist the need for the world's approval.

You cannot allow others to define you. Whether you *let* them or not is your choice. People are fickle; their opinions will shift with the wind. That is why it is essential that you grow confident in the path God lays before you and take full responsibility for your choices. You must be

YOU—unapologetically, authentically, and purposefully.

Others may not understand your decisions when you follow God's leading, and it is not your responsibility to make them understand. Your job is to obey God, not to win the approval of spectators.

Live by Matthew 6:33 (TPT) - *So above all, constantly seek God's kingdom and his righteousness, then all these less important things will be given to you abundantly.* And if someone presses you with a "why?" when they don't understand your choices, you can simply answer, "Matthew 6:33," and let that be enough.

They'll either understand…or they won't.

But the two who matter—you and God—will.

I love you, son. I hope you always know it. —Dad

Your Identity in the Father's Heart

CHAPTER NINE
God Doesn't Abuse His Kids

Son,

It is vitally important that no matter what circumstances come your way, you settle this truth deep in your heart: **God is good.** The enemy will do everything he can to pull you away from that reality, because if he can convince you that God is somehow complicit in your tragedy, then he knows it becomes difficult—if not impossible—for you to fully trust Him.

I don't think I'm overstating it when I say that many Christians, though they believe God sent Jesus to die for their sins, admit He loves humanity, and acknowledge His grace and forgiveness, still have an underlying belief that God is abusive (or at least harshly punitive) when His children fall short.

"God gave me cancer."
"God took my loved one."
"God is punishing me for messing up."

None of these reflect the character Jesus modeled. And the Bible is clear—Jesus said, *"If you've seen Me, you've seen the Father."* In other words, if you want to know what the Father is like, look directly at Jesus. His actions, His compassion, His healing, His mercy—that is who Father God is too.

God does **not** abuse His children. On the contrary, Scripture says over and over again that **God is love.**

1 Corinthians 13 describes love in a way that reflects God's own nature:
Love is incredibly patient.
Love is gentle and consistently kind to all.
Love refuses to be jealous.
Love does not traffic in shame or disrespect.
Love is not easily irritated or quick to take offense.
Love celebrates honesty and takes no delight in what is wrong.
Love is a safe place of shelter.

Love never stops believing the best in others.
Love never takes failure as defeat.
Love never gives up.
Love never stops loving.

Now go back and read those characteristics again—but replace the word *love* with *God*.

That is who your Heavenly Father truly is.

He is not an abuser. He is not the source of your pain. He is a good Father who gives good gifts to His children, and nothing the enemy whispers to you should ever be allowed to distort that truth.

Guard this revelation. It will anchor you through every storm.

I love you, son. I hope you always know it. —Dad

Your Identity in the Father's Heart

CHAPTER TEN
I Trust You Daddy

Son,

Today as I was praying, I whispered the words, "I trust You, Lord." The moment they left my mouth, I heard your voice—your small, nervous voice—as a little boy sitting on a sled behind a four-wheeler on a frozen lake in Edmonton, Alberta.

You had never experienced anything like that before. I grew up playing on ice, but you hadn't even walked on a frozen lake until that day. You understood that beneath that ice was frigid water far over your head, and falling through could have been dangerous. Your fear made sense. But I was right there with you, and I assured you everything would be alright.

Just before we took off, you looked at me—wide-eyed, unsure—and said loud enough for me to hear you, "*I trust you, Daddy.*"

When I prayed those same words today, I said them for a very different reason. I wasn't feeling brave or confident. I was disappointed. I thought something good was finally about to happen—something I had prayed for, that seemed to be falling right in alignment with my prayers. The door looked like it was opening... and then it closed without explanation.

That's when the Lord brought your voice to my memory.

Walking by faith and not by sight means trusting that God knows more than we do, even when our stomachs are tight and our hearts are confused. Even when we don't understand. Even when we thought things were supposed to go a different way.

Sometimes faith is simply sitting on the sled and letting God drive the four-wheeler. Holding on. Letting Him lead in the direction He knows is best.

It may not always feel easy. It may not always feel fun. But you are His child, and He will never take you anywhere meant to harm you. Trust Him. Don't lean on your own understanding. He will make your path straight—just like He promised.

I love you, son. I hope you always know it. —Dad

Healing Pain and Growing in Emotional Maturity

CHAPTER ELEVEN
You Are Worth the Fight

Son,

I was praying for you today. This "fathering" thing isn't easy. There are so many moments when I feel like I don't know what to do. There are always several options in front of me, and the pressure of choosing the right one can feel overwhelming.

I've said your whole life, *"I'm not raising a child—I'm training a man."* And that carries a weight I don't take lightly. Every difficult moment, every hard conversation, every consequence, every challenge… all of it is meant to help shape you into the man God has called you to be. But son, there are days I still feel under-equipped.

Scripture tells me to *"train up a child in the way he should go."* That means God expects me to consider your future, your destiny, your wiring, your calling—not just what I might want for you, but what God desires for your life. It obligates me to seek His wisdom on your behalf, to strategize for your future, to handle my role as your father with intentionality.

And I'll be honest with you—sometimes it's a lot. Sometimes it weighs heavily on my heart, my mind, and my emotions. I don't always know if I'm doing the right thing. I often look back wishing I had said something differently or handled a situation better. Parenting feels like a war at times—internally and externally—and buddy, it ain't easy.

But hear me clearly: you are worth the fight.

There is greatness inside you. You are becoming an incredible man. Every difficulty, every frustration, every failure—each one carries an opportunity to grow if you're willing to look for God's wisdom in the middle of it. Growth won't happen by accident. It requires intentionality and maturity on your part.

I told you recently, and I mean it with everything in me: I don't love anything in this world more than I love you. And that will never change.

I love you, son. I hope you always know it. —Dad

Healing Pain and Growing in Emotional Maturity

CHAPTER TWELVE
Don't Let Fear Lead You - The Rockwall

Son,

One of my proudest moments as your father came on a day that might look ordinary to anyone else. It was a picture snapped of you at the top of the rock wall in Mission Beach. Just a simple climb. Just a happy kid. But you and I know there was a whole story behind that moment.

When you were little, you were fearless. Trampolines, dirt bikes, skateboards, jiu-jitsu—whatever challenge was in front of you, you attacked it. But I'll never forget that birthday when you were just little at the indoor playground. You clipped into the climbing harness, jumped from pillar to pillar, and then halfway up... you froze. I saw fear hit you like a punch in the gut. It surprised you, and honestly, it surprised me too.

I wasn't frustrated with you—I was angry at the fear. I had grown up being afraid of everything, and it tormented me. I never wanted that for you. From the time you could barely talk, I would ask you, "What are you afraid of, boy?!" and you would respond, "Nothing!" Then I would ask, "Why not?" and you would say, "Because God doesn't give me a spirit of fear!" And you had lived that out—until that moment.

You came down that day disappointed, and you thought I was disappointed in you. The truth is, I felt like I failed you. I didn't want you to carry the same enemy of shame I had fought growing up. So I didn't push you after that. I let time do its work. You faced fear in every other area of your life—but the fear of heights lingered in the background.

Then that day at the amusement park came. We walked past a rock wall, and something in me knew the moment had come. You tried to brush it off when I told you that I thought you needed to conquer that rock wall, but when we sat down, the tears behind your sunglasses told me everything. I explained to you the difference between reasonable caution and the kind of fear that tries to control a man. And I told you the truth: even at ten years old, you were standing at a crossroads. If you got used to backing down when you felt afraid, it would set a ceiling of limitation on your whole life.

You buried your head in your arms, wrestling with it. And then, after a long moment, you popped up, took a deep breath, and said, "Let's do this." Right then, I saw the warrior in you stand up.

We went to the wall. You clipped into the rope, nervous but determined. Every step, I coached you—left foot, red rock, reach higher, push with your legs. And then, step by step, you climbed higher than your fear. When you reached the top, I snapped the picture that means more to me than most people will ever understand.

You came down smiling, chest out, eyes bright.

"I did it, Daddy."

"You sure did, son."

"But you always knew I could... didn't you?"

"I did. But it was more important that *you* knew."

Son, listen to me—fear is loud, but it's a liar. Courage isn't about feeling brave; it's about moving forward even when you don't. You faced a giant that day, and you beat it. And that victory will follow you into every hard moment of your life if you choose to remember it.

I love you, son. I hope you always know it. —Dad

Building Godly Character and Integrity

CHAPTER THIRTEEN
The Gold That Really Matters

Son,

There are two very different "golden rules" people live by in this world:

1. **The Golden Rule:** *Do unto others as you would have them do unto you.*

2. **The Gold Rule:** *He who has the gold makes the rules.*

Both statements reveal something—but not about money. They reveal character.

In her article *Rules and Common Sense*, Peggy Sanders wrote, *"How someone applies the rule demonstrates their character."* I couldn't agree more. You don't have to tell me what you believe—your actions show me. Character is always lived out in plain sight.

So let me ask you questions every man should wrestle with:

What are you willing to do to win?
Who are you willing to step on in pursuit of your goals?
Do you value people, or do you value profit?
Does success matter more than integrity?

Son, the world is full of people who sacrifice integrity for advantage. They compromise honor for gain. They climb ladders by stepping on others. And even if they "win," they lose something far more valuable—their name, their honor, their soul.

Money can open doors, but character determines whether they stay open. Wealth can give opportunity, but integrity determines whether you deserve it. Anyone can chase success. It takes a man of God to pursue success without losing himself.

Your choices—both small and large—are shaping who you are becoming. They are building the reputation others will remember. More importantly, they are building the legacy your future family will inherit.

So ask yourself often: Who do I want to be? How do I want to be remembered?

Live by the Golden Rule, not the Gold Rule. Lead with honor. Protect your integrity. Value people over profit. Let your character speak louder than your ambition.

If you do that, God will trust you with favor far greater than anything this world can offer.

I love you, son. I hope you always know it. —Dad

Discipline, Consistency, and Spiritual Growth

CHAPTER FOURTEEN
Guard Your Thoughts, Guard Your Future

Son,

Positively or negatively, visualization is a powerful extension of faith. I'm convinced you can actually extend faith toward both positive *and* negative outcomes in your life. As the old Henry Ford quote says, *"If you believe you can or you believe you can't—you're right."* What you focus on, and what you extend belief toward—whether hope or doubt—shapes what ultimately becomes your reality.

Faith in the promises of God has the power to manifest His purposes into your life. But extending faith toward doubt, fear, or negative expectations can just as easily collapse those outcomes into your world as well.

It's so easy to write off an entire day because of a single moment of difficulty, when the truth is, you didn't have "a bad day" … you had a bad 15 minutes, and you chose to indulge in it.

The Bible instructs us to *take every thought captive to the obedience of Christ* because what we dwell on becomes the seed of our outcomes. Your thoughts are not harmless—they are formative. They are prophetic in the sense that they create momentum toward what you expect.

When the devil tempted Jesus, he waited until Jesus was hungry—physically weak—and then he attacked His thoughts, trying to influence Him away from believing who He knew God created Him to be. *"If you really are who you say you are… then prove it."*

Satan's strategy hasn't changed. He still attacks with the same doubt-filled questions, attempting to shift your faith away from God's promises and onto his lies—even though you are bound to God in a covenant relationship. Like a marriage covenant, that bond carries rights, authority, and security. The enemy's aim is not to break the covenant, but to convince you to live as if it doesn't exist.

Don't fall for that trap, Son. God's promises are for you. You are a child of God with covenant rights, covenant identity, and covenant authority. Do not allow doubt or unbelief to steal from you what God intends for your life. Do not let the enemy frame your potential into a lesser version of yourself because you entertained a lie long enough for it to take root.

Guard your thoughts... they shape your faith, and your faith shapes your future.

I love you, son. I hope you always know it. —Dad

Discipline, Consistency, and Spiritual Growth

CHAPTER FIFTEEN
Don't Draw Back - Draw In

"So now the case is closed. There remains no accusing voice of condemnation against those who are joined in life-union with Jesus, the Anointed One."
—Romans 8:1 (TPT)

Son,

Over the years as a pastor, I've seen a certain pattern play out countless times. I can almost spot it instantly.

Someone who normally sits in the first few rows—full of joy, singing their heart out, worshiping with freedom—is suddenly sitting quietly toward the back. Their posture changes. Their expression changes. And you can see the war happening inside them. Something in their life has made them believe that God is disappointed in them… or worse, that He's distancing Himself from them.

We've all heard the phrase, "sin separates us from God," and although before salvation our sin did separate us from God, and the consequences of sin does produce death in our lives, most people interpret it in the most damaging way possible. The moment they step into a place where God's presence is usually felt—worship, prayer, church—they no longer feel Him. All they feel is guilt. Shame. Condemnation. And they assume God must be behind that feeling.

Son, listen to me carefully: that is a lie straight from the enemy.

Shame does not come from your *Father*.
Condemnation does not come from your *Father*.
Rejection does not come from your *Father*.

You belong to Him. Messing up does not disqualify you from His love. Yes, the Holy Spirit will correct you when your actions are out of alignment with God's will—but correction and condemnation are not the same thing. One leads you *toward* God; the other pushes you *away* from Him.

God never pushes you away.

A good father doesn't reject his child when they make a mistake. He draws them close. He teaches them. He restores them. He loves them right through it.

Son, when you stumble—because all of us do—make it a habit to run *to* Him, not from Him. Don't draw back. Draw in.

The Bible calls King David "a man after God's own heart." It wasn't because he lived a flawless life. He made some devastating mistakes. But when he fell, he didn't hide. He didn't withdraw into shame. He ran to God with a repentant heart. He leaned into God's love instead of embracing the spirit of rejection.

That's why God honored him.

And I want you to understand this: God doesn't hate sin because it offends Him—He hates sin because it harms *you*. Every time. His heart is always to protect you, not punish you.

The enemy knows that if he can distort the way you think that God feels about you, he can make you spiritually vulnerable. When you believe the lie, you empower the liar. But when you believe God's truth, you disarm every attack.

Son, God is who He says He is. *Love.* Faithful. Merciful. Patient. Kind. And He loves you far more than you will ever fully grasp.

So in those moments when guilt tries to suffocate you, when shame whispers that you're unworthy, when you feel the urge to withdraw—do the opposite. Run straight to Him.

He will finish what He started in you.

I love you, son. I hope you always know it. —Dad

Leadership, Authority, and Kingdom Influence

CHAPTER SIXTEEN
Lead or Support — Know Your Moment

Son,

Sometimes it's your moment to lead, and sometimes it's your duty to assist. The wisdom is in discerning *which moment you're in* and responding appropriately.

When I was a detective and assigned a case, I was the lead. In that role, it was my responsibility to call the shots, organize teams, and delegate assignments. But there were other times when I wasn't the lead—and in those moments, my job was to do whatever the lead investigator needed, because the goal was never about *me*. The goal was to solve the case.

Football works the same way. Sometimes the running back carries the ball, and sometimes he throws a block so someone else can score. Both roles matter. Both are essential to the win.

It's important to remember that success is about the *team*, not the spotlight. Stay intentional. Keep yourself in check. Never become a "diva" leader who believes contribution only matters when they are the one out front.

Last year, a Christian business conference rented our building for their event. Afterward, the organizer expressed how shocked she was by the way I served—stepping in wherever I could to help. She said they expected to be handed the keys and left alone, and they couldn't believe that I treated the event as though it were my own.

I told her, "What would you do if Jesus sent His sister to your house to minister to people in your city?" Because that's exactly what happened—and I took it personally to make sure she felt welcomed, supported, and honored.

Son, most people never see the bigger picture hidden in the smaller moments. But leaders must. Be intentional. Be present. Be humble.

Sometimes it's the rookie's moment to score the touchdown. When that happens, throw the best block you've ever thrown and celebrate their win louder than everyone else.

Everyone you serve alongside is on a journey. Just like you, they have a God-given purpose—and God loves them every bit as much as He loves you. Sometimes your assignment is to lead; other times your assignment is to support. Never be so prideful that you think blocking is less important than running the ball. The whole point is the win—the final *"Well done, my good and faithful servant."*

In his book *And David Perceived He Was King*, Dale Mast writes a line I've read nearly every day: *"There is a David in a field near you. He needs you to make it. He doesn't know he's the next king of Israel."*

A true leader doesn't just advance their own calling—they empower others to rise into theirs.

I love you, son. I hope you always know it. —Dad

Deepening Faith and Intimacy with God

CHAPTER SEVENTEEN
Anchored in the Truth of God's Word

Son,

Pain has a way of molding perspectives that may or may not be truth.

This is why it is essential for you to be able to reference **THE TRUTH** when life seems void of it.

The Bible says, *"You shall know the truth, and the truth will make you free," "My people are destroyed for lack of knowledge," "I am the way, the truth, and the life,"* and so on.

Faith is often not even activated until our circumstances contradict God's Word and we are forced to choose whose voice we are going to believe.

Many times, the only way to truly walk by faith and not by sight is to resolve that the Bible is the only source of truth for life. Circumstances may contain elements of fact, but when they contradict **THE TRUTH** of God's Word, you must go back to the Word and place your faith in **THE TRUTH**.

We wouldn't need His peace if we never encountered stress or difficulty.
We wouldn't need the joy of the Lord to be our strength if we never battled sadness.
We wouldn't need His grace if sin were never an obstacle.
We wouldn't need His healing if sickness were never a hurdle.
We wouldn't need His power if there were no enemy to overcome.
And we wouldn't need **THE TRUTH** of His Word if we never had to believe it *instead* of a lie.

There are many voices that have a form of godliness but are void of—or deny—the power. No matter how good those voices sound, if they contradict God's Word, they are not the source of truth.

Jesus said that He was going to the Father and would send the Holy Spirit, whose power would fill us with the ability to do what He did—and even greater things. That is **THE TRUTH** of His Word.

So when you can't rationalize your circumstances into comprehension, you have the gift of God's Word and God's Spirit to reveal **THE TRUTH** in spite of what you see or feel.

Don't rewrite your theology to accommodate your tragedy. Truth is truth—even when you don't understand it—and it will set you free when contrary voices seek to convince you to believe a lie that would otherwise rob you of the blessing that only comes through faith in **THE TRUTH**.

I love you, son. I hope you always know it. —Dad

Deepening Faith and Intimacy with God

CHAPTER EIGHTEEN
When Your Experience Doesn't Meet Your Expectation

Son,

There is a part of me that would prefer to wait until the test is over and all that remains is the testimony—but I think there is a deeper lesson found in writing this now, right in the middle of it. Sometimes the most important truths are revealed when your experience doesn't match your expectation.

Nearly 18 months ago, I stepped down from pastoring at a church I had faithfully served for 20 years. I knew my season there was finished. It was painful because I genuinely loved the people, but I also felt the excitement and anticipation that comes from finishing an assignment well. Naturally, I expected God to immediately open the next door. I had sown faithfully, served with integrity, and done everything I believed God asked of me. But it didn't unfold the way I imagined. Instead of clarity and wide-open doors, nearly every hopeful opportunity was met with confusion. Relationships that didn't develop. Opportunities that fizzled out. Direction that never fully materialized.

Nine months later, two different people—who did not know each other—called me on the same day and said the exact same words: "God says your whole life you've kicked doors down and made things happen... but this next thing He has for you is something *you cannot make happen*. You need to climb up in your Father's lap, rest, and let Him do it." Statistically, two people sharing that exact message hours apart is nearly impossible. I knew it was God.

Another nine months have passed. Today I'm working my sixth fourteen-hour shift this week in a job that looks nothing like what I feel called to do. From the outside, none of it makes sense. But here's the strange beauty—I still have peace. I know God's Word. I know His promises. I know His character. Setbacks don't change His faithfulness, and silent seasons don't change His goodness. He is always working, even when we can't see it.

Son, when you don't have all the answers, remember this: you *do* know the One who is the answer. Trust Him. He is working all things together for your good—even in the middle, even when it feels uncertain, and even when the path doesn't look anything like you expected. He is a good Father…and He loves you.

I love you, son. I hope you always know it. —Dad

Deepening Faith and Intimacy with God

CHAPTER NINETEEN
When Your Experience Doesn't Meet Your Expectation Part 2

Son,

To finish my thought from the last post, I mentioned that part of me would prefer to write this from the position of already experiencing the victory. But the truth is, when we are in covenant with God and heirs of His promises, even in the middle of the test we are already victors. That's the beauty and certainty of God's Word.

The Scriptures make it clear that God's promises are not fragile or conditional based on our circumstances. *"Jesus Christ is the Son of God, and He is the one whom Timothy, Silas, and I have preached to you—and He has never been both a 'yes' and a 'no.' He has always been and always will be for us a resounding 'YES!' For all of God's promises find their 'yes' of fulfillment in Him. And as His 'yes' and our 'amen' ascend to God, we bring Him glory! Now it is God Himself who has anointed us, and He is constantly strengthening both you and us in union with Christ."* (2 Corinthians 1:19–21 TPT)

Another passage speaks into this so powerfully: *"When God made His promise to Abraham, He backed it to the hilt, putting His own reputation on the line. He said, 'I promise that I'll bless you with everything I have—bless and bless and bless!' Abraham stuck it out and got everything that had been promised to him. When people make promises, they guarantee them by appealing to some authority above them so that if there is any question they'll make good on the promise, the authority will back them up. When God wanted to guarantee His promises, He gave His Word, a rock-solid guarantee—God can't break His Word. And because His Word cannot change, the promise is likewise unchangeable. We who have run for our very lives to God have every reason to grab the promised hope with both hands and never let go. It's an unbreakable spiritual lifeline, reaching past all appearances right to the very presence of God where Jesus, running on ahead of us, has taken up His permanent post as high priest for us..."* (Hebrews 6:13–18 MSG)

Son, if God promised it, it's as good as yours. Your part is to place your agreement—your "amen"—in what He has already declared. That agreement connects your faith to His unbreakable promise, and nothing in this world can sever what God has already secured.

I love you, son. I hope you always know it. —Dad

Healing Pain and Growing in Emotional Maturity

CHAPTER TWENTY
"But Did You Die?" — The Perspective That Keeps You Going

Son,

As I pulled up to the gas pump today, I glanced over at a black Jeep that looked almost identical to mine, and on the side window was a sticker that read, *"But did you die?"*

I've lived through a lot of tough seasons. More than some people, less than others—but enough to leave a mark. And interestingly, just *before* I turned and saw that sticker, I had been replaying some of those difficult seasons in my mind.

Earlier at lunch, I was telling a friend about one of those seasons—the one that cost me more than a million dollars. As I drove into the gas station afterward, I was replaying that conversation and feeling a bit frustrated as I reconsidered the loss.

Then I turned and saw those words: *"But did you die?"* I actually laughed out loud. And in that moment, I felt the Holy Spirit add His own commentary to the joke by saying, *"You're a victory statistic. You've made it through 100% of your worst days."*

Son, here's the lesson:
Yeah, it was hard.
Yeah, it cost a lot.
Yeah, it hurt like heck.

But I'm still here.
I'm still fighting.
I'm still an overcomer, and I still have the promises of God that He will work everything together for my good.

The key is this: **You can't quit.**
You can recalibrate.
You can reassess.
You can cry, hurt, and feel it—but **you cannot quit**.

I heard a man today say, *"Your perspective can be your prison or your passport."* Then he asked, *"Are you buried, or are you planted?"*

Every deed is a seed. And your perspective is the soil it grows in.

So don't let your perspective become your prison. Keep your thoughts, words, and actions aligned with the Word and promises of God. Hold fast to what He says about you. Remember—you are more than a conqueror.

You've survived 100% of your worst days. And today? It's just another day you get to win—even if winning hurts a little on the way.

I love you, son. I hope you always know it. —Dad

Leadership, Authority, and Kingdom Influence

CHAPTER TWENTY-ONE
The Marks of a Leader of Leaders

Son,

There are thousands of books written about leadership, but life has taught me something the books rarely touch. You can know all the right information, quote all the right sources, and recite all the right material—but if you are missing three essential qualities, weaker, younger, less-experienced men may follow you, yet **strong, battle-tested leaders will not**. They'll see through the hype, and you'll be left with nothing but underdeveloped yes-men, because strong leaders do not follow weak leadership long-term.

The first quality a leader of leaders must have is scars.
Scars are the evidence that you've survived what you want others to trust you to lead them through. No seasoned warrior will follow someone into battle whose mettle has not been tested. Now, if you ever find yourself promoted beyond your experience, then you'd better be clothed in humility and willing to receive instruction from those who *do* have the scars. Without humility, the promotion will crush you.

The second quality is integrity.
Your men must know—without hesitation—that your word is your oath. That what you say is true, trustworthy, and consistent. Without that trust factor, seasoned leaders will never fight beside you. Their wisdom will cause them to stay on guard around you, protecting themselves from being misled by someone whose character wavers.

And the third quality is a willingness to get into the trenches with your men.
If you ask people to do what you are unwilling to do yourself, you will be viewed with disdain. When a leader gives the impression that he is "past that" or only shows up when it benefits his image, he loses the respect of the very men who could have been his strongest supporters. Simon Sinek highlights this in *Leaders Eat Last*—true leaders sacrifice first, serve first, and demonstrate through action that the mission and the team matter more than their comfort.

Son, I don't share these perspectives from a place of assuming I have mastered leadership, but from the place of one who has endured enough battles to know what strong men will and will not follow. And you *are* a strong man. If you want to lead strong leaders, you must rise to a standard worthy of their respect.

Lead with humility. Lead with integrity. Lead with scars—and earn theirs.

I love you, son. I hope you always know it. —Dad

Resisting Comparison and Cultural Pressures

CHAPTER TWENTY-TWO
Seeing Like God Sees – The Comparison Deception

Son,

In many of these chapters I've talked with you about leading well, but I want to teach you something just as important: **your ability to advance in life will often depend on how you honor God-appointed leadership when it isn't easy.**

I remember a season when I was frustrated with leadership decisions that were making my life much harder. Deep down, I believed I could do it better. When I finally stopped venting long enough to listen, God confronted me in a way I didn't expect:

"Are you judging My choice? Because if you are, you're functioning in an Eliab spirit..." (I'll explain that in a minute.)

I didn't like that. But He was right.

God's choices rarely look the way we imagine they should. Where people only saw a small, unimpressive shepherd boy—David—God saw the king who would slay giants. Meanwhile, David's oldest brother, Eliab, seemed like the perfect candidate for leadership: the oldest, the strongest, the one trained for battle. But when God bypassed him and chose David instead, something sour formed in Eliab's heart.

He thought he could do it better.
He judged what God saw.
He assumed his perspective was superior.

Right before David killed Goliath, Eliab confronted him and told him to go home, insisting he had no purpose on the battlefield. We usually teach this story from the perspective of God using the unlikely underdog—but the day God corrected me, He showed me something else:

We often don't know what we don't know.

God is always working behind the scenes in ways we cannot see. He is developing people, shaping them, strengthening them—and if we're not careful, we'll judge what God is doing because it doesn't look the way we think it should. That's why it's so important to keep your heart right and support what God is doing in others, even when you believe you could lead better.

As an oldest brother myself, I can understand Eliab's reaction. Until the moment he saw David kill Goliath, he probably believed that *he* was the more qualified one. But every person—no matter how ordinary they appear—is in a process where God is molding them into who He already knows they can become.

Training yourself to see through that lens will transform how you serve under leaders and how you lead others. You'll be able to work with people who are still growing, empower those around you without insecurity, and avoid the trap of comparison.

Son, everyone has something to contribute to the whole. Discern the season you're in, fill YOUR lane with excellence, empower others with your support, and never get misdirected by ego or comparison. Honor where God has placed you, and He will honor the path He has prepared for you.

I love you, son. I hope you always know it. —Dad

Leadership, Authority, and Kingdom Influence

CHAPTER TWENTY-THREE
Title and Leader Are Not Synonymous

Son,

It's not uncommon for someone to do what they're told while having no honor in their heart for the authority they're submitting to. In other words, they may comply with the rank while quietly despising the leadership behind it. This often happens when people feel unseen, misused, belittled, disrespected, or dishonored.

People know when their leader is asking them to do something the leader believes they're "too good" to do themselves. And when someone feels like leadership views them as *less-than*, resentment forms and respect evaporates. Strong people will not follow weak leadership for long—and nothing reveals weak leadership faster than a leader who fails to honor the ones submitting to them.

A leader may receive outward compliance, but underlying resentment guarantees minimal results. They might have the title, but they won't have the heart of their team.

Simon Sinek wrote *Leaders Eat Last*, a book that powerfully outlines how people will go to the ends of the earth—even into hell itself—to follow a leader they trust, a leader who truly prioritizes them. Sadly, many leaders find more identity in their rank than in their responsibility to their team. And when leaders elevate themselves above those they lead, the team sees it clearly—and they will resent it.

Son, be the kind of leader who makes sure your men eat before you do. Be the one who prioritizes their well-being above your own. Be present. Sweat with them. Carry the weight when the work is heavy. Take interest in their lives. Let them know, without question, that you would take a bullet for them if it came to it.

A leader who loves his people will produce a team that honors him—not just one that complies with him.

Be the leader they love, and they will become the team you need.

I love you, son. I hope you always know it. —Dad

Leadership, Authority, and Kingdom Influence

CHAPTER TWENTY-FOUR
Honor the Gift, Honor the Giver

Son,

Leadership is a responsibility. What you esteem, celebrate, and are thankful for, you multiply in your life. What you murmur about, resent, and complain about, you also multiply in your life.

When we honor the gifts God has given us, we honor the Gift Giver. When we celebrate, esteem, and appreciate the relationships He places in our lives, that gratitude becomes worship—an acknowledgment of the One who has blessed us with those gifts.

If each gift is a work of art crafted by the Master Artist, then displaying that artwork on the wall of your life honors the Artist Himself. When you notice the brush strokes, the intricate details, the intentionality behind the masterpiece He created, you give glory to the One who made it.

When you recognize the value and esteem the worth of the gifts God has entrusted to you, you create an environment where the Master knows His finest pieces will be cared for. He trusts His most meaningful treasures to the collector who understands the value He places on each one. He gave you the gift for a reason—don't hide it in the closet.

Whether we're talking about the gifts *in* people, the gift *of* people, opportunities, positions, or possessions—remember: **the Gift Giver gives good gifts to those who steward them well.**

Son, those who are faithful in the little things will be made ruler over much. Be thankful in everything. Celebrate and steward each gift well, and God will multiply what you choose to honor.

I love you, son. I hope you always know it. —Dad

Leadership, Authority, and Kingdom Influence

CHAPTER TWENTY-FIVE
They're Looking for What You Already Have

Son,

Last week we went to see your favorite band in concert. It wasn't a Christian event, and three other bands played before them. The lead singer of the opening band *The Used* stepped up between songs and said, "If you've followed me for the last 20 years, you know I struggle with depression and anxiety..." He went on to encourage the room to not submit to depression and to choose life because he loved them.

The crowd cheered, and as I looked around the room I almost cried. I saw hundreds of young people who, in almost any other environment, would be considered misfits. Yet in that moment, they felt unified—connected through a shared struggle and the music that spoke to them.

Their identity seemed intertwined with the singer, the lyrics, and with others in the crowd who carried the same pain. They felt seen. They felt like they belonged. And still, all I could feel was a deep compassion—because the despair in the singer's words and the way the crowd responded revealed just how many of them were hurting.

As the next songs played, I watched hands lift, voices shout, and people sing with a passion that felt almost *church-like*. They were reaching for something—connection, meaning, hope. For a moment, it was overwhelming to witness.

The world is desperately searching for three primary things wherever they can find them: **love, joy, and peace.** They chase after them in fleeting moments of emotional connection but almost always leave still wanting.

But Son, those three things—the very ones the crowd was craving—are the first three listed as an inheritance for those who belong to the Spirit of God. And as I stood there, I couldn't stop thinking, *"If all these people just knew the love of Jesus... if they could find this same sense of belonging within the church... how many could be set free from their pain?"*

We carry what the whole world is trying to find, and most of them don't even know it exists. They aren't resisting God—they simply don't know the truth yet. They're searching in the only places they've been told to look.

Son, always try to see people through the lens of their pain, not their presentation. Look beyond the tattoos, the style, the music, the attitude. Everyone is carrying a story. Everyone is longing for what you already have.

Choose compassion. Show them Jesus.

I love you, son. I hope you always know it. —Dad

Your Identity in the Father's Heart

CHAPTER TWENTY-SIX
The Lie of Sin Consciousness

Son,

I've often heard people say that *sin separates us from God*, but that's not actually true. **Sin-consciousness** does.

God's Word tells us that He is **not** holding the sins of His children against them. Yet so often, when we mess up, we pull away from God—not because He moved, but because *shame* convinces us that we're unworthy to approach Him. When we focus more on what we've done wrong than on what Jesus has done right, our own sin-consciousness becomes the barrier, not the sin itself.

Romans 8 and 1st Corinthians 3 both talk about our authority over "things present and things to come." Notice what's missing? **The past.**

Why?
Because the past no longer belongs to you.

Jesus bought it—with His blood. The sins of yesterday are no longer yours to carry, revisit, or feel condemned by. You can do something about *today*, and you can influence *tomorrow*, but you can do **nothing** about what you already surrendered to Christ. Focusing on what's been forgiven can sabotage what God is trying to grow in you right now.

Think of it this way: if you sold your car to someone, then later found the spare key in a drawer, you wouldn't drive to their house and take the car for a spin. That would be illegal—and you'd know it. The same is true of your past. It is **paid for, owned by Jesus**, and **no longer your property** to pick up again.

This is why Scripture declares: *"There is now no condemnation for those who are in Christ Jesus."* (Romans 8:1)
Your sin has been removed from you as far as the east is from the west—infinitely, irreversibly.

Son, your ability to pray, praise, worship, and communicate with God is a privilege—a blood-bought one. Don't let shame, guilt, regret, or sin-consciousness rob you of that privilege even for a moment.

What melts mountains of shame? **His presence.**

What dismantles guilt? **His love.**

What restores confidence? **His truth.**

When sin-consciousness tries to push you away from God, *run to Him instead*. Nothing—absolutely nothing—can separate you from His love, but sin-consciousness can trick you into withdrawing your affection, communication, and closeness. Don't let that happen.

God is not mad at you.

He loves you fiercely, fully, and faithfully.

I love you, son. I hope you always know it. —Dad

Building Godly Character and Integrity

CHAPTER TWENTY-SEVEN
Don't Be That Guy

Son,

There's something I've watched for years—something subtle, something most people never slow down long enough to notice—but it can cost a man more than money, more than reputation, and more than opportunity. It can cost him his character.

In business, people study ethics because there's a code, and if you break that code, it hits your wallet fast. But in relationships, there's another kind of code—relational ethics—and the cost of violating them is far greater. It reveals who you truly are when no one is watching.

Living in a city like Nashville, I've met so many people who are either trying to "make it" or terrified of losing what they think they've already gained. And here's a pattern I've noticed again and again:

When someone is struggling, their phone lights up with calls to their friends. They lean heavily on relationships. They need support, encouragement, and presence. In those seasons, you'll hear from them frequently.

But the moment they taste a little success—The moment a door cracks open—Suddenly, your phone goes silent.

You can call.
You can text.
You can check in.
And somehow, you no longer exist.

When that happens a few times, I simply stop reaching out. And I can't recall a single one who ever contacted me again—until they needed something. Then suddenly, out of the blue, my number still works for them.

Here's the truth they tell themselves:
"It's just the grind."
"It's just business."

"I'm busy."

But son, underneath those excuses, it's something entirely different. They're giving their attention to the people who can still benefit them… and quietly discarding those who no longer can.

They don't see it, but it's parasitic.
Leeching.
Convenient loyalty.

One season you were useful to them. The next season, someone else is. And they move on without ever realizing the relational damage they leave behind.

Now listen to me closely: relationships *do* change with seasons. That's normal. People grow, move, shift, and transition. But no matter where God takes you—no matter how high you climb, who you meet, or what opportunities open—never forget the people who stood with you when you had nothing to offer them in return.

Relational success is not measured by what you gain. It's revealed by how you treat people when you no longer "need" them.

Son, don't ever become the kind of man who prioritizes people only by what they can do for you. That way of living corrodes a soul. It isolates. It blinds. And it turns good men into hollow ones.

I'm not telling you this because I'm hurt. I'm telling you this because I've watched too many "good people" become selfish people without ever realizing it.

So hear my heart:
Don't be that guy.
That guy loses more than friendships.
That guy loses himself.

Walk with integrity.
Honor people.
Be loyal even when there's no benefit in it for you.
And remember—success without character isn't success at all.

I love you, son. I hope you always know it. —Dad

Your Identity in the Father's Heart

CHAPTER TWENTY-EIGHT
Grace Is Stronger Than Your Shame

For by grace you have been saved by faith. Nothing you did could ever earn this salvation, for it was the love gift from God that brought us to Christ! So no one will ever be able to boast, for salvation is never a reward for good works or human striving.
Ephesians 2:8-9 (TPT)

Son,

Have you ever made a mistake—cut someone off in traffic, said something dumb, reacted too quickly—and then felt that uncomfortable knot in your stomach when you finally faced the person you wronged? That awkward feeling of staring straight ahead, pretending you don't notice them, hoping the light turns green so you can escape?

That's what sin-consciousness feels like. And too many believers live their entire spiritual lives stuck at that red light—avoiding God, afraid to look at Him, convinced He's disappointed, frustrated, or just plain tired of dealing with them.

But son, that is **not** who God is. And that's not how grace works.

We mess up. We know it. And we know God knows it. But instead of running to Him, we hide. We distance ourselves. We skip church. We avoid prayer. We lower our heads and let shame drive the car.

But shame is not from God. Shame is the very thing Jesus died to break off of you.

Grace wasn't given because you earned it. Grace was given because you *couldn't*. Scripture says salvation is a gift—freely given so no one can ever brag that they deserved it. If you have to pay for it, work for it, or prove you're worthy of it…it stops being a gift.

Imagine giving someone a car, and they spend the next year walking to work and handing you a few dollars every time they see you, hoping they'll eventually "pay off" what you already gave them. You'd shake your head and say, "Why won't you just drive it? It's yours."

That's how many believers treat grace. They keep trying to earn what God already fully paid for.

When your failures become louder in your mind than God's love, you slip into a works-based life where you will *never* measure up. That's exactly what the enemy wants—distance between you and the only One who can transform you.

But the Bible says **nothing** can separate you from God's love. *Nothing* means what it says—**nothing**. Your sin isn't the exception. You aren't the one person in history who accidentally found the limit of God's grace.

Son, God isn't waiting to punish you. He's waiting to restore you. He's not counting your sins against you—Scripture says He actually chooses to remember them no more. His grace is the truth that sets you free, not your perfect performance.

So when you blow it—don't run away from God. Run straight toward Him. Let His love melt away the shame that tries to keep you at arm's length.

You are forgiven.
You are loved.
And because of Jesus, you are clean in God's eyes.

I love you, son. I hope you always know it. – Dad

Building Godly Character and Integrity

CHAPTER TWENTY-NINE
Don't Assume — Be Intentional

Son,

Read these words with the voice and emphasis of Everett in *O Brother, Where Art Thou* when he says, *"Do not seek the treasure!"*

Do. Not. Assume!

Generations of men have been raised to hide their feelings, bottle their emotions, and assume that the people they love "just know" how they feel—without communication, without affirmation, without expression. **DO NOT ASSUME.**

I read a study last week about children: the ages when they disconnect from their parents, stop showing affection, and withdraw emotionally. What the study revealed was heartbreaking. It is **almost never** the child who disconnects first. It is nearly always the *actions of the parent* that make the child feel questioned, unsafe, or unwanted in their expressions of affection.

The examples they cited were simple but devastating: —A child shows emotion or affection, and the parent responds with rejection or embarrassment, or reframes the timing as "inappropriate." —A child tries to open up, to share their heart, but the parent is distracted—on the phone, buried in work, or mentally somewhere else. The child is shut down, ignored, or silenced. Those moments create a divide. Children learn very quickly where it is unsafe to share their hearts.

But—on the flip side—the study showed that the child who is consistently embraced, hugged, seen, affirmed, and lovingly responded to... **that child never "grows out of" showing affection.** They don't disconnect because there is nothing unsafe for them to disconnect *from*.

Son, be intentional—*aggressively intentional*—to show your feelings, speak your affection, and express your love to your wife and children. Those old sayings, "Real men don't cry," "Real men hide their emotions," "Real men tough it out"—those sayings were created by broken, wounded, emotionally stunted men.

Real men LOVE.
Just like their Father…God.

You can be strong—fierce, even—and still love exceptionally if you are intentional.

Don't ever assume your loved ones know how you feel. Don't assume your wife knows you think she's beautiful—**tell her.** Don't assume your child knows you're proud of them—**say it every day.** Don't assume your mother knows how much you appreciate her—**thank her, intentionally and specifically.**

There's an old saying, *"When you assume, you make an ass out of u and me…"*

But in this case, son—it would just be you.

I love you, son. I hope you always know it. —Dad

Deepening Faith and Intimacy with God

CHAPTER THIRTY
The God Who Fights Beside You

Son,

Isaiah 41:10 is one of the most quoted comfort verses in the Bible: *"Fear not, for I am with you; be not dismayed, for I am your God."*

Most Christians stop reading right there and interpret it to mean, "Don't worry—God is nearby, watching over you while you go through something difficult." But when you read the *entire* verse in context, the meaning becomes far more powerful than passive reassurance. It's actually a warfare passage—one filled with strength, strategy, and supernatural empowerment.

"I will strengthen you, Yes, I will help you, I will uphold you with My righteous right hand."

Here's what God is really saying:

"I will strengthen you." The Hebrew word *amats* doesn't mean "I'll encourage you." It means: *I will make you strong. I will fortify you. I will make you brave and steadfast in battle.* It's the same word used in Deuteronomy 31:6 and Joshua 1:7: *"Be strong and courageous."*

"I will help you." The Hebrew word *azar* means: *I will surround you with protection. I will support you. I will rescue you in combat when you are about to collapse.* This is battlefield language—God stepping into the fight on your behalf.

"I will uphold you." The word *tamak* means: *I will tenaciously grasp you. I will hold you up in battle. I will sustain you under pressure.*

"With My righteous right hand." In ancient warfare, the right hand held the weapon—symbolizing power, strength, and decisive victory. God is saying: *My weapon hand is holding you.*

Son, this passage is not describing a passive Father patting you on the back. It is describing the God of angel armies standing beside you in formation—fortifying you, rescuing you, sustaining you, and strengthening you with His own battle-ready right hand.

We do not serve a God of passivity. We serve a God of power. A God who equips us with His armor, His strength, and His authority.

This is why Scripture tells us: *"After you have done everything to stand… stand firm."* (Ephesians 6:13) Because no weapon formed against you can prosper when the One holding you is the same One who commands victory.

So don't lose heart in the fight. You are not outmatched.
You are not alone.
And you are not fighting in your own strength.

The One who lives within you is greater than anything that comes against you.

I love you, son. I hope you always know it. —Dad

Healing Pain and Growing in Emotional Maturity

CHAPTER THIRTY-ONE
Don't Live Your Labels

Son,

If you believe you are a sinner, you will sin by faith. Faith is simply the extension of action in agreement with what we believe. I've always said, *"You don't have to tell me what you believe—your actions show me."* If I accept a label about myself, I will act out the characteristics of that label in everyday life.

This is why I refuse to accept the common Christian phrase, "a sinner saved by grace." It's unbiblical. I am not currently a sinner. I *was* a sinner—defined by my failures and enslaved to the old nature—but Scripture tells us we were transformed. The word used in the New Testament is the same word for "metamorphosis," like a caterpillar becoming a butterfly. Once transformed, the butterfly is no longer defined by what it used to be... and neither are we.

Like the children of Israel after 400 years in slavery, if you don't see yourself as a child of God, you will continue to respond like a slave. If you lose your identity in Egypt, you can't overcome the giants in your promised land. Then the wilderness becomes your future and not the place of your transition. People rarely come to the realization of who He is in them if they don't first understand who they are to Him. Until you understand that God loves you, you'll probably never experience what His love provides you.

You must understand that sin no longer defines you, so you must refuse to embrace the label of something Jesus has already delivered you from.

As long as you accept that you are bound by sin, you will continue to live a life that believes more in your human disposition than in your God-ordained position. And if you believe that is who you are, then—whether you realize it or not—you will begin to live out that belief.

In other words, you will *sin by faith*... simply because you placed your agreement in the wrong thing.

Son, guard your identity. Believe what God says about you, not what religion or guilt tries to label you as. You are a new creation, a son of God, and you will live according to the identity you choose to embrace.

I love you, son. I hope you always know it. —Dad

Deepening Faith and Intimacy with God

CHAPTER THIRTY-TWO
The Power of a Surrendered Will

Son,

Have you ever heard someone say, *"I will do that…"* or *"I won't do that…"*?
Every person surrenders their will to something, and as a result, they face the consequences—good or bad—of the choices they make.

I've often said, *"You don't have to tell me what you believe; your actions speak louder,"* because actions reveal the true condition of the heart. Simply put: your actions expose your will. What you value is displayed not by your words, but by what you consistently do.

The Bible instructs us, *"Submit yourself to God, resist the devil, and he will flee."* (James 4:7) There is divine order in that scripture. First and foremost, we must submit ourselves to God—period. You cannot expect to defeat the devil if you are still in partnership with him. Many people attempt to resist the enemy in their own strength, yet they have not first submitted their desires, attitudes, or decisions to God. This creates a futile battle, because without submission, the power to resist remains locked away.

We see this tension clearly in the life of King David. The same man who conquered Goliath—Israel's greatest external threat—was defeated by Bathsheba, the internal desire he had not surrendered. Our greatest giants are not always "out there." Often, they are the unsurrendered desires within us.

Proverbs 21:21–23 says, *"Whoever pursues righteousness and love will find life, prosperity, and honor. The wise can conquer the strongest city and bring down its defenses. Those who guard their words and actions keep themselves out of trouble."*

Son, every one of us wants to defeat the enemy in our lives. But victory does not begin with trying harder—it begins with surrendering deeper. When you place your will beneath God's will, when you honor His Word above your impulses, when you align your desires with His ways… the battle becomes the Lord's. And when it's His battle, you cannot lose.

Put things in the right order: **Submit first. Resist second. Win always.**

I love you, son. I hope you always know it. —Dad

Discipline, Consistency, and Spiritual Growth

CHAPTER THIRTY-THREE
Go Deep, Son

Son,

When you were very little, you pointed to a magazine on the coffee table and asked, *"Daddy, is that Jesus?"* The cover showed Brian "Head" Welch—a rockstar with tattoos and dreadlocked hair who had radically given his life to Jesus. Without even thinking, I replied, *"Son, that is the only Jesus some people will ever see."* He was using his influence to point people toward Christ.

Every one of us has a choice: live for ourselves or live for something bigger than ourselves. That decision shapes destiny, fulfillment, and impact. Living shallow—living only for yourself—will always leave you feeling empty, especially once you get even a glimpse of what deeper purpose looks like.

I remember driving halfway up the mountain north of Kapalua, Maui, when I spotted a stunning horseshoe-shaped cove. Instantly I said, *"I have to snorkel there!"* We parked along the road, hiked through the trees, and found one of the most breathtaking snorkeling spots I'd ever seen. About 40 yards out, the coral suddenly dropped off, forming 30-foot walls around a basin of bright white sand.

As I floated on the surface, I happened to look straight down... and there, 40 feet below, were two scuba divers exploring the depths.

I wanted to be down there *so badly*. In that moment I decided: I would never again be satisfied with the shallow surface if the deep was possible. I dreamed of it. I envisioned it. I got scuba certified. And the next time I went back—I went deep.

Son, the surface is safe... but the deep is exhilarating. The surface is predictable... but the deep is powerful. The surface is comfortable... but the deep is where your destiny lives.

God has deep things for you—exhilarating, powerful, fulfilling things. But you must choose them. You have to let your mind envision the life you can live, the lives you can touch, and the Kingdom impact you can have when your obedience (your natural) touches His supernatural. That's when miracles happen.

Don't settle. Don't quit. Don't accept a shallow existence when God designed you for depth. People's lives—and their eternal destinies—are waiting on you to show up with courage, boldness, and the fullness of who God created you to be.

You may be the only Jesus they ever see… so show up strong.

Go deep, Son.

I love you, son. I hope you always know it. —Dad

Healing Pain and Growing in Emotional Maturity

CHAPTER THIRTY-FOUR
The Heart of a Warrior

Son,

There are three natural responses to dangerous situations: fight, flight, and freeze. From the time you were old enough to form the words, *"Fight, Daddy, fight,"* your instinct was already clear. Even as a little boy, something in you leaned forward when most people lean back. That wasn't accidental—it was woven into your design.

You are wired to be a warrior.

As a warrior and a future leader, God will require things of you that He may never require from others. When other people face danger and feel permission to run away, God will often call *you* to run directly toward it. And the truth is, deep down, you wouldn't be fulfilled doing anything else. It's who you are. People may look at you and wonder how you carry the strength to confront what they avoid. But you must be careful, son—never judge them for not being built like you. You are wired differently, intentionally, by God. That difference isn't superiority; it's assignment. And with that assignment comes both responsibility and weight.

Yet even warriors must understand this truth: **choose your battles wisely.** Because when your nature is to fight, everything can begin to look like an enemy. To the hammer, everything resembles a nail. There is a time to war and a time to lay down your weapons. A time to speak boldly and a time to keep your mouth shut. A time to advance and a time to wait. And sometimes, those moments are only seconds apart.

There will be seasons when the Holy Spirit is training you in timing, and He will whisper, "WAIT… wait… NOT YET… now." That moment—*now*—is everything. Warriors often struggle not with courage, but with timing. When your instinct is to *charge*, sometimes the most spiritual thing you can do is to *hold, stay still,* and *trust* God's voice even when every part of you wants to fight. Wait for the *now*.

And son, equally important is this: **you must learn to rest in times of peace.** Warriors often feel unsettled when they are not battling something. The quiet can feel foreign, even uncomfortable. But peace is not the absence of purpose. Peace is a different kind of assignment—one that requires you to be present, grateful, and intentional. If you do not learn how to rest, you will eventually burn out in seasons where God intended you to recover.

Every breath you take is a gift. Every person you meet, every place you set your feet, every moment you walk into—there is purpose in all of it when you are led by the Spirit of God. Don't rush past peaceful moments because you're waiting for your next fight. Learn to let the peace of God be as meaningful to you as the battles He calls you to win.

Son, you are a warrior by design, but a son of God by identity. Fight when He says fight. Wait when He says wait. Rest when He gives rest. And lead in every season with wisdom, humility, and courage.

I love you, son. I hope you always know it. —Dad

Your Identity in the Father's Heart

CHAPTER THIRTY-FIVE
The Father Who Dreams Over You

Son,

You couldn't have been two months old yet. I was lying on the floor beside you as you slept, and I began to whisper in your tiny ear all the places I dreamed of taking you one day…

"One day Daddy is going to take you to Hawaii." "One day I'm going to take you scuba diving and snorkeling on the Great Barrier Reef." "One day I'm going to take you to the Great Wall of China."

As you slept, I dreamed about all the incredible experiences I wanted you to have. I imagined the joy of watching you encounter each one for the very first time. Those whispered promises were my heart overflowing with hope for your future.

Today, sitting alone in my office, that memory flooded back to me—so vivid it felt like yesterday. And in the stillness of that moment, I heard *the Father* whisper to my heart:

"The heart of the Father expressed through His child to his child…"

And I knew exactly what He meant:

"Son, that's how I have always felt about you."

Matthew 7:11 reflects this same truth: *"If you want to give good gifts to your children, how much more does your heavenly Father want to give good gifts to His children?"*

Sometimes, when we view Him only as the mighty "God of the universe," we unintentionally lose sight of His more intimate nature—the heart of a loving Father who actually delights in dreaming over His children. He anticipates our joy. He treasures our laughter. He loves to watch us experience the goodness He designed for us.

I'll be honest, I often find myself wrestling with how to reconcile the simplicity and the mystery of this Father/God dynamic. How can the

God who spoke galaxies into existence love me with such personal, fatherly affection? It's almost too much to comprehend. And in my own heart, I can't imagine anyone loving anything more than I love you.

Yet Scripture is clear: **God's love far surpasses our greatest measure of love.** It is deeper, stronger, purer, and more constant than we can fathom.

They didn't understand this about God in Jesus' day—many still don't today. But son, grasping this truth is *foundational* to truly knowing Him. When you understand His love:

—It changes how you approach Him.
—It changes how you serve Him.
—It changes how you see yourself.
—It changes how you love others.
—It changes how boldly you extend faith.
—It changes the impact you leave on the world.

God loves you. He's not mad at you. He dreams over you. He wants good things for you. And He delights in watching you live the life He designed for you.

I love you, son. I hope you always know it. —Dad

Leadership, Authority, and Kingdom Influence

CHAPTER THIRTY-SIX
You're Just the Ass

Son,

I'm going to teach you one of the most important lessons a godly leader can ever learn. When you are called by God to lead people—in whatever arena your calling takes you—there is always a temptation to form a mental image of what "making it" looks like and then become prideful once you feel like you've arrived.

I've seen it in every vocational field I can think of. The waitress becomes the manager and suddenly treats former peers like they're beneath her. The kid who was bullied becomes a police officer, and the authority goes straight to his head. The "extra" finally lands a great role and starts acting as though they're better than everyone else. The pastor who spent years struggling to build a church finally sees growth and instantly assumes that blessing is proof of his superiority and correctness.

Scripture says, *"Pride comes before destruction, and a haughty spirit before a fall."* (Proverbs 16:18) Pride is subtle. It's an effective weapon of the enemy. It quietly creeps in—often riding on the back of insecurity—and convinces a person to adopt a mindset that will ultimately destroy their progress.

If you aren't intentional, pride will sink its claws into even the best of us and deceive us into our own downfall.

No story communicates this truth better than the story of the colt Jesus chose to ride when He entered Jerusalem.

Imagine the "honor" the donkey must have felt being *chosen* by the Master. As he carried Jesus into the city, crowds waved palm branches and laid them at *his* feet. They cheered! They shouted! They sang, "Hosanna!"

How special that donkey must have felt as he began to strut through the celebration. But the moment pride entered and he started to "strut," he revealed the depth of his foolishness. The cheers, the praise, the celebration—it had nothing to do with him.

He was receiving praise that belonged only to the Master.

In his immaturity, the donkey failed to recognize the truth: **he was just the ass the Master chose to ride that day.**

Son, never lose sight of the fact that even your greatest talents are simply an expression of the One who rests His hand upon your life. The calling is honorable—but every gift, every open door, every bit of influence comes from God alone.

Stay humble. Stay grounded. Stay submitted. And remember who the praise actually belongs to.

I love you, son. I hope you always know it. —Dad

Building Godly Character and Integrity

CHAPTER THIRTY-SEVEN
Excellence is your Standard

Son,

Don't settle for average. You're better than that! You'll have no difficulty in life looking around and seeing how easily average people are content to live average lives with average outcomes. You'll notice how some are lazy, unmotivated, or simply indifferent—just getting by. And when you compare your life to theirs, you may be tempted to put in less effort simply because nobody else is striving for excellence. But son, leaders don't settle for average.

There's a scripture that says to *"do all things as unto the Lord."* In essence, it's talking about stewardship—how you conduct your life, your responsibilities, and the opportunities entrusted to you. The parable of the talents makes it unmistakably clear: God is not pleased with the servant who refuses to work, grow, multiply, or increase what he has been given.

Several years ago, I was positioned as an interim pastor while the church searched for their next full-time pastor. I asked God, *"How do You want me to handle this assignment?"* His response was simple and unmistakable: *Treat it like it's yours, and leave it better than you found it.*

Every circumstance and every season offers opportunities to build character, strengthen disciplines, and plant seeds of excellence that will impact your future. Steward those moments well. If you borrow a car, return it in better condition than when you received it—wash it and fill the gas tank. If you commit to something, show up on time and honor your word. Put the grocery cart back where it belongs. Don't drive past a long line of cars waiting to exit and then cut in at the last second. When you complete work, review it—make sure it's excellent, complete, and presentable. Don't leave the small things undone, because the small things reveal the heart behind the big things.

The Bible says that when you're faithful with little, you will be made ruler over much. Excellence matters. Integrity matters. Faithfulness matters. And when you live that way consistently, God Himself will reward you.

Aaron D. Davis

I love you, son. I hope you always know it! —Dad

Building Legacy and Finishing Strong

CHAPTER THIRTY-EIGHT
Intentional Fatherhood

Son,

A few years ago, I was speaking with the teenage son of an executive. I mentioned to him that I try to be very intentional to participate with you in the things you're interested in—even when those things aren't really *my* thing. I explained that what matters to you matters to me simply *because you* care about it.

When I said this, I watched something shift in him. He broke eye contact, looked down, and quietly said, "*I wish my dad would do that...*" His words hit me hard.

One day you'll be a father—and for the record, I believe you will be an amazing one. When that day comes, I want you to consider this truth: **as a parent, you have your entire life to do what *you* like to do.** But your window to invest in your children's world is short. At the time I'm writing this letter, you'll be 18 in three years, and truthfully, I'm already dreading the day I have to miss you as an adult.

As your father, I have not regretted *one single moment* I've prioritized you or spent time appreciating what makes you unique. I determined early that I would not be the dad who looks back wishing he had been more present, trying to make up for lost years once his child is grown.

One day, you'll have your own family. Your time will be divided. Your responsibilities will increase. Your priorities will shift—as they should. But this season right now? This time of watching you grow, discovering what you love, pursuing what you're passionate about... that is a gift I refuse to take for granted.

When you look back on your childhood, I want your memories to be filled with the reassurance that your father supported your passions, encouraged your dreams, and showed up as often as he possibly could. Whether or not you remember every moment, *I will*.

Live with that same intentionality when you have a family of your own. I promise you—you will never regret choosing presence over

Aaron D. Davis

preference, investment over convenience, and love over busyness.

I love you, son. I hope you always know it. —Dad

Leadership, Authority, and Kingdom Influence

CHAPTER THIRTY-NINE
People Before Process

Son,

You are a natural-born leader. Your whole life, people have watched you, followed you, and taken their cues from you. From a very young age, it was evident that leadership is wired into your DNA. But hear me clearly—*natural-born leadership is not enough to lead well.* You must intentionally decide the kind of leader you want to be and consistently audit your own heart to make sure you're living up to that standard.

There's an old saying: **"People before process."**

When you lead, there will always be a temptation to let people pour themselves out as much as possible to accomplish *your* vision. But true leadership prioritizes people above the process. Look out for them and their well-being. Don't use people. Don't take advantage of them. Don't see them as beneath you simply because they follow your lead.

The truth is, people can be a blessing to you—and you can be a blessing to them—but *only* if you lead well.

Far too often, what is modeled as "leadership" in the world looks more like using people as stepping stones, leaving behind exhausted, resentful hearts in the wake of achievement. That is not the Godly model of leadership.

Jesus changed the world, but He did it while prioritizing people—seeing them as the beloved children of God they are. His influence didn't rise from using people, but from valuing them.

Son, be known as a wise leader who treats people honorably. Protect them, empower them, and lift them. Let the way you lead reflect the heart of Jesus, and you will not only accomplish great things—you will shape people's lives in the process.

I love you, son. I hope you always know it. —Dad

Discipline, Consistency, and Spiritual Growth

CHAPTER FORTY
The Wisdom of Right Now

Son,

This scripture from Proverbs 10 jumped off the page at me today: *"KNOW the importance of the season you're in and a wise son you will be. But what a waste when an incompetent son sleeps through his day of opportunity!"* (TPT)

It amazes me how easy it is to lose sight of *right now*. Most people live trapped somewhere between yesterday's regrets and tomorrow's worries, and because of that, they miss the opportunity that is standing right in front of them today. But wisdom is learning to recognize the weight of the present moment—the one moment you actually have the authority to shape.

Even when you don't fully understand *why* a particular season matters, you need to be intentional to look for purpose in it. If you aren't watching for it, you'll overlook it. And missing what God is trying to show you today is one of the most unnecessary losses a man can experience.

You will never have today again. Today is the only place where faith can be acted on, where choices can be made, and where growth actually happens. Don't throw away the power of today because your mind is stuck replaying yesterday—or trying to live in a future that hasn't arrived.

Matthew 6 says it this way: *"So above all, constantly seek God's kingdom and His righteousness, then all these less important things will be given to you abundantly. Refuse to worry about tomorrow, but deal with each challenge that comes your way, one day at a time. Tomorrow will take care of itself."* (TPT)

God is faithful. He is already in your tomorrow, but He meets you *in* your today. Trust Him with what's ahead, honor Him with what's in front of you, and He will guide every step.

I love you, son. I hope you always know it. —Dad

Leadership, Authority, and Kingdom Influence

CHAPTER FORTY-ONE
"Who" You Ask? They.

Son,

In 1938, a comedy duo named Abbott and Costello released a baseball sketch called **"Who's on First?"**—a routine that *Time Magazine* later called the greatest comedy sketch of the 20th century. In the skit, "Who" is on first, "What" is on second, and "I Don't Know" is on third. The audience understands these are the actual names of the players, but the duo ends up in a hysterical wordplay argument because Costello thinks Abbott is asking questions rather than stating names. (Look it up on YouTube—it's worth watching.)

I remembered that sketch—one I watched with my own father when I was little—when this thought dropped in my heart for you: *"Son, They are waiting for you to lead them."*

Who, you ask…? *They*. Right now, "They" are faceless, but make no mistake—they are real. They're waiting for you to step into your calling. They will remain faceless until you accept your role in their story. There's a phrase your grandfather used to tell me growing up: *"When the student is ready, the teacher arrives."* In parallel, I would say to you: *when you accept your responsibility to lead, "They" will come.* And when they come, remember—every deed is a seed. Someone is always watching, and what you model will matter more than you realize.

As I discussed in an earlier letter, when you were about three years old, you saw a magazine on my table with Brian Welch on the cover—a rockstar who had radically given his life to God. You pointed to the picture and asked, *"Daddy, is that Jesus?"* I answered, *"Son, that is the only Jesus some people may ever see."* You were too young to grasp the depth of that statement then, but it remains true today.

In almost every environment you step into throughout your life, someone— *"they"*—will be present who needs to encounter the Jesus in you. Romans 10 puts it this way: *"How will THEY call on Him in whom THEY have not believed? How will THEY believe in Him whom THEY have not heard? And how will THEY hear without a preacher?"* Whether you realize it or not, someone in the room is looking for a leader. You are that leader. And *they* are waiting.

Lead well.

I love you, son. I hope you always know it. —Dad

Mastering Your Mind and Inner World

CHAPTER FORTY-TWO
Choose To Sow Life

Son,

Sowing and reaping is a very real thing.

People will misuse you at times. They'll take what they need, speak highly of you while it benefits them, and then distance themselves or discard you when they're finished. When their motives finally become clear, it hurts—it really hurts. These are the challenges of living in a world where people's integrity, values, and character won't always match yours.

But hear me clearly: **live with integrity anyway.**

There is a spiritual law woven into the fabric of the universe called **sowing and reaping**. Scripture says in Galatians, *"God is not mocked. Whatever a man sows, that is what he will reap."* This is inevitable. It applies to *them*, and it applies to *you*.

How others treat you will return to them, for better or worse. But how you choose to respond also plants seeds that will produce a harvest in your own future. If you choose kindness instead of bitterness… peace instead of strife… love instead of retaliation… obedience instead of emotional impulse… you will reap the fruit of those choices. So be intentional.

A few years ago, I was deeply wounded by someone I cared for immensely. I had never experienced that kind of betrayal and pain before. I was angry, heartbroken, confused, and grieving. And to make it even more difficult, I had to help address—spiritually and practically—the very behaviors that had hurt me so badly. I hadn't healed. I was still bleeding inside.

So I reached out to a minister friend for a perspective outside my pain. His words were simple but life-changing: *"If you are not careful, you can do the right thing from the wrong place in your heart. Whatever you do, make sure you do it in love."*

That sentence echoed inside me for weeks. Every time my emotions tried to drag me backward, I pulled myself forward and chose love again. It wasn't easy. It took real effort, real intentionality. And while I'm not sure I got it perfect, I know I kept redirecting my heart toward love every time it drifted.

Son, life will give you many opportunities to choose blessing or cursing… life or death… love or retaliation. **Choose life. Choose love.** It will always produce the better harvest.

I love you, son. I hope you always know it. —Dad

Building Godly Character and Integrity

CHAPTER FORTY-THREE
Listen For the Lesson

Son,

The Bible says there is wisdom in a multitude of counselors. This morning, I was speaking with your grandfather, and he shared something he felt God was teaching him as he watched a program on TV. As he explained what he felt God was revealing to him and the parallels in life, he paused and said to me, *"I wish I had better words, like you, to convey what God was showing me, but I just have a hard time explaining it."* Unbeknownst to him, I had been thinking moments before, *Where do thoughts like his even come from? I would have never seen that parallel with as much insight or wisdom.*

When I was a young man, I genuinely thought I knew more than those who had trailblazed before me. In my heart, I believed their perspectives and lenses were dated—even irrelevant to what God was doing *"today."* I know now that was a huge miss, influenced only by my inexperience and naivete.

While it is true that some of the *"boomers"* (as I've heard you call them—us) can have ideals that are rigid or archaic, especially when they are deeply rooted in a legalistic, religious spirit, there is still something those old-timers have that you don't: insight that is only revealed by experiences seasoned with time. The only way you will ever learn what they know is to either get old yourself or be willing to put your own thoughts, pride, and lack of experience aside and ***listen for the lesson.***

Sometimes the lesson is hidden in a glance of the eyes or a tear as they recall a memory—pay attention. Sometimes it's disguised in many words as they struggle to express something that feels just out of reach—be patient and listen for what's not being said. Sometimes the lesson only begins with their words as a catalyst, and the Holy Spirit takes that lesson to the next level—don't disregard it.

When someone who has many more years of experience than you takes the time to share what they've learned and what they know is important for you to hear, *listen for the lesson.* Don't just hear out of obligation or polite respect. With full intentionality, focus on what they are saying and learn the lesson God will speak to you through those who have gone before you.

I love you, son. I hope you always know it. —Dad

Building Legacy and Finishing Strong

CHAPTER FORTY-FOUR
Training Them to Live Without You

Son,

Since you were a little boy, whenever I had to teach you a difficult lesson, I would tell your mother, *"I'm not just raising a child, I'm training a man."* Recently, I came across a parallel quote that struck me deeply: *"Parenting is training the one person you would never want to live without… to live without you."* I always knew this was true, but I'd never heard it expressed so simply and so accurately.

Being your father, and having the privilege of raising you, is one of the greatest joys of my life. Of all the titles I've ever carried, **"Dad" is my favorite.** Psalm 127:3 says, "Children are a gift from the Lord," and in every stage of your life, that has proven true.

My encouragement for your future is this: in every season, be intentional to be present and grateful for the time you have. It will pass far faster than you expect, and you cannot get it back. Don't let your attention be consumed by things—work, responsibilities, pressure, or even people—that are not as important as your family. I can't tell you how many men I've heard express deep regret because they prioritized what they *did* over who they *were* as fathers… and lost what mattered most. Money can provide opportunities, but it does not secure your legacy. The greatest resource you will ever give your family is your love—expressed through your time, your consistency, and your intentional presence. A good father impacts his children far more through his example than through his earnings.

I've watched you step out of the role of "child" and grow confidently into the man God created you to be, and I want you to know I am genuinely proud of you. Keep putting God first in every area of your life—your character, your decisions, your future family—and the blessing of the Lord will follow you through every season.

I love you, son. I hope you always know it. —Dad

Leadership, Authority, and Kingdom Influence

CHAPTER FORTY-FIVE
Famous to Me

Son,

So many perspectives weren't clear to me until I became a father. I didn't understand the weight of responsibility to do the right thing or lead you in the right direction. I didn't understand the pain I would feel when you hurt. I simply couldn't comprehend the joy that would come from doing simple things—wrestling on the floor, teaching you to ride a skateboard, or watching you compete in sports.

I never understood how just hearing you laugh could lift my spirit, or how having you lay your head in my lap could bring peace when my world felt chaotic. So many things made more sense to me once I became a father... especially love. There's just no perspective that compares to the love you feel when you're a dad.

As my absolute favorite athlete, musician, actor, student, and person—no matter what level you eventually reach—you are already, and will always be, **famous to me**. I could not be more proud or more excited to see you step into your destiny and become who you were created to be. I am your biggest fan.

I'd be willing to pay any price to help you live your dreams. As your father, my hope is that my ceiling becomes your floor—that you go further, climb higher, and experience more than I ever have. I would sacrifice my ambitions to see you live yours. I would fight to defend you. I would lay down my life without hesitation to save yours.

Why? Because you are my son, and I love you.

Understanding the love of a father—*as* a father—has given me more insight into the nature of God than anything else in my life. Matthew 7:11 (TPT) says, *"If you, imperfect as you are, know how to lovingly take care of your children and give them what's best, how much more ready is your heavenly Father to give wonderful gifts to those who ask Him?"*

I'm more convinced than ever that God desires a close, personal relationship with us as a Father. I didn't fully understand it before, but

I do a lot more now. If I, in all my imperfections, can love you this deeply, then imagine the magnitude of God's love for you. Don't ever let anyone or anything convince you otherwise.

I love you, son. I hope you always know it. —Dad

Mastering Your Mind and Inner World

CHAPTER FORTY-SIX
What's In Your Hand?

Son,

You don't have to wait until everything is perfect to make a difference. In fact, that mindset probably robs more people of blessing than anything else. Waiting for ideal conditions usually means doing nothing—and *nothing* cannot be multiplied. Zero times infinity is still zero. A seed that stays in your hand can never produce a harvest, even though its potential is limitless. The question is rarely *can* you make a difference, but *will* you.

God has a way of empowering and multiplying whatever you are willing to surrender to Him.

In Scripture, when God asked Moses to do something that looked impossible, Moses started making excuses. But God interrupted him with one simple question: *"What's in your hand?"* All Moses had was a shepherd's staff—ordinary, unimpressive, insignificant. But when he released it to God, that simple staff became a tool heaven used to part seas, confront kings, and deliver nations. God took something natural and put His *super* on it. And when God puts His super on your natural, the result is limitless.

So, Son—**what's in your hand today?** What do you already carry that seems too small to matter? What skill, gift, resource, opportunity, or moment can you surrender to God *right now*? Don't wait for something bigger. Don't wait for something easier. Don't wait for *"one day."*

Obedience is better than delay disguised as preparation.

If you wait until you feel like you have *"enough for God to use,"* you've forgotten the nature of the One who fed thousands with a kid's lunch. God multiplies what is surrendered. He breathes on whatever you make available.

Walk by faith, not by sight. Faith is the catalyst for the miraculous.

And when your hands feel empty, remember—if the Spirit of God lives in you, you still have something to give. A word of encouragement. A prayer. A blessing. A moment of compassion. These aren't small things—they are supernatural seeds that God loves to multiply.

Just put something in His hands… and watch what He does with it.

I love you, son. I hope you always know it. —Dad

Deepening Faith and Intimacy with God

CHAPTER FORTY-SEVEN
God of the Watch

Son,

I've always liked watches. Honestly, it's dangerous for me to walk through a jewelry department because if a watch jumps off the shelf at me, I might end up taking it home. A few years ago, I was passing by the counter when a six-foot display caught my eye. It was a blown-up image of one of the best-looking watches I had ever seen—gunmetal gray with just a few touches of blue on the second hand and some of the chronograph details. It stopped me in my tracks.

I immediately told the salesperson, "*I want to see that watch!*" She pulled it out of the case, and as I tried it on, the price tag slid down and dangled from the band. My heart sank. It was way out of my price range. Truthfully, in that season *anything* was out of my price range. But man... that watch was sharp. I handed it back, walked past the display again, pulled out my phone, took a picture of it—and then life went on. I completely forgot about it.

A few months later I was meeting my friend Greg for lunch. The second he walked in, I noticed his watch—like I said, I like watches. He sat down and said, "*I just left the jewelry store and got this new watch!*" Then he took it off and handed it to me so I could get a closer look.

"*That's a good-looking watch, Greg,*" I said.

But as I handed it back, his whole expression shifted. He hesitated for a moment and then said, almost reluctantly, "*God just told me... that's your watch. I bought it for you, not me.*" I argued with him for a minute, but in the end, I walked out of that restaurant wearing his brand-new watch.

A couple of weeks later, I walked past that same jewelry counter at the mall. The same six-foot display was still there. It caught my eye again—only this time something clicked. I looked down at my wrist...

That was the same watch. The exact watch I took a picture of months before.

I had forgotten all about it… but *God hadn't*.

Son, here's the lesson: **God cares enough to watch the little things.** Sometimes life makes us feel unseen or overlooked, but heaven is never indifferent. God sees. God remembers. God cares. His eye is on the sparrow—and the same Scripture (Matthew 6:26–34) says you matter far more to Him than that.

God's got you. He sees you. He loves you. And so do I. I hope you always know it.—Dad

Deepening Faith and Intimacy with God

CHAPTER FORTY-EIGHT
God of the Watch — Part 2

Son,

Make giving your lifestyle. Scripture teaches, *"Obedience is better than sacrifice,"* meaning this: always do what God directs you to do—even when it's uncomfortable, costly, or doesn't make sense to anyone else. No harvest ever grows without a seed being planted.

For years now, I've worn a watch that holds deep sentimental value. The story behind it made it one of my most treasured possessions (go back and read "God of the Watch" for the full story). But here's the short version:

I once saw that watch in a store—sleek, beautiful, and nearly $1,000. Way beyond my budget at the time. Days later, I felt God prompt me to give my current watch to a man who admired it. I obeyed. A few weeks after that, a friend walked into our lunch meeting straight from the jewelry store with a new watch on his wrist. He handed it to me to look at, paused, and with a stunned expression said, *"God just told me this isn't my watch—I bought it for you."* It was the exact watch I had admired.

That moment marked me. On some of my hardest days, just seeing that watch reminded me that **God sees me** and He is always faithful.

This week, I saw a man I only encounter every year or two. But the last two times I've seen him, I've felt God say, *"Give him your watch."* I wrestled with it—because he collects luxury watches worth far more than mine. It felt embarrassing, like giving a used Honda to the owner of a Ferrari dealership. And honestly, if he had offered to trade me one of his expensive watches for mine, I would have refused because the sentimental value of mine was priceless.

But God pressed on my heart again: **"It's not about him. It's about you. He's good soil—SOW THE WATCH."**

So the next time I saw him, I placed the watch in his hand.

Son, here's the lesson: **Your job is not to understand—your job is to obey.** Give when God says give. Sow when He says sow. Act when you feel His nudge, even when logic argues against it. God is faithful, and obedience always produces a harvest.

Plant the seed.

I love you, son. I hope you always know it. —Dad

Deepening Faith and Intimacy with God

CHAPTER FORTY-NINE
God Is Still Good

Son,

Sometimes we do everything we know to do, and the circumstances still don't end the way we expected or hoped they would. **God is still good.**

Sometimes we walk through pain that has absolutely nothing to do with anything we caused or contributed to. **God is still good.**

Sometimes we mess everything up and make choices that cost us far more than we ever wanted to pay. **God is still good.**

Sometimes bad things happen, and it feels painfully unfair. **God is still good.**

Sometimes our heart breaks, and God feels distant. But even then, He is still there—and **He is still good.**

In the middle of darkness, disappointment, or deep confusion, it can be extremely difficult to perceive God's love or His goodness. But regardless of how it *feels*, you must anchor yourself in this truth: **God is still good, and He loves you very much.**

Your faith must be bigger than your feelings. Your faith must be rooted deeper than your circumstances.

Everyone—without exception—will have opportunities for their faith to be tested. Life will make sure of it. And your enemy, who wants to see you lose, will make sure of it too. But you, son... you must dig deep, stand firm, and hold fast to the truth no matter what life throws at you:

God. Is. Always. Good.

You will not always understand the *"why"* or the *"why not"* behind the pain you experience, but I promise you this: **none of it is ever the result of a lack of God's goodness.**

We live in a fallen world. You have a real enemy who comes to steal, kill, and destroy. Sometimes you will get blindsided and never fully understand how it happened. **But God is still good.**

And when you are hurting—when confusion or grief hits so hard that you don't even know what to pray—don't run *from* God. **Run to Him.**

I've watched many believers walk through discouragement, disappointment, and disillusionment, and then turn on God in bitterness because they assumed their pain was God's failure. But over the years (through a lot of my own pain), I've learned this: things are rarely as they appear, and many times, my assumptions were wrong.

We simply don't see the whole picture from here.

Son, even if you live to be a hundred, that long life is still only a blink compared to eternity. People place far too much weight on this temporary sliver of time we call *"life,"* as if it is all there is. They treat death as final—but neither of those perspectives are true.

Don't let your heart grow cold toward God over things you don't yet understand during such a short season of existence. There is so much more ahead—more to learn, more to discover, more to experience, and far more joy than this world could ever offer.

Keep your eyes on eternity, son. That's the real prize.

I love you so much! I hope you always know it. -Dad

Wisdom, Discernment, and Godly Decisions

CHAPTER FIFTY
Choose Your Counsel Wisely

Son,

The advice you take to heart can make you—or it can break you. That's one of the reasons I love reading Proverbs. It's packed with wisdom that can save you from a lifetime of unnecessary pain. Proverbs 15:22 (KJV) says, *"Without counsel purposes are disappointed, but in the multitude of counselors there is safety."* That one verse has kept me steady through more seasons than I can count.

I believe I'll be around for a very long time to offer you sound, honest, level-headed feedback whenever you need it. But if, for some reason, life doesn't allow that, you must be intentional about who you allow to speak into your life. Not everyone who offers advice should be listened to, and very few people are as wise as they make themselves out to be.

If your buddy has never walked through what you're facing, navigated it successfully, and come out on top, he's not the voice you need in that moment. He might be a good friend, but if he hasn't lived it, he can't lead you in it. And when the blind lead the blind, somebody ends up in traffic.

When you need clarity or direction, there are **three primary sources of counsel** you should keep close:

1. The Holy Spirit. He will reveal things you have no natural way of knowing—especially when a decision is important. Pay attention to peace. Peace is often the place where the Holy Spirit speaks most clearly and quietly. He often leads you with the *"gut feeling"* of peace.

2. The Word of God. Scripture is full of wisdom, direction, and correction. If wisdom is what you're after, Proverbs is a gold mine. The Bible will keep your heart aligned and your steps steady in alignment with God's will for your life.

3. Wise Counsel with Like Values. Talk to people who have been through similar battles, who carry experience, maturity, and success—and **who share your values**. That last one is crucial. There's more than one way to accomplish a goal, but don't ever compromise your integrity to get there. Plenty of people have become millionaires by stepping on others to climb higher. That's not your path, and someone with that heart will steer you wrong.

Seek first God's way of doing things. Trust in the Lord with all your heart. Follow peace. Surround yourself with wise people who love God and live with integrity—and He will make your path straight.

I love you, son. I hope you always know it. —Dad

Leadership, Authority, and Kingdom Influence

CHAPTER FIFTY-ONE
Include God in the Fight

Son,

For years I lived with a mindset of, *"I'm smart enough, I'm wise enough, I'm strong enough."* But after a lifetime of fighting from that perspective, I've learned the hard way that as long as I rely only on myself—my strength, my logic, my abilities—I'm setting myself up for disappointment and disillusionment. Eventually every man reaches the end of his own capacity. And nothing reveals our insufficiency faster than the moments when we try to be "enough" and fall flat on our face.

You were never meant to fight alone. You *can't* be enough without God—and you don't have to be.

If you need wisdom, His Word says to ask, and He will give it generously.
If you need peace, He provides a peace that doesn't even make sense.
If you need strength, He empowers you to do all things *through* Him—not through yourself.

The key is this: invite Him into the fight before the battle even starts. Most people only turn to God when the weight becomes unbearable, but He was never meant to be your last resort. Scripture says to *seek first* God's way of doing things, and *then* everything else will fall into place. That is a divine order—one that never fails.

If you insist on fighting in your own strength, your ceiling will always be limited by your natural ability. But when you humble yourself, when you ask God for direction *first*, you open the door for supernatural intervention and results that could never be accomplished by your strength alone.

Make it a habit to talk to God about *everything,* son—the small things and the big things. Nothing is too insignificant for Him, and nothing is too overwhelming for Him. He sees what you can't. He knows what you don't. And He will lead you further than your own strength ever could.

I love you, son. I hope you always know it. —Dad

Wisdom, Discernment, and Godly Decisions

CHAPTER FIFTY-TWO
Relationships Will Make or Break You

Son,

A mentor of mine used to say, *"When God wants to bless you, He will send a relationship into your life... and when the devil wants to distract you, he will send a relationship into your life."* I've also heard some of the most successful people in the world say, *"The key to success is not what you know, but who."*

Who you choose to walk with can build you—or break you. Aside from your relationship with God, I'm convinced the most important decisions you will ever make revolve around who you surround yourself with.

The Bible warns us clearly: **"Bad company corrupts good morals."** — 1 Corinthians 15:33 **"Guard your heart above all things."** —Proverbs 4:23

As a pastor who has counseled countless people, I can tell you that the relationship with the greatest power to bring pleasure—or bring pain—is the one you choose to love and eventually marry.

I remember a young man I once knew. The first time I saw a picture he posted of the woman he was dating, I thought, *"Wow, she's beautiful!"* On a superficial one to ten *"looks"* scale, she was an eleven! I could understand why he was drawn to her.

They married, had children, and then life took a devastating turn. I don't know every detail, but I do know she kept his kids from him and, when he fought for them, accused him of something horrific. He is in prison today because of those accusations. He denies them, and those close to the situation—people I trust—believe wholeheartedly he is innocent.

If he could speak to you today, I'm convinced he would say: **"Your relationships can destroy you. Choose wisely."**

Son, God knows the desires of your heart, and He delights in blessing His children. He will send the right people into your life—people who build you, strengthen you, sharpen you, and walk with you. But you must be patient enough not to settle for anything less than His best.

Matthew 6:33 says: *"Seek first God's way of doing and being, and everything else will be added to you."*

When you rush God's timing, you end up birthing an *"Ishmael"*—like Abraham did. When you are blinded by beauty or desire, you end up like Samson—betrayed and literally blinded because he ignored the warning signs. When jealousy is allowed into the heart, you see the tragedy of Cain and Abel. When insecurity rules a person, you see Saul attacking David without cause. When someone chooses ungodly relationships, even the wisest man in the world—Solomon—had his faith and destiny corrupted.

I could list example after example.

I've heard it quoted many times that Jim Rohn said, *"You become the average of the five people you spend the most time with."* If that's true, then be extremely intentional with your inner circle. Prioritize close relationships with people who share your convictions, your values, and your vision. Be kind and gracious toward those who don't—but keep them at a wise distance.

The right relationships will build your life. The wrong ones can unravel everything.

Choose wisely, Son.

I love you, son. I hope you always know it. —Dad

Discipline, Consistency, and Spiritual Growth

CHAPTER FIFTY-THREE
See Beyond What You See

Son,

What we see with our natural eyes influences so much of how we respond. But if you only rely on your five senses to discern what's happening, you'll misperceive situations, misdiagnose problems, and ultimately miss the greater truth.

Scripture tells us plainly that **we do not wrestle against flesh and blood**. That means what you see in the physical almost always has a spiritual catalyst behind it. But most people respond only to the physical symptom and never discern the spiritual root. That's one of the enemy's greatest deceptions.

Something happens in the natural... You *see* it... Your emotions react... And then you respond physically—never realizing the real issue wasn't physical at all.

This is why 2 Corinthians 10 reminds us that **the weapons of our warfare are not physical**, but mighty through God. The first battleground is the mind—casting down thoughts, imaginations, and internal narratives that don't align with the Kingdom of God. What looks like a physical battle is often a spiritual one, and if you don't discern that, you'll fight the wrong enemy.

If you believe the deception, you empower the deceiver. (If you believe the lie, you empower the liar.)

Jesus told us in Luke 10 that He has given us **power over all the works of the enemy**. But Son, you can't exercise that authority if you're aiming at the wrong target. Most people have no idea they're being influenced, manipulated, or puppeted by spiritual realities behind the scenes. If we don't shine a light on that truth, many will live their entire lives fighting shadows, never realizing God has more for them.

It's God's perfect **love** that casts out fear.
It's the **measure of faith** He gave you that helps you overcome.
It's His **peace and joy** that strengthen you.

It's His **goodness and patience** that break the power of sin.

These are spiritual tools—fruits of the Spirit—not physical weapons. And you'll never walk in victory if you try to fight spiritual battles with physical responses.

Son, the real battle is almost **never** as it appears on the physical surface. See clearly. Discern deeply. Respond spiritually.

I love you, son. I hope you always know it. —Dad

Resisting Comparison and Cultural Pressures

CHAPTER FIFTY-FOUR
Don't Compare Your Way into Compromise

Son,

I've seen many over the years excuse their ungodly behavior with something like, *"I know what I'm doing isn't right, but everyone I know is doing things worse than what I'm doing…and they look like they are doing fine."*

There will always be a temptation to compare your choices to the actions of people whose behavior is worse and then use that comparison as justification—almost as if sin is graded on a curve and God determines righteousness by looking at the person next to you.

But that's not how it works. Comparison is one of the enemy's most subtle traps, because it convinces you that compromise is harmless. It whispers, *"At least you're not as bad as them,"* while quietly coaxing you into planting seeds that will eventually produce a destructive harvest.

Son, you must understand this: **your harvest is not determined by someone else's seed in someone else's field.** When sin matures, *you* will deal with the consequences—not the person you compared yourself to. That's why comparison is such a deceptive bait. It lulls you into believing the seed won't grow, that the compromise won't catch up to you. But a seed ignored still sprouts, and sin unaddressed always matures.

God's grace toward you is limitless, but there is still a standard—and it is found only in the Word of God.

This is why the enemy pushes compromise so aggressively. He knows that even **small compromises, repeated and watered over time, grow into significant destruction.**

Two scriptures make this clear:

- *"The wages of sin is death."* — Romans 6:23
- *"Faith without works is dead."* — James 2:14–26

Sin produces death. Grace produces freedom. Both bondage and freedom are rooted in choices we make.

Choose freedom, Son.

Choose obedience. Choose the path that leads to life.

Prioritize God first in your life, and everything else will fall into place.

I love you, son. I hope you always know it. —Dad

Leadership, Authority, and Kingdom Influence

CHAPTER FIFTY-FIVE
The Leadership That Washes Feet

Son,

I read a meme today that said, *"If I knew today was my last day, what would I do?"* Then came the line that really struck me: *"Jesus knew His last day... and He washed feet."* The natural comparison is obvious—if Jesus is our example, then our highest aim should always be to become more like Him.

Many years ago, I was leading an incredible team of people. Every Monday morning we'd cram into my office for a time of teaching and discussion—call it a devotion, a meeting, or just a moment of sharpening. But during that particular season, everything felt uncertain. Honestly, each week I wondered if this would be the last chance I had to pour into those men and women.

So every Monday, before I walked into that room, I asked myself: *"If today is your last opportunity to influence your team, what leadership lesson matters most... what would you want to model?"*

I've made a lot of mistakes in leadership. I've learned from both the good and the bad, and—if I'm honest—I've learned *as much about what NOT to do* from many leaders I've served under as I have from what *TO* do. Because of that, I always tried to lead from a posture of security, balance, and honor. I tried to protect my team when I could and empower their gifts whenever possible. I didn't always get it perfect, but I tried.

When I read that meme today—*"He washed feet"*—it reminded me of a particular Monday morning years ago when I felt the Lord say, *"That's the lesson today."* And Son, I truly believed that week might have been my last chance to speak into my team.

So I grabbed a bowl, a towel, and—just as Jesus did—I knelt down and washed their feet.

Not as a performance. Not as a gimmick. But as a living picture of what leadership is supposed to be.

I wanted them to remember that the greatest leadership is not standing above people but kneeling below them. It's not demanding honor but giving it. It's not being served—it's serving.

Son, God calls leaders to **serve** people, not to rule over them. But too often leaders forget this. They see themselves as the pinnacle—the top of the pyramid. But Jesus flipped that pyramid upside down. His shoulders carried the weight of everyone above Him.

In the Kingdom of God, the higher you rise, the more you serve. The greater your influence, the heavier your responsibility to lift others. The more authority you carry, the more grace you're called to extend.

This is the leadership model that transforms lives.
This is the leadership that reflects Christ.
This is the leadership I pray you choose.

Be a man who washes feet… even on your *"last day."*

I love you, son. I hope you always know it. —Dad

Building Godly Character and Integrity

CHAPTER FIFTY-SIX
It's So Much Harder to Keep Your Mouth Shut Than It Is to Fight

Son,

HEARTBROKEN is the only word I can use to describe the pain I felt. I've wanted to write this lesson to you for a long time because I knew it belonged in these letters, but I simply couldn't find the right words without risking dishonoring anyone. Today, I believe I finally have some clarity. The details are irrelevant but the lesson is vital.

There were only a handful of people who knew the full story. Your mother once asked me if I would tell her everything, and I told her I couldn't. Not because I wanted to hide anything, but because revealing the whole truth would have unnecessarily tainted her perspective of those involved—far beyond where it already was—and it would have violated confidences I refused to betray. She knew enough, but not everything, and I wasn't willing to destroy others with my words.

During that season, people who knew only fragments—pieces fed to them by others or assumptions built on partial information—judged me harshly. They spoke badly of my character because they believed the narrative they had been handed. Some thought I should have done something they *believed* I didn't do. Others thought I shouldn't have done something they *believed* I did. The hardest part? None of them knew what they didn't know. Even some who were closest to the situation didn't know the full story they were convinced they understood.

In just a few paragraphs of explanation, I could have completely vindicated myself. I could have restored my reputation, silenced the lies, corrected the rumors, and shut down every false assumption.

And that would have been the easy road.

But I refused—because to defend myself publicly, I would have had to wound other people publicly. I would have had to expose details that would harm them, and even if they were wrong, I wasn't willing to do that. Not even to save my own reputation.

As I've told you your whole life: ***integrity is what you do when no one is watching.*** And even if no one else knew the truth, *I* knew. *God* knew. And I maintained my integrity through the entire ordeal.

Did it cost me? Yes.
It cost me relationships.
It cost me influence.
It cost me opportunities.
It cost me pain—deep, gut-level pain.
But the one thing it did *not* cost me was my integrity.

And Son, that mattered more than anything else.

Would I have preferred a different outcome? Absolutely. But keeping my integrity was worth the cost—even though it was incredibly hard.

The truth is, it's usually much harder to keep your mouth shut than it is to fight. But wisdom is often found in restraint.

There are layers of lessons and life parallels woven into every paragraph of this letter. The ability to share them with you came at a great personal cost, and the truths they reveal about integrity rise above any single circumstance. Learn from it. Glean from it. Build on it.

You are amazing, and I'm so proud of the man you're becoming. I pray my ceiling becomes your floor.

I love you, son. I hope you always know it. —Dad

Healing Pain and Growing in Emotional Maturity

CHAPTER FIFTY-SEVEN
Don't Let Pain Set the Ceiling of Your Faith

Son,

A couple of days ago I was talking with a friend, and I told him something I've realized over the years: ***most people have already set the ceiling of their faith because they refuse to pursue deeper understanding when challenges come.***

Instead of seeking God for clarity or wisdom, they default to the belief that whatever happens must simply be "the sovereign will of God." It becomes a passive, *que sera sera* approach to life—*"whatever will be, will be."* And son, I believe that mindset keeps countless people living far beneath what God intends for them.

Scripture says, *"If anyone lacks wisdom, let him ask of God, who gives freely."*
Nothing exposes where we need wisdom like pain. Pain confronts us. Pain reveals gaps in our understanding. And pain often becomes the place where people create entire belief systems about what is or isn't possible.

If someone goes through something devastating and walks away convinced that situations *"like that"* are hopeless, then that belief becomes the new boundary of their faith. From that point forward, their expectation of what God can do is limited by their past disappointment.

Son, I am convinced that faith is a real force—just as real as gravity. It's woven into the fabric of how God designed the world. Faith has the ability to defy logic, shift outcomes, and collapse the space between what looks impossible and what God says is possible.

But Scripture also says that ***faith is the substance of things hoped for.*** So hear this: **If you decide something is hopeless, you've already shut the door on activating faith in that area.** Your faith won't reach for what your heart doesn't believe is possible.

Most people don't pursue answers because they don't expect any. Pain told them a story, and they accepted it as final. But disappointment should never have the last word—God should.

So when life doesn't go the way you expected, don't let pain define your future. Don't sacrifice hope on the altar of discouragement. Instead, press into God and ask Him *"why,"* not from a place of accusation, but from a desire to understand. Let Him expand your faith instead of letting pain shrink it.

Let God and His Word—not hurt—set the ceiling of your expectations.

I love you, son. I hope you always know it. —Dad

Discipline, Consistency, and Spiritual Growth

CHAPTER FIFTY-EIGHT
Make Decisions in Faith, Not Fear

Son,

I want you to think about something: **Does a poor decision made in faith have more potential for success than a good decision made in doubt and unbelief?**

I've watched so many people get stuck in life because they are terrified of making the *wrong* choice. They freeze. They hesitate. They wait... and wait... and wait—until opportunity passes them by. They convince themselves they're being *"wise,"* when really, they're being paralyzed by fear.

Now, don't misunderstand me—you should always seek God's wisdom. You should listen to wise counsel and take time to pray. But if the only reason you're making *no* decision is because you're afraid of making the wrong one, then fear—not faith—is leading you.

And son, fear is a terrible leader.

I can't help but wonder if sometimes a *less-than-perfect* decision made with genuine faith might carry more blessing than what appears to be a *"good"* decision made in doubt, hesitation, and unbelief. Faith moves mountains. Faith activates God's promises. Faith steps into the unknown trusting that God will meet you there.

The Bible tells us plainly: **We walk by faith, not by sight.**

Faith doesn't guarantee that everything will be easy—but it positions you for God to guide your steps. Fear guarantees nothing except missed opportunities and a life lived smaller than what God intended.

Son, press past fear. Don't let it dictate your choices or shrink your future. Make decisions with a heart that's leaning toward God, not away from Him. If you move forward in faith, even if it's imperfect, God has room to direct you, correct you, and bless you.

I love you, son. I hope you always know it. —Dad

Building Godly Character and Integrity

CHAPTER FIFTY-NINE
Be A Man of Integrity

Son,

There was a time when a man could look another man in the eyes, make a commitment, and it *meant* something. A time when a handshake was as binding as any contract. A time when a man would defend his reputation if someone even insinuated, he was a liar. There was a time when integrity mattered.

Actions reveal nature. The Bible says to let your word be your oath. Somewhere along the way, integrity was traded for convenience. Where men once showed up on time because it was the right thing to do, many now only do so when it benefits them. Where people used to work with excellence *"as unto the Lord,"* now they work according to the standard of complacency. Where they were once self-disciplined, today many are simply self-indulged. And where honor once required a life worthy of respect, many leaders now want the *title* without the *character* that should accompany it.

Son, in a world where integrity is so rare, hear me clearly—**INTEGRITY STILL MATTERS.** Set a standard that is uncommon. Become a man you can be proud of. Keep your word. Do what is right and do it well. Live in such a way that when people see your actions, they never have to question your motives.

Scripture promises this:

"For the Lord has a hidden storehouse of wisdom made accessible to His godly ones. He becomes your personal bodyguard as you follow His ways, protecting and guarding you as you choose what is right. Then you will discover all that is just, proper, and fair, and be empowered to make the right decisions as you walk into your destiny." —Proverbs 2:7–9 (TPT)

Be a man of integrity. It will carry you further than talent, gifting, or charisma ever could.

I love you, son. I hope you always know it. —Dad

Building Godly Character and Integrity

CHAPTER SIXTY
Stewarding Your Talent

Son,

I've had many opportunities in life to observe gifted people. And I'll be honest—there were times I thought it felt unfair. One person can pick up an instrument and play it beautifully in record time, while another has to grind for years to reach the same level. Some can sketch a portrait with almost no effort, while another can't even draw a stick figure with straight legs. Some people can read something once and it becomes permanent memory, while others can study for hours and still struggle to recite what they just learned.

But Scripture gives us a powerful perspective on this.

Jesus told a story about three men who were entrusted with *talents*—a measurement of money, though I love the modern meaning because it creates such a perfect parallel. The master returned after some time and asked what each man had done with what he was given. Two men used their talents and multiplied them. One man buried his to keep it safe, thinking that simply returning what he was given would please the master.

It didn't. The master was furious. Why? Because he didn't give that man the talent to sit on it—He gave it to him to grow it.

There's a strong caution here for the naturally gifted:

God expects you to grow what He gave you.
Not bury it.
Not coast on it.
Not "get by" with minimum effort.

Some people who are gifted drift into laziness simply because they *can*—they can deliver decent results with half the effort. But Son, that is just another form of burying your talent. It dishonors the gift and the Giver.

Scripture says, *"To whom much is given, much is required."* That means God places an expectation on you—not to just *possess* your talent, but to *develop* it. To build on it. To steward it with gratitude and excellence.

I read a quote recently that perfectly sums this up:

"*The gifts and calling of God are irrevocable. Character, on the other hand, must be chosen and developed. Character is what enables you to steward your gifts well.*"[1]

Gifts may get you noticed—but **character** will determine whether you can sustain what your gifting opens the door to.

Integrity is doing what is right when no one is watching. Steward well.

I love you, son. I hope you always know it. —Dad

Deepening Faith and Intimacy with God

CHAPTER SIXTY-ONE
Choose His Way First

Son,

It would be *easier* to follow their advice. People won't understand why you don't do it *their* way—after all, their way makes sense on paper. It would be *easier* to prioritize money over people. It would be *easier* to value personal success more than relationships. It would be *easier* to choose your friends based on how they benefit your goals. It would be *easier* to view life like a business transaction—measuring every decision by its return on investment and giving preference only to what increases your bottom line.

And Son, there *are* times when some of that logic contains a measure of practical wisdom. But there is a variable infinitely more important than any earthly benefit: **you must follow the leading of the Holy Spirit above everything else.**

God won't always lead you down the road the millionaire leadership author recommends. He won't always guide you along the path society—or even your mentors—claim is the road to success. And there will be moments when everything in you wants to choose what *"makes sense,"* because you *know* you could do it and it would probably work… yet you also know the Holy Spirit is whispering, *"Don't do that. Not now. This is the path I want you to take instead."*

People won't understand. Sometimes *you* won't understand. There will be tears, frustration, and seasons that feel painfully lonely. There will be times you feel used or taken for granted because God asks you to stay quiet when everything in you wants to speak up and fight back. People will mistake your kindness for weakness and assume they can take advantage of you.

And yes… it would be *easier* to do it their way. But doing it the *"easier way"* would change who you are.

Be God's man first, Son. Choose His way first, even if it means you stand alone.

It will not always be applauded, but it *is* honorable—and God sees it even when no one else ever will. People matter most to Him. Never allow anything—not success, ambition, comfort, or logic—to shift your priorities away from that truth.

I love you, son. I hope you always know it. —Dad

Deepening Faith and Intimacy with God

CHAPTER SIXTY-TWO
Listen for His Voice

Son,

As I was driving today and pondering a letter to write to you, the words *"Listen for His voice"* came to me. In the lives of believers, many prioritize reading their Bible or praying on a regular basis, but I believe far fewer actually take time to *listen for His voice* when they do. Much like going to church, prayer and Bible reading can become habits—good habits—but still incomplete if we simply check the box without including God in our daily decisions and interactions.

I believe God is always speaking, but so often we are not really listening. When you read the Word, stop and ask God what He is saying to *you* in that moment. Sit with it for a few minutes. Ponder it. Listen. When you pray, ask God for direction, wisdom, and clarity—and then be quiet. He may show you a picture in your mind. He may speak words to your spirit. He may give you an idea or a gentle nudge in a specific direction. In those moments, be intentional to listen—and then act.

Call the person who suddenly comes to mind. Pray for the person who pops into your thoughts while you're driving. When you ask God for guidance and are presented with multiple options, choose the hardest one. That's usually the one that requires faith, and God works in the arena of faith—where what He's calling you to do would be impossible without His involvement.

Go where God tells you to go. Do what He tells you to do. Listen for His voice, and then respond.

Yesterday, I had to run some errands. While I was out, I felt prompted to stop by the mall. I didn't really want to go, but I had about twenty minutes to burn and decided to walk through and see if God placed anyone in my path. After a few minutes, it seemed like nothing was happening, so I headed back to my car. Just as I was about to exit, I glanced over my shoulder—and there was a friend I hadn't seen in months. Our eyes met at the same time.

We talked, and he began sharing some health issues he had been dealing with. We prayed together right there in the food court, and then I left. That was why I was supposed to be there. I didn't know it going in, but because I listened and responded, I was able to be present for someone who needed it that day.

Sometimes you'll listen, respond, go to the mall—and leave wondering why you were there because no one showed up. That's okay too. Maybe God was simply training you to hear and respond more clearly. Maybe He was protecting you from something you'll never know about. Maybe He needed to shift your routine so He could speak to you in a different headspace. Your job is not to figure out *why*—your job is to listen and respond.

"Stop here."
"Don't go that way—go this way."
"Did you notice the pain in her eyes? Go tell her God loves her."
"Ask your waitress if there's anything you can pray for."

God is always speaking. Learn to listen for His voice—and then move when He speaks.

I love you, son. I hope you always know it. —Dad

Deepening Faith and Intimacy with God

CHAPTER SIXTY-THREE
Praise Is a Weapon

Son,

Praise is a countercultural protest.

The Bible tells us to *enter His gates with thanksgiving and His courts with praise.* Thanksgiving and praise are powerful—and often untapped—weapons against the attacks of the enemy. Many times, when people come under spiritual attack, their first response is fear, followed by a self-empowered plan to fix the problem. The issue is this: **you cannot fight spiritual battles with natural strength.** Spiritual warfare requires faith, and that is where thanksgiving and praise become effective.

When fear tries to take hold and, instead of retreating or scrambling to fix things in your own power, if you begin thanking God for His blessings and praising Him for who He is, faith is released into the situation. Praise shifts the atmosphere because it shifts your agreement. You are literally creating and changing environments with your words, thanksgiving, and praise.

When you thank the Lord that He is your Healer, praise Him for being your Provider, and acknowledge Him as your Deliverer, you are declaring the truth of God's power over your life above the lies of the enemy—who comes only to steal, kill, and destroy.

"I thank You, Lord, that Your Word tells me You are Jehovah Jireh—my Provider. I praise You that You are Jehovah Rapha—my Healer. In the midst of the storm, You are the God who is more than enough. You prepare a table before me in the presence of my enemies. You promise You will never leave me or forsake me. You are a friend who sticks closer than a brother. Though a thousand fall at my side and ten thousand at my right hand, Your Word says it shall not come near me—so I will not fear. You protect me. You lift me above my circumstances. When the enemy comes in like a flood, the Spirit of the Lord raises a standard against him. So today, I rest in Your provision, Your strength, and Your might."

You see, son, you always have a choice. You can agree with the fear that is attacking you—or you can fight fear with faith by choosing praise and thanksgiving. Agreement gives power. What you agree with will determine what you experience.

Faith is not usually sparked by what feels natural. It is ignited when you intentionally direct your focus toward the goodness and faithfulness of God and choose to thank Him and praise Him *in advance* for what He has already promised to do in His Word. When you do that, things shift in the spirit—even when nothing has changed yet in the natural.

Praise reminds your soul who God is.
Thanksgiving anchors your heart in truth.
And faith rises when fear loses its voice.

Never forget: *praise is not your retreat—it is your resistance.*

I love you, son. I hope you always know it. —Dad

Deepening Faith and Intimacy with God

CHAPTER SIXTY-FOUR
Keep Praying Anyway

Son,

A few years ago, I was having lunch with one of our young adults—he's a pastor in Arizona today. While we were eating, a young blind man walked by. At that time God had been moving so powerfully in my life that praying for the sick had become *normal* for me. I had watched God rebuild knees, open deaf ears, and perform miracles I had only dreamed of seeing. I was excited… and sometimes excitement exposes areas where we still need to grow.

We got up from our table, walked straight over to the man, and I abruptly said, *"Excuse me, can we pray for you?!"* If I put myself in his shoes, my approach lacked tact. Being blind, he had no idea we were even there and he was startled responding sharply, *"WHO ARE YOU?!"*

I felt terrible. We prayed, but we didn't see a miracle that day. Had I allowed the embarrassment of that moment to shame me, I might never have prayed for anyone again. But I learned from it—and I kept going.

Fast forward to just recently. I approached a man who was limping, clearly in pain. We talked, and I asked how I could pray for him. He told me he had recently had knee surgery and could barely stand on it. I knelt down, placed my hands on his knee, and began to pray. When I looked up, he had the most bewildered expression on his face. I asked, *"How's the pain?"*

Shaking his head, he said, *"It's gone… NO SH*T, IT'S GONE!"* And then he started doing squats right there in front of me. I just laughed. He wasn't faking—his shock even came out in his wording. It was real and raw.

Here's the lesson, Son: *don't allow fear, embarrassment, or the memory of what didn't happen to keep you from obeying God.* When I pray for someone, occasionally I'm tempted to remember the moments of felt *failure* when I didn't see what I hoped to see. But if the embarrassment of that *blind-man encounter* had stopped me, that man with the healed knees today would still be walking in extreme pain. You often have to press through disappointment when stepping into faith.

God uses *willing vessels*. Not perfect ones. Willing ones. *"In Him we live, and move, and have our being."* And sometimes the reason you're in a certain place at a certain time is because God intends to flow through you.

Be bold. Be compassionate. And when God nudges you—move.

I love you, son. I hope you always know it. —Dad

Deepening Faith and Intimacy with God

CHAPTER SIXTY-FIVE
God's Will, Your Part

Son,

I believe one of the most harmful doctrines in all of Christianity is the idea that *God's sovereign will* is responsible for every tragedy. When you read the New Testament as a whole, you simply cannot arrive at that conclusion without twisting what is written.

Many people, in the middle of heartbreak, will simply shrug and say, *"Well, God is sovereign,"* as if their tragedy must somehow be *God's doing*—even when their experience stands in direct contradiction to His promises. It becomes a way to cope, but not a way to stand in faith.

The truth is, God is absolutely sovereign—but He was sovereign when He spoke His promises. He was sovereign when He gave us His Word to record those promises. And He was sovereign when He said in 2 Corinthians 1:20 that *"ALL the promises of God are YES in Christ, and we speak the AMEN"*—meaning that His promises are established by Him, but activated in our lives when we place our faith and agreement in them.

God's sovereignty does not nullify His promises; it guarantees them. (READ THAT SENTENCE AGAIN AND AGAIN UNTIL IT LANDS IN YOUR SPIRIT) It's our agreement (amen) that brings them into our reality.

This morning, I was reading Ephesians 3:20, and I noticed something most people overlook. They quote the first part:

"Now to Him who is able to do exceedingly abundantly above all that we ask or think…"

But they leave out the most important part:

"…according to the power that works in us."

God's ability is limitless—but its manifestation on the earth is connected to the *power at work in us*. In other words, **our agreement and cooperation are essential variables** in seeing God's will become reality in our circumstances. Our lack of participation can restrict what God desires to do.

It's like baking a cake. You can have all the ingredients laid out on the counter—but if you never mix them together, you'll never have a cake. You'll only have a mess. Many people's lives are a mess not because God didn't give them what they needed, but because they expected Him to bake the cake for them.

God gave you the *ingredients* (His power), and the *recipe* (His Word), but the *"exceedingly abundantly"* shows up when **you** take responsibility to use what He gave you.

Son, don't ever let anyone convince you that God isn't for you simply because something didn't go your way. The issue is rarely God withholding—more often, it's us failing to follow the recipe.

Walk in the authority He gave you. Believe what He said about you. And cooperate with the power that works in you.

I love you, son. I hope you always know it. —Dad

Deepening Faith and Intimacy with God

CHAPTER SIXTY-SIX
Live, Move, and Have Your Being in Him

Son,

God is not just the One we pray to when life gets hard. If that's the only way you know Him, then you're missing out on so much of what He wants to be in your life.

Acts 17 (TPT) says it beautifully: *"...He has done this so that every person would long for God, feel their way to Him, and find Him—for He is the God who is easy to discover. It is through Him that we live and function and have our identity."*

God is not distant. He's not detached. And He's not limited to answering prayers in crisis. When you learn to hear His voice, you discover how close, faithful, and involved He truly is. You begin to recognize His whispers in the simplest moments—and that's when your relationship with Him becomes real, not just religious.

Recently, He showed *you* His faithfulness. You were facing something heavy, and I felt prompted to stop what I was doing and text you: *"Hey dude... Just thinking about you. Your dad loves you and I'm praying for you. God has an awesome plan for your life. Partner with Him and you're gonna have an amazing ride."* I had no idea what you were dealing with in that moment—but God did. And He used me to speak strength into you right when you needed it.

That's what it looks like to *"have my being in Him."* I've practiced hearing His voice enough to know when to pause and obey—even when it feels small or random.

And Son, when you live that way—responding to His nudges, trusting His impressions, leaning into His voice—you will experience things other people only wish for.
He'll tell you to:
"Turn here."
"Go home this way."
"Call that person."
"Send that text."

It won't always make sense in the moment. But in dangerous, pivotal, or life-changing situations, that same voice becomes your protection, your guidance, and your advantage.

Through trial, practice, and even mistakes, I've learned to trust those moments—and God has never failed me.

Pursue Him with that same intentionality, Son. It will save you unnecessary pain, open doors you never expected, and anchor your life in ways nothing else can.

I love you, son. I hope you always know it. —Dad

Building Godly Character and Integrity

CHAPTER SIXTY-SEVEN
Do It Well

Son,

Several years ago, a man who had worked for me for a few years walked into my office and gave his two-week resignation notice. I asked him to use his remaining time wisely—to put together a simple instruction booklet for his replacement outlining the daily processes he handled so we could maintain continuity after he left.

I was frustrated and disappointed by his answer: *"Why would I do that?! No one ever did that for me!"*

Son, that mindset is the difference between people who merely *do a job* and people who *do things well*. And that difference is everything when it comes to your future, your habits, your integrity, your character, and your contribution.

It's not enough to *"just do it,"* like the Nike slogan says. Many people do the bare minimum and call it good enough. But anything worth doing is worth doing well. Scripture says it this way: *"Do all things as unto the Lord."* (Colossians 3:23-24) That means excellence isn't for your boss, your team, or your reputation—it's your offering to God.

Integrity is mostly about intentionality toward excellence. It's choosing to leave things better than you found them.

If you borrow someone's car, return it clean and with a full tank. If you splash water on the sink brushing your teeth, wipe it up. If a gum wrapper falls out when you grab your keys, pick it up. If you eat at the food court, clean your table when you leave.

It's the small things that reveal who you truly are.

The moment you think, *"That's not my job,"* or *"Someone else gets paid to do that,"* you've stepped out of excellence and into mediocrity. And mediocrity never produces greatness. You're better than that. Do things well—consistently and intentionally—and you will reap a harvest of excellence in every area of your life.

The Bible says: *"A beautiful reputation is more to be desired than great riches, and to be esteemed by others is more honorable than immense investments." Proverbs 22:1 (TPT)*

Build that reputation now. It will carry you further than talent ever will.

I love you, son. I hope you always know it. —Dad

Building Godly Character and Integrity

CHAPTER SIXTY-EIGHT
Guard Your Heart Without Hardening It

Son,

Many years ago you asked me, *"Daddy, why don't you trust people?"* You were too young then for me to explain what I've seen as a cop, as a pastor, and as a man who has walked through his share of betrayal. All I could say was, *"Son, Daddy has seen the evil that men do, and I just want to protect you from it."* That moment hurt my heart, because I never wanted you to inherit my lenses. But you are far too discerning to stay unaware of the reality of evil in this world.

As your father, I want to challenge you with two lessons that took me years to learn and even longer to balance:

1. Don't let painful realities rob you of the joy of loving people in spite of themselves.

2. Don't let pain callous you to the voice and presence of the Spirit of God.

Son, you're like me in ways I wish you weren't—especially in your ability to disconnect from emotion. I've watched you do it. I understand it. I did it for years. But hear me: *it's not healthy, and it will cost you more than it protects.*

You have an empathic gift. You can sense environments the moment you walk into them. That's a strength few people possess. But if you turn off your emotions to keep yourself safe, that choice will affect every other aspect of your discernment. Emotions aren't your enemy—God designed them as part of your navigation system. Don't run from them. Learn from them. Use them. Embrace them.

The real danger of shutting down emotionally is that it builds a wall between you and others—one they will feel even if you never say a word. And that barrier cripples your influence. As the old saying goes, *"People don't care what you know until they know that you care."* You are a natural leader. It's in you. But if you stop caring—even when caring hurts—you lose the very thing that makes people want to follow you.

Pain and joy are both part of leadership. They're part of loving people. They're part of carrying God's heart.

And Son, here's the deeper danger: **When you allow your heart to become calloused toward people—whom God deeply loves—it becomes far too easy for your heart to grow calloused toward God as well.** If your heart hardens, it won't just affect your relationships. It will affect your marriage, your children, your friendships, your calling, and your ability to hear God clearly in the moments that matter most.

This is why Scripture tells us, *"Above ALL else, guard your heart." (Proverbs 3:23 NIV)* A guarded heart is not a hard heart. One protects. The other isolates.

Real manhood—and real leadership—isn't about being tough or untouchable. It's about being willing to feel, willing to love, willing to sacrifice, and willing to care even when it costs you something.

Keep your heart soft toward God and tender toward people. If you choose that now, early in life, you will go further than I ever have. I want that for you more than anything.

I love you, son. I hope you always know it. —Dad

Leadership, Authority, and Kingdom Influence

CHAPTER SIXTY-NINE
The Power that Confirms the Message

Son,

Courts have long recognized the weight of a person's last words. They know those final statements often carry deeper meaning than anything said before. With that in mind, consider this: in Mark 16, Jesus chose these words as His final instructions before ascending to heaven. They were His last earthly message to His disciples—and to us. That alone makes them profoundly important:

"And these signs shall follow them that believe; In my name shall they cast out devils; they shall speak with new tongues; they shall take up serpents; and if they drink any deadly thing, it shall not hurt them; they shall lay hands on the sick, and they shall recover." (Mark 16:17-18 KJV)

I get frustrated when I hear people argue theology—not because questions are wrong, but because so much of the debate is fueled by a powerless experience. People read Mark 16, look at their own lack of supernatural fruit, and reshape theology to accommodate their disappointment. They convince themselves that these words were only for the early church, and in doing so they strip the gospel of the very power Jesus promised.

But the Bible warned us this would happen. 2 Timothy says many would have *"a form of godliness but deny the power thereof." (2 Timothy 3:5 KJV)*

Son, you've seen with your own eyes that God still heals people when we pray. You've witnessed miracles that no logical argument can explain away. That's why I'm of the resolve that **theology without the display of power is limited to/by the intelligence of the person presenting or opposing it.** The true gospel has never been just intellectual—it has always been supernatural. It doesn't always make natural sense.

When someone's faith rests only on mental assent, they can be swayed by debate. But once you have experienced the power Jesus promises—once you've seen the impossible bow to the name of Jesus—

someone else's contrary argument becomes irrelevant. As the old saying goes:

"The man with an experience is never at the mercy of the man with an argument."

Life will bring moments where questions arise. Doubt will knock. Circumstances will challenge what you believe. When that happens, remember the miracles you've seen. Remember the moments where God moved in ways that defy logic. Let those memorials fuel your faith when your mind searches for answers.

I love you, son. I hope you always know it. —Dad

Building Godly Character and Integrity

CHAPTER SEVENTY
Don't Do It—Even If They Deserve It

Son,

Pain is a powerful teacher... and I'm hoping some of mine can spare you from learning things the hard way. Over the years there have been a handful of moments that still grieve me when I think about them. One situation in particular resurfaces just about the time I think I've healed from it—only for word to come back that my name is being dragged through the mud again, both publicly and privately. Partial truths get twisted into weapons meant to damage my reputation.

Every now and then someone who knows more of the *real story* will come to me and apologize for the injustice of what they've seen. My response has been, *"If they need a target to shoot at to process their pain, I'm a good one... because I won't hold their arrows."*

Son, this was not always my response. Age and experience have tempered me. My justice and integrity values run deep, and I've always tried to guard my reputation, love people well, and do the right thing because it was right. And truthfully, it would be easy—*so* easy—to shred their accusations by revealing details that would exonerate me in the court of public opinion. But doing so would hurt people, and in that moment my motive would not be righteousness—it would be self-preservation.

If you can't do something in love, most of the time you shouldn't do it at all.

I don't want to cause pain, even when I'm justified. If people believe lies about me because of someone's misrepresentation... then that's simply something I have to release to God.

Scripture says God is your defender. Your emotions will tempt you to defend yourself. Sometimes that's the right thing to do, but many times it isn't. When you're unsure, submit it to God and let Him handle your defense. Your responsibility is to guard your integrity—not by winning arguments, but by choosing righteousness over retaliation.

It's not always easy. But son, doing what is right *because* it is right—that's real integrity. Love people, even when they lash out. Most of the time their attack is rooted in their own pain. Be big enough to see that pain with compassion instead of offense. As Jesus said on the cross, *"Father forgive them, they don't realize what they are actually doing."*

I love you, son. I hope you always know it. —Dad

Leadership, Authority, and Kingdom Influence

CHAPTER SEVENTY-ONE
Forgiveness is a Choice

Son,

There are few things in life that require more strength than forgiveness. And I want you to understand this clearly from the beginning—forgiveness is both an event and a process. There is often a moment where you choose to forgive, and then many moments afterward where you must continue choosing it again and again. **That's because forgiveness isn't a feeling. It's a choice.**

Living according to God's ways means walking in forgiveness, but what many people have been taught about forgiveness is incomplete. Sometimes we imagine forgiveness as something reserved only for deep wounds, while at other times we excuse ourselves for holding onto resentment over things that should have been released long ago. Whether the wound was devastating or seemingly small, forgiveness is essential—and it must be addressed honestly.

Let me be clear about something important: forgiveness is not excusing what happened to you. Forgiveness does not mean abuse was acceptable. It does not mean betrayal was justified. It does not mean manipulation, neglect, or harm was okay. It wasn't okay when it happened, and it never will be.

In fact, real healing—emotionally, spiritually, and even psychologically—begins when you are willing to acknowledge the truth of what happened and the weight it carried. Naming the wrong matters. Admitting that something caused real damage is not weakness; it's courage. That recognition is often the doorway to restoration.

Forgiveness doesn't minimize the pain—it relocates it. It shifts the weight from your heart to God's hands. It's not telling the offender their actions were acceptable; it's telling yourself that you are no longer willing to carry what you were never designed to carry forever.

You've probably heard the phrase *"forgive and forget."* That sounds good, but it's not realistic—and it's not required. As human beings, we are not wired to simply *"forget"* and if you're waiting to forgive until you feel *okay* about what happened, or until the memory *disappears*, you may wait a lifetime. Trauma doesn't work that way. Memories don't simply vanish because we wish them to.

God, in His divine nature, chooses not to remember our sins. That is grace. But He does not require you to erase your memory in order to forgive. **Forgetting is not the prerequisite—release is.** You can remember and still choose to forgive. You can acknowledge the pain and still choose to release it to God.

The truth is, you will feel things. Some emotions will linger longer than you want. That doesn't mean you haven't forgiven—it means you're human. Forgiveness is proven not by what you feel, but by what you *choose* when the feelings show up.

At its core, forgiveness is an act of faith and obedience. When you *choose* to forgive—even when it doesn't feel right—you align yourself with God's Word and refuse to let offense define your future. Freedom often comes after obedience, not before it.

Choose forgiveness, son. Not because what happened was okay—but because you deserve to live free from the bondage of what happened.

I love you, son. I hope you always know it. —Dad

Building Godly Character and Integrity

CHAPTER SEVENTY-TWO
The Elevation of Title Above Capacity

Son,

People often point to someone with a crowd following them and say, *"That guy is a natural-born leader."* But a following doesn't make a man a leader any more than getting a woman pregnant makes one a father. In my lifetime and the multiple fields I've worked in, I've met many people with influence—people others blindly followed—who were terrible at leading. From them, I often learned more about what *not* to do than what to do.

Some were manipulative. Some were narcissistic. Some were liars, users, or driven entirely by ego. They had followers, but they weren't leaders. They were simply skilled at using people to elevate themselves.

This is what I call the *elevation of title above capacity.* It happens when charisma is valued more than integrity—when being charming is mistaken for being trustworthy. A conman knows how to get people to like him too, but that doesn't make him a leader. The same could be said for many *"leaders"* I've studied.

Jesus showed us a completely different model. His life demonstrated that the higher the level of influence, the *greater the level of service.* True leadership is not measured by how many people follow you, but by how many people you lift. (Read that last sentence again.)

Our culture often gets this backward. We applaud charisma, spotlight giftedness, and assume popularity equals capacity. But when influence grows faster than character, the risk of corruption increases exponentially. History—and Scripture—are full of examples.

Son, you cannot allow the praise of people to become your compass. The moment a leader believes they have risen *"above"* serving others, pride has already begun its work. From politics to pulpits, the downfall usually begins when a leader sees themselves as the exception to the standards they once upheld.

That's why the Bible doesn't tell others to humble you—it tells *you* to humble yourself. It tells *you* to bring every thought into the obedience of Christ and the Word of God. These responsibilities can't be delegated. Only you can guard your own heart.

And don't ever fall into the trap of telling stories about how you *"used to"* serve—as if serving was just a stepping stone to something *more important*. Jesus washed His disciples' feet. The higher He went, the deeper He stooped. Leadership dues don't decrease—they increase.

If your focus is climbing to the top instead of helping others rise, you're not leading… you're advancing yourself and those two are very different.

Someone once said, *"Be the leader you wish you had."* Son, it's one thing to know that truth, and another to live it. I'm still growing too. We all are. Aspire to be your best version of you!

I love you, son. I hope you always know it. —Dad

Leadership, Authority, and Kingdom Influence

CHAPTER SEVENTY-THREE
Keep Your Eyes on the Right Battle

Son,

Some time ago we talked about *knowing your enemy*, and I asked you, *"If you were the devil, where would you attack you to divert your destiny?"* That's an important question, and it *is* wise to understand how the enemy operates. But hear me clearly—awareness is not the same thing as focus.

I'm a fighter by nature, and I am deeply grateful for the authority God gives us to stand against the enemy. But a major mistake many believers make is living more aware of what the devil is doing than what God is doing. They study the enemy, follow every distraction, fill their minds with fear-driven news, and then wonder why they feel defeated. If the devil gets more of your attention than *the Father* does, he's already won half the battle.

Son, the God who lives in you is greater than anything happening in the world around you. Your energy, your attention, and your faith must be rooted in what *God* is saying, what *God* is doing, and what *God* is assigning you to do today. You have a post in His Kingdom, and you cannot fill it while primarily staring at the enemy's camp.

Teams that only play defense rarely score. In the same way, Christians who only react to the devil never advance the Kingdom. Jesus said, *"Seek first the Kingdom of God,"* not *"Study everything the enemy is plotting."* Proverbs 25 tells us it is the glory of kings to search out the matters God conceals—not the chaos that the enemy stirs up. And Psalm 37 says the wicked plot against the righteous, but God laughs at their plans.

So here's my challenge: Pay attention, yes. Be wise, yes. But don't obsess over the enemy. Redirect your primary focus toward what your King is doing. Ask Him, *"Lord, what is Your assignment for me today? What battle plan are You unfolding? Where do You want me positioned?"* That's where your strength, clarity, and authority come from.

Just some food for thought.

Aaron D. Davis

I love you, son. I hope you always know it. —Dad

Leadership, Authority, and Kingdom Influence

CHAPTER SEVENTY-FOUR
Be Known for Love, Not Division

Son,

For centuries the Church has operated under a mindset of division—denominationalism, protest, and separation. The irony is that the very word *Protestant* comes from the root word *protester*. When disagreement arises, history has taught believers to divide, label, ostracize, and excommunicate instead of love. And sadly, many Christians still mirror that pattern today.

We slap people with alienating titles the moment they think differently than we do—politically, spiritually, socially. But the Bible is clear: *"Though I speak with the tongues of men and angels and understand all mysteries… if I have not love, I am a resounding gong and a clanging cymbal."* (1 Corinthians 13 - Paraphrased NIV)

Son, we are Christians. We are supposed to be known for our **love**—for blessing those who curse us, praying for those who mistreat us, and walking in unity even when we disagree.

Love doesn't mean you approve of someone's beliefs. It means you choose *connection over division* for the sake of Christ.

Daniel is one of the greatest biblical examples of this. He was enslaved by an evil king, likely castrated, renamed after a pagan god, and labeled a *"magician"* instead of his calling of a *prophet*. Yet when it came time to interpret the king's dream, Daniel wasn't vengeful or spiteful. He said: *"O king, I wish this dream were about your enemies…"*

He responded with honor—even to a man who had wounded him deeply.

Later, when King Darius threw him into the lion's den, Darius stayed up all night fasting in fear for him. At dawn he ran to the den shouting, *"Daniel, has your God saved you?"* And Daniel—without bitterness—answered, *"O king, live forever."*

Think about that. He blessed the man responsible for his suffering.

I'm convinced Daniel didn't influence Babylon because he prayed or prophesied—though he did both. He influenced Babylon because he **loved** the people God placed him among. His love gave him authority. His character gave him credibility. His compassion gave him a voice in a dark and hostile culture.

Son, if you want influence—real Kingdom influence—choose love over being *"right."* The *kindness* of God draws men to Him, not the *correctness* of His followers.

Don't become a loud, clanging noisemaker who wins arguments but loses hearts. Lead with love. Speak truth with humility. And let your life reveal Jesus even where your words are not welcome.

I love you, son. I hope you always know it. – Dad

Discipline, Consistency, and Spiritual Growth

CHAPTER SEVENTY-FIVE
Garbage In Garbage Out

Son,

There's an old saying you've probably heard a thousand times: *"You are what you eat."* Physically, that makes sense—what you put in your body affects your strength, your health, and your well-being. But the same truth applies to your spirit, your mind, and your heart.

Jesus warned His disciples to *"beware of the leaven of the Pharisees and of Herod."* (Matthew 16) He wasn't talking about bread. He was talking about **mindsets**—religious mindsets and political mindsets that sound righteous but are rooted in **self-righteousness**, not God's righteousness. Those mindsets don't draw you closer to God; they distract, distort, and eventually derail your focus.

This is why Scripture also tells us, *"Whatever is pure, lovely, of good report—whatever is virtuous or praiseworthy—think on these things."* (Philippians 4:8) In other words: **guard what gets into your mind.**

There's a lot of garbage floating in the atmosphere around us—opinions, outrage, fear, pride, anger, entitlement, cynicism. It's toxic. But it doesn't affect you until it gets *in* you—through the gate of your eyes, your ears, your focus, and your meditation.

That's why the Bible says, *"Above all else, guard your heart, for out of it flow the wellsprings of life."* (Proverbs 4:23 NIV) Your heart is the command center of your life. Whatever you let in will eventually come out. Whatever you feed will grow (sin or righteousness).

You can't always control what happens around you, but you always have authority over what you dwell on, what you meditate on, and what you allow to shape your internal world. Choose wisely—because son, it truly matters.

Just like your body: Too much junk creates sickness. Too many toxins create imbalance. And too much negativity creates spiritual disease.

Garbage in, garbage out! But the opposite is also true: Truth in, peace out. Grace in, strength out. God's Word in, wisdom out.

Practice a healthy *"focus diet."* Feed your heart what builds you, not what breaks you.

I love you, son. I hope you always know it. —Dad

Building Godly Character and Integrity

CHAPTER SEVENTY-SIX
The Detail of Obedience

Son,

God honors every investment you make—your time, your talent, and your treasure. Scripture is clear: *"Whatsoever a man sows, that shall he also reap." (Galatians 6:7-9 KJV)* Nothing you pour out in obedience ever goes unseen by Him.

In the military they call an assignment *a **detail***—and sometimes God's *details* don't make sense to your natural mind. I've walked through seasons where my heart felt heavy and discouraged, and on the surface, it looked like my life was moving in the opposite direction of my dreams. But God promised that He works **all things together for our good** when we love Him and walk according to His purpose (Romans 8:28 *paraphrased*). Notice it **doesn't say** everything *is* good or everything that happens *comes from* God. It says He will weave it together for our benefit.

I'll never forget a moment when, after a long season of struggle, I asked God, *"Lord, don't You think I've been in this season long enough?"* He answered, *"Aaron, you had a lot to unlearn."*

Another time I cried out, *"God, this is so hard. What do You want me to do?"* He responded, *"Man your post."* In the military, that means a soldier stands watch—alert, faithful, responsible—protecting the rest of the unit. In other words, God was telling me: *"Do what you know to do. Guard the assignment I gave you until I relieve you. Stay faithful where I placed you."*

And in a different season, I asked Him how to steward a responsibility that I knew was temporary—something I wouldn't personally harvest the fruit from. That *"post"* felt like restoring a classic car you'll never get to drive. God said, *"Treat it like it was yours."*

So, I did. I washed it, waxed it, polished it, cleaned the windshield every time a bird left its mark. I detailed it because I wasn't doing it *for people*—I was doing it *as unto the Lord* (Colossians 3:23). The *detail* became worship.

That's the thing about sowing and reaping: that promise in Galatians 6:7 begins with, *"Don't be deceived, God is not mocked..."* He sees the late nights. He sees the unseen obedience. He sees the extra effort nobody else will ever know about.

And according to His Word, *you will reap exactly what you've sown.*

Son, be faithful in the *detail* God assigns you. Follow His direction even when you don't understand it. Honor Him in the unseen places, and He will make your path straight.

I love you, son. I hope you always know it. —Dad

Building Legacy and Finishing Strong

CHAPTER SEVENTY-SEVEN
Legacy Lives Through You

Son,

I watched a movie (Top Gun: *Maverick*) recently where Maverick thanked the son of his former partner, Goose—who had been killed in a tragic accident more than twenty years earlier—for saving his life, and the son simply replied, *"It's what my dad would have done."* That line hit me in the feels. It made me think about legacy, honor, and example—the things a father leaves behind that outlive him through his children.

You're your own man, and one day you'll make choices that shape your legacy… **our** legacy. Your children will watch how you respond when they fail. They'll see how you react when you're angry. They'll pay attention to how you treat their mother, how you speak to a waitress, how you correct an employee, and how you express love, appreciation, and grace in everyday moments.

Whether you realize it or not, they'll take notes. And much of what you model—good or bad—they will replicate.

I don't know that I valued that truth as deeply as I should have when you were young. I've made mistakes, and when I realized them, I apologized. My challenge to you is to take everything I've modeled—the strengths and the shortcomings—and learn from it. Build on what was good… and be better where I fell short.

As your father, my desire has always been to impart love, integrity, wisdom, justice, truth, and mercy. If my ceiling doesn't become your floor, I've missed part of my purpose as your dad. I want you to go further than I ever did. I want you to avoid some of the failures I walked through because I taught you how to walk around them instead of through them.

That's part of why I'm writing these letters—to give you something that will outlive me. Maybe one day your children, and their children, will have more than just a picture. They'll have my voice, my heart, and the lessons God taught me—all preserved for them.

Legacy matters, son. Be intentional to build a healthy one.

There's so much more I could say, but I'll save it for another day. Stay teachable. The more you learn, the more you'll realize how much you still don't know.

I love you, son. I hope you always know it. —Dad

Deepening Faith and Intimacy with God

CHAPTER SEVENTY-EIGHT
The Reward of Putting God First

Son,

When your mother and I first moved to Nashville, we were broke newlyweds just trying to survive. We were driving two dying vehicles—one of them a manual Plymouth Horizon with first and second gear completely burned out. I literally had to feather the clutch just to get the car moving in third gear. Finances were tight, and every bill felt like a mountain.

During that season, a man named Ron was one of the most successful people I had ever known. He lived in a house I could only dream of owning, and he carried himself with the peace and stability I desperately wanted to build for our family. One day I asked him, *"Ron, what advice would you give a young couple like us—newlyweds just starting out?"*

He didn't talk about work ethic, financial strategies, investments, or bold risks. He said, *"Be generous with what you have, and always be faithful to tithe. God is not mocked—whatever you sow, you will reap."*

That advice stuck with me. His message was simple: **Seek God's ways first, and everything else will come in time.**

Five years later, something surreal happened. Ron moved out of that *dream home*—and I moved into it. I bought the very house I once admired, the one I never believed I'd be able to afford. At that time, we had no children, yet I was driving a new Escalade, parking my 24-foot boat outside, keeping two motorcycles in the garage... You get the picture. God had blessed us just like He blessed Ron—just like He promised He would.

Now hear me: since then, life hasn't always been full of Cadillacs and motorcycles. I've walked through deep valleys and difficult seasons. But through every mountain and every low place, God has been faithful. He honored His Word, because He always does.

Son, the Bible says, *"Where a man's treasure is, there his heart will be also." (Matthew 6:21)* If you want your life aligned with God's blessing, put your treasure—your generosity, your trust, your priorities—in His hands.

    Be generous.
    Honor God with your whole heart.
    Live open-handed, not tight-fisted.
    And He will make your paths straight when you trust in Him.

    I love you, son. I hope you always know it. —Dad

Deepening Faith and Intimacy with God

CHAPTER SEVENTY-NINE
Discerning God's Voice

Son,

Everything in life isn't black and white. Some of the most important decisions you'll ever make won't come down to logic, proof, or what makes sense on paper—they'll come down to **discernment**. You must learn to recognize the voice of God for your circumstances.

There have been many times in my life when something simply didn't sit right with me. I couldn't explain it. I couldn't justify it. I had no evidence to back it up—I just *knew* something was off. That kind of knowing is often the Holy Spirit whispering to your spirit.

A few years ago, you landed a game-changing acting gig in Canada. It was a dream opportunity, but something about it felt wrong in my spirit. I told you my concern—that the country might close its borders and that you and your mom could get stuck there. I had zero substantiation, no data, no news reports—just a deep, unsettling knowing. Naturally, that was disappointing for you.

Two months later, I showed you the newspaper article: the borders had closed. People were trapped inside the country for months—some for eight months, including people I personally spoke to. I still can't explain how I knew. I just did. And truthfully, this kind of thing happens to me often.

But Son, being *right* has the capacity to create its own danger. Here's the lesson:

When you're *right* a lot, you can start *assuming* you're right—every time. And assumption creates *blind spots.*

That's why I'm careful. I don't jump on bandwagons. I don't rush to judgment on world events. I don't cling too tightly to my own interpretations. Because I know that without the Holy Spirit, my insight has limits—and my biases can cloud my vision.

Things are not always as they appear. And sometimes what *appears* obvious to you may actually keep you from seeing the truth you're unknowingly blinded to.

So seek God first. Ask Him, *"Lord, what do You say about this?"* Let His voice anchor you before you form your conclusions. There is wisdom in His reply that no human intuition can match. Seek Him first and let God show you what you might not otherwise know.

I love you, son. I hope you always know it. —Dad

Leadership, Authority, and Kingdom Influence

CHAPTER EIGHTY
You Can't Lead the Unwilling

Son,

One of the most important lessons you'll ever learn in leadership is this: *you can't lead people who don't want to be led*. It doesn't matter how wise, compassionate, or gifted you are—if someone chooses misery, you cannot drag them into freedom.

There's a saying, *"misery loves company,"* and it's true in two ways. Miserable people either want to surround themselves with others who are just as miserable, or they want to be around someone who will listen endlessly while they stay exactly the same. As a leader, you need a compassionate heart, an approachable spirit, and a posture that makes people feel safe—but **you also need boundaries**.

If you're not careful, people who refuse to change will see your compassion as a place to dump their problems without any intention of growing. They don't want wisdom—they want an audience. They don't want transformation—they want validation for staying stuck.

But Son, great leaders help people **heal**, not just **hurt out loud**. And you can usually tell very quickly which kind of person you're dealing with.

Whenever someone comes to me asking for mentorship, coaching, or guidance, I meet with them once—and then I give them a simple assignment. Usually, I ask them to read a book that speaks directly to the issue they're dealing with. I do this because if they're serious about growth and wanting my input in their life, they'll take responsibility for their own healing and follow my instruction.

The next time they ask to meet, I ask one question: *"Did you read the book?"*

Their answer reveals everything.

If they didn't do the assignment, it's almost always a sign that they don't really want change—they just want attention. My time, my energy, and my emotional bandwidth are too valuable to invest in someone who refuses to invest in themselves. This doesn't mean you stop caring—it means you lead wisely.

Of course, every rule has exceptions, and sometimes compassion calls for patience. But as a general principle, this one truth will save you from a great deal of unnecessary frustration.

The Bible says, *"Above all else, guard your heart, for out of it flows the wellspring of life."* Setting healthy boundaries is part of *guarding your heart*. Be compassionate—but be wise. Help those who *want* help. Love everyone—but don't let everyone drain the strength God gave you. Finally, be aware that the Holy Spirit may ask you to do the exact opposite of what I have advised in this letter. If that happens, always follow the leading of the Holy Spirit. What I am sharing here is a *"rule of thumb"* not an absolute.

I love you, son. I hope you always know it. – Dad

Discipline, Consistency, and Spiritual Growth

CHAPTER EIGHTY-ONE
Lead with Strength, Not Fear

Son,

When I was a child, fear controlled a lot of my life. I carried that fear into adolescence, but by then I had gotten big and strong. That's when I discovered something: other people were afraid too. And when I felt powerless or out of control, anger seemed to make people submit. For the ones who didn't, violence usually did. So I became a big, fear-filled *man-child* using fear to keep from *feeling* fear. It was a broken system—and it shaped me in ways I wish it hadn't.

Because of that, I never wanted you to live the way I did. That's why the first scripture I ever taught you—before you could even speak clearly—was, *"God has not given us a spirit of fear."* (2 Timothy 1:7 NLT) I'd ask, *"What are you afraid of, boy?"* You'd grin and say, *"Nufin!"* (2-year-old speak for "nothing") *"Why not?" "Because God has not given me a spirit of fear!"* Those moments were powerful. They mattered.

But here's the truth I have to own: when you misbehaved or pushed back in ways that triggered my own insecurity, I didn't always lead with love—sometimes I led with fear. I fell back into old habits. I demanded control. I intimidated. I governed you with the same spirit I hated growing up. And Son... that was wrong. I modeled something I never wanted to pass down.

You may or may not grow to be my size physically, but I already know you'll be stronger, wiser, and better than me in all the ways that matter. So hear me clearly: **Never lead anyone—your future wife, your children, or your team—by fear, intimidation, or control.** Don't feed those fear demons while you're young. Don't let fear become your leadership style.

Use your strength the way God intended:
—Let your arms and hands be a place of protection, not punishment.
—Let your shoulders be a platform where your children stand taller than you ever could.
—Let your ceiling be their floor.

—Let love—not fear—govern your home.

God didn't give them a spirit of fear, and you shouldn't either.

I know I did many things right, but in this area, I know I sometimes modeled something wrong. Learn from my mistake. Break the pattern. Lead differently. Lead better.

I'm sorry for the fear you felt in moments when I should have given you peace. I was navigating my own brokenness while learning how to be your father. You deserved better, and my prayer is that you will *be* better.

You are an incredible young man. I'm so proud of who you are, and even more excited about who you're becoming.

I love you, son. I hope you always know it. – Dad

Leadership, Authority, and Kingdom Influence

CHAPTER EIGHTY-TWO
Stay in Your God-Given Lane

Son,

One of the things you'll discover as you grow is that people called by God into different areas—different spheres of influence—often see the world through very different lenses. And if you're not called to their assignment, it's incredibly easy to misunderstand, misjudge, or even criticize their choices, approach, or associations.

Scripture gives a perfect example of this. Daniel was called to serve and *advise* a wicked king. Elijah, on the other hand, was called to *confront* and challenge the king of his day. Both were prophets. Both were anointed. Both were obedient. But their roles, audiences, and strategies were nothing alike—and they weren't supposed to be.

If the Elijahs of Daniel's day had evaluated Daniel, they probably would have accused him of compromise. And the Daniels of Elijah's day may have thought Elijah was reckless or too harsh. But here's the truth: **one was called to be honey, and the other was called to be vinegar.** Different assignments. Different approaches. Same God.

Problems start when someone called to one lane tries to copy another's lane—usually out of insecurity or comparison. I've studied how men in ministry sometimes abandon the very thing God created them to do because they were overly impressed or intimidated by someone else's success. Son, that's a fast track to frustration and burnout.

Learn from others. Take wisdom from their victories and lessons from their failures. But never—**never**—trade your identity for someone else's calling. You're not graced for their assignment, and they're not graced for yours.

And remember this: the same God who calls you to your lane expects you to honor the calling of those He places in theirs—even when their lane looks nothing like yours.

So where does that leave you? It means you have a responsibility to discover who God created *you* to be. To know your assignment. To stay focused on your purpose. Because when you're busy being faithful to your calling, you don't have time to criticize someone else's.

Find your lane. Fill it with integrity. And celebrate those who fill theirs.

I love you, son. I hope you always know it. —Dad

Wisdom, Discernment, and Godly Decisions

CHAPTER EIGHTY-THREE
Choose Thankfulness in Every Season

Son,

Just before you were born, my life took a turn I never expected. Because of some tragic circumstances, I lost my job after an attempt on my life and spent years healing—physically, emotionally, spiritually. I was still hurting when you entered the world, and suddenly I found myself in a role I had never imagined: a stay-at-home dad caring for a newborn while your mom worked ten- to twelve-hour days, six days a week, just to help us get by.

I didn't know how to take care of a newborn. I didn't know how to slow down after working since I was fourteen. I didn't know how to navigate that season with any sort of grace or confidence.

I felt out of place. Uncertain. And honestly... emasculated.

If I could do it over again, son, I would do it very differently.

Instead of throwing myself a pity party, instead of focusing on what *wasn't*, I would have been intentionally thankful for what *was*. I would recalibrate my focus to be thankful for every second that I had with you. I would have thanked God daily that you were healthy and growing. I would have recognized that—even though it wasn't how I imagined—God was still providing for our needs. I would have been grateful that I was alive, recovering, and able to pour into your life. I would have taken more time to appreciate the friends and family who stood beside us when we needed it most.

I didn't do everything wrong in that season, but I know this: ***I could have done so much better if I had simply been present and thankful.***

Son, life happens. Disappointments happen. Setbacks happen. Sometimes *"manure occurreth"*—but if you process it through the right lens, it becomes ***fertilizer***. It grows you. It nourishes your seed in the difficult season. It produces something far better in the long run.

Knowing what I know now, I wish I had more of those early moments with you back—not because I wasted them, but because I wasn't as thankful as I could have been. Gratitude would have changed my attitude, my peace, my smile, and how I handled the little frustrations that didn't really matter.

I can't rewrite that chapter—but *you* can learn from it.

Be intentional. Be present. And every day—**every single day**—look for something to be thankful for. There is always something if you're looking for it.

I love you, son. I hope you always know it. —Dad

Wisdom, Discernment, and Godly Decisions

CHAPTER EIGHTY-FOUR
Choose Grace Over Judgment

Son,

Today at work I remembered a conversation we had when you were six or seven. I was trying to explain God's grace to you—how He doesn't hold your sin against you, how He loves you no matter what, and how His heart toward you never changes even when you mess up.

Well, the very next day you came home from school after getting in trouble again. That season felt like every day your teacher was calling, and every night ol' Dad had to lay down some discipline. You walked through the door, dropped your backpack, and said, *"Dad, I'm gonna need you to show me some grace. I got in trouble again today."*

I tried so hard not to laugh… because you were learning something important.

Like your father, you have a strong sense of justice. You don't like to see unfair things happen, and you feel things deeply when they do. People with high justice values need to understand grace even more than most—because your strength can also become your struggle.

As you grow and eventually lead your own family, ministry, business, or team, you'll face moments where someone's mistake gives you a choice: *Will you lead with judgment, or will you lead with grace?* Unless a mistake requires legal consequences, I recommend you choose grace as often as possible.

There's something else you need to pay attention to. People with strong justice values often withhold their love when they're hurt—as a way of *"balancing the scales."* It feels like the natural response, but it doesn't reflect *the Father's* heart.

God doesn't pull away from you when you mess up. He doesn't give you the silent treatment. He doesn't withhold affection to make a point.

He loves, corrects, guides, and restores—without withdrawing His heart.

Son, when you get hurt, mirror God's way. Don't withhold love from your wife to make a point. Don't withhold love from your children to prove a lesson. Don't withhold love from people you lead in order to emphasize their mistake.

Correct in love. Lead with compassion. Show grace the way Jesus did.

Remember *the woman caught in adultery* from John chapter 8. The law, religion, and the crowd said she deserved death. Jesus said, *"He who is without sin, cast the first stone."* And when she looked up, He asked, *"Where are your accusers?"* Then He said, *"Neither do I accuse you. Go and sin no more."*

That's grace. Correction wrapped in love. Truth wrapped in kindness. Leadership wrapped in compassion.

Son, I'm still learning this myself every day. But I'm convinced that grace and love are the closest expressions of God's heart we will ever demonstrate.

Mirror Him as best as you can. Your life will be richer, and everyone you lead will be better because of it.

I love you, son. I hope you always know it. —Dad

Leadership, Authority, and Kingdom Influence

CHAPTER EIGHTY-FIVE
How You Fill Your Lane Matters

Son,

How you fill your lane matters.

God told Jeremiah, *"Before I formed you in your mother's womb, I knew you and I called you."* That truth is just as real for you today. In every season of your life, you will be part of a team—with a role to play and a lane to fill. As you've grown, your mom and I have placed certain expectations on you, not as chores to check off, but to help you learn responsibility, integrity, and time management. Those expectations are your contribution to our family team. You're not just living in this house—you're helping carry the responsibility of it.

To whom much is given, much is required.

Son, I carry a lot on my shoulders. What I do, how I act, and the choices I make all affect our whole family. If I failed to fill my lane, it would impact you and your quality of life in ways you might not see now but would absolutely feel later. In that same way, when you cut the grass or take on your responsibilities, it's one less weight that I have to carry. Your contribution is a blessing—to me, to your mother, and to our whole home.

But this lesson is bigger than our house. It carries into every environment you will ever be part of. You represent your team wherever you go—your family, your future family, your church, your career, and ultimately the Kingdom of God. The way you conduct yourself can either bless or hinder the team you are called to serve. This is why Scripture tells us, *"Do everything as unto the Lord."* (Colossians 3) When you understand that what you do is ultimately for God, the small things don't feel so small anymore.

The truth is, you won't always want to *"cut the metaphorical grass."* You won't always feel like doing the right thing. You won't always want to lead, to sacrifice, or to carry responsibility. Some mornings the alarm will go off and your flesh will want to check out. But your contribution still matters—and when you do it through the lens of *honoring God*, He honors your faith and your faithfulness.

Son, what you do matters. How you do it matters. Your lane matters. Fill it with integrity, humility, and love.

I love you, son. I hope you always know it. —Dad

Your Identity in the Father's Heart

CHAPTER EIGHTY-SIX
You Are Enough

Son,

When people mess up, the typical church response is to shepherd them back into *"right relationship"* with *the rules*. Leaders often mean well, but many forget that our connection to God isn't rooted in performance—it's rooted in love. Character and integrity matter, and they will always help you steward what God entrusts to you. But never confuse that with the idea that God's love or blessing must be earned. They aren't. They never were.

Our relationship with God is not a relationship with *the law*. Scripture says, *"The law of the Spirit of life in Christ Jesus has set you free from the law of sin and death."* (Romans 8:2) That means your standing with God is not determined by rule-keeping—it's determined by relationship.

Under the old system, everything was built on fear of punishment. Under the new covenant Jesus gave us, everything is built on love. Jesus showed us the Father's heart when He told the story of the prodigal son. The son came home dirty, broken, guilty—yet his father ran to him, embraced him, restored him, and blessed him before he could even apologize. None of it was based on performance. It was based on sonship.

And Son, that's exactly how I feel about you. I don't love you because you earn it. I don't love you because you behave well. I don't love you because you impress me. I love you because you are my son. Nothing changes that. Nothing threatens that. Nothing takes that away.

If I—a flawed human being—feel that way, how much more does your heavenly Father love you with a perfect, unshakable love?

It's the kindness of God that draws people to repentance. Repentance isn't about fixing behavior—it's about changing your mind about who He is and who you are. When people encounter His kindness, they naturally want to live for Him. Love transforms what law could never touch.

So when you lead others, Son, never lead them to the rules. Lead them to *the Father*. Lead them to His mercy seat. Help them encounter His love—because once they know He cares, their desire to walk with Him will grow from the inside out.

You're His son before you're His servant. Never forget that.

I love you, son. I hope you always know it. —Dad

Your Identity in the Father's Heart

CHAPTER EIGHTY-SEVEN
You Don't Know God

Son,

There's an old saying: *people don't sing because they're happy—they're happy because they sing.* In the same way, people aren't separated from God because they sin—they sin because they are separated from God. Their behavior is a symptom, not the root issue. So why would we expect anything different from someone who doesn't know the One who transforms hearts? The Bible says we don't wrestle against flesh and blood. People are not the enemy.

Religion has often tried to fix people from the outside in—clean up their actions, fix their behavior, make them *"look"* holy. But sin isn't the real issue. The world doesn't have a *sin condition*—it has a *heart condition*.

And that heart condition has two sides.

One side is filled with people who don't know God at all and desperately need to understand His love. The other side is filled with people who *do* know God, yet still don't understand His love. Those on this second side often become so focused on the symptoms—sin, behavior, politics, culture—that they completely miss the heart underneath. They correct, condemn, and get offended at actions without ever seeing the person behind them.

But Scripture says it is the *kindness* of God that leads men to repentance—not anger, not outrage, not correction. And repentance doesn't mean *"change your actions."* It literally means *"change your mind."* When you think differently, you behave differently. When you truly understand the kindness and love of God, that love becomes the force that changes everything else.

Last night I saw someone write, *"God save us from Your followers."* At first it irritated me. But the more I thought about it, the more I understood. There are a lot of people who claim to love God, yet act nothing like Him. They weaponize truth but never show love. They act offended, superior, and judgmental toward anyone who doesn't fit their mold. But the Bible is very clear—*God is love.* And if love isn't present,

God isn't either.

Son, people will always matter more than systems, processes, arguments, or being right. Remember that. **See the heart before you see the behavior.** Love before you correct. **And always choose compassion over condemnation.**

I love you, son. I hope you always know it. —Dad

Building Godly Character and Integrity

CHAPTER EIGHTY-EIGHT
Better Than Fear

Son,

When you motivate, manipulate, or control people with fear, you trap yourself into leading that way forever. Fear may work for a season—but eventually, especially in strong people, it breeds rebellion. And honestly, I believe that rebellion to fear is *God-inspired.* Scripture says God has not given us a spirit of fear, but of power, love, and a sound mind. Deep inside every person created in God's image is a resistance to anything that tries to control them through fear.

Think about the heroes we admire—David facing Goliath, Shadrach, Meshach, and Abednego standing before the furnace, the unknown man in Tiananmen Square, William Wallace, Rosa Parks. What inspires us is not their strength alone, but their refusal to bow to fear. That's why fear-based leadership always collapses. Eventually people rise up and say, *"I won't live like this anymore."* And I believe that fire inside comes from the One who created us for freedom, not bondage.

There is a better way to lead—**you lead with love.**

There's a saying I've told you many times: *people don't care what you know until they know that you care.* Son, I know this to be absolutely true. I've led people through storms, chaos, and dangerous seasons—places where the outcome wasn't guaranteed. And I've followed leaders into situations where I wasn't sure I would walk out. The difference was always the same: *I was willing to follow leaders who I knew cared about me more than they cared about themselves.*

I heard someone say this week, *"People don't quit jobs; they quit bosses."* For the most part, I believe that's true. That's why I challenge you—be the leader you would want to follow.

There's another saying worth holding onto: *"Leaders eat last."* It means you make sure your people are fed, protected, empowered, and supported before you think of yourself. The world may not always recognize that kind of leadership, but your men will. When people know you genuinely care, they'll walk with you through anything.

And remember this: the Bible says it's *God's kindness* that leads men to repentance—not fear. Love transforms hearts in a way intimidation never could.

Just a few thoughts from your dad today, because I want you to lead well, love well, and represent *the Father* well.

I love you, son. I hope you always know it. —Dad

Building Godly Character and Integrity

CHAPTER EIGHTY-NINE
Humility Will Take You Further Than Pride Ever Will

Son,

Just before you were born, I released my first book, *The Spirit of Religion*. It took me several months to write. The day I typed the final sentence, I sat back, smiled, and felt proud—I had finished what I started. But almost instantly, I heard that still small voice say, *"Good job, but it's not My heart."*

The truth is, I wrote that book out of anger. My first draft sounded more like the rebuke of an Old Testament prophet than the heart of a New Testament *father*. The content wasn't necessarily wrong—there were good lessons there—but the delivery lacked love. My tone didn't reflect Jesus. It reflected my frustration.

Scripture tells us that Jesus came to *reveal the Father*. The religious leaders of His day didn't understand who God really was, so Jesus showed them: a God of compassion, mercy, kindness, and grace. A God who healed the broken, restored the outcast, and embraced the sinner. Jesus said, *"If you've seen Me, you've seen the Father."*

Son, that truth matters. Any time a leader—pastor, politician, police officer, or anyone in authority—says something about God that doesn't look like Jesus, you have every right to question it. Jesus is the perfect representation of His Father. If it doesn't look like Him… it's not Him.

I had to humble myself and admit that parts of my book didn't reflect the heart of God. That realization allowed me to rewrite it for the future with a different spirit. But it required humility. It required the willingness to say, *"Maybe I was wrong."*

And that's something many leaders today refuse to do.

I've seen it in every arena—people clinging to old positions, old opinions, old attitudes because admitting they were wrong would cost them pride… or work… or reputation. But the Bible says, *"Humble yourself in the sight of the Lord, and He will lift you up." (James 4:10 NKJV)* God elevates the humble, not the proud.

Son, if you ever want to step into your fullest leadership potential, you must confront your own humanity. You must be willing to admit when you missed it. An unwillingness to acknowledge fault will place a ceiling on your influence faster than anything else.

Every week I see men stand behind pulpits or in positions of authority sounding like Old Testament prophets—loud, harsh, and convinced their tone represents God. But all they're doing is echoing 1 Corinthians 13… a clanging cymbal without love.

Don't ever be that man. On whatever platform God gives you—big or small—represent Him well. Use your words and actions to reveal Jesus, not your pride.

I love you, son. I hope you always know it. —Dad

Leadership, Authority, and Kingdom Influence

CHAPTER NINETY
Call Out the King in Others

Son,

Somewhere out there is a David standing alone in a field, completely unaware that he carries the heart of a king. And he will need someone—*maybe you*—to see what others overlooked and call out the greatness that was always inside him².

So many leaders miss this. They think their calling is about their own success, their own recognition, their own ascent. But the greatest aspect of leadership is often this: being the reason someone else rises into the fullness of what God created them to be.

David's own father and brothers stood close enough to influence him, yet failed to recognize the king right in front of them. They prioritized wrongly. They judged by appearances. They looked for outward qualifications instead of seeing the heart.

Son, don't ever be that kind of leader. See people with God's eyes. Look for the hidden potential others overlook. Call out greatness where it has never been spoken.

When you build a team without needing the credit... when you celebrate others' victories as if they were your own... when you choose empowerment over comparison... you create an exponential legacy that insecure leaders will never experience. Because insecurity chokes destiny, but encouragement unleashes it.

Here's what I want you to remember: When you play a role in someone else's success, their victory becomes part of your legacy. When you empower the greatness in another for the sake of the Kingdom, the whole team wins.

So when God puts people under your leadership, be intentional. Speak life into them. Call out their gifting. Affirm their purpose. Your words matter more than you know.

Ask God to show you what they cannot yet see in themselves. And when He does, declare it boldly. Sometimes one encouragement from the right person at the right time can change the entire trajectory of someone's life.

And son—don't stop there. Teach the ones you lead to do the same. Encourage the giant-slayers you raise to become *legacy-minded*—men and women who will one day identify and empower other giant-slayers after them.

That's how Kingdom legacy is built. That's how generations are shaped. That's how kings are discovered in fields.

I love you so much, son. I hope you always know it. —Dad

Discipline, Consistency, and Spiritual Growth

CHAPTER NINETY-ONE
Guard Your Heart from Entitlement

Son,

Scripture says, *"Above all else, guard your heart, for out of it flow the wellsprings of life."* That verse has confronted me more times than I can count—but one moment stands out vividly.

A few years ago, when I broke my leg, I was given a handicap parking placard. I used it when I needed it, mostly at church. But I was careful. I left the closest spots for people who truly needed them.

Eventually, my leg healed. I didn't *need* that spot anymore—but I liked the convenience of it. And because I was the executive pastor, I convinced myself it was fine. So, one Sunday morning, I pulled right into that handicap space like it still belonged to me.

As I got out of the car, Jim looked at me with a half-joking, half-serious grin and said, *"You're just gonna park right there, huh?"* I smirked and said, *"Yep,"* and walked toward the doors.

But before I could step inside, that quiet voice between my ears spoke loud and clear:

"So because you have a little authority, you think you can do what would be illegal for anyone else? Do you really believe you've earned a right that sets you above the people you're leading? That's entitlement. That's pride. That's the opposite of godly leadership."

It hit me like a punch to the chest.

God wasn't upset about a parking space. He was showing me a heart issue—an attitude that said, *"It's okay for me but not for anyone else."* And son, that kind of mindset will destroy a leader from the inside out.

So I hung my head, walked back outside, and quietly moved my car.

The Bible says, *"Out of the abundance of the heart, the mouth speaks."* But I'd add this parallel: *out of the abundance of the heart, our actions reveal us.* That day, my actions revealed entitlement—something I never wanted in my heart. God, in His mercy, knocked me off the little pedestal I had placed myself on.

It's the little foxes that spoil the vine. It's the small compromises that plant seeds of something ugly. Pride. Arrogance. Entitlement. These things creep in quietly but grow quickly—and they will always hurt the people you lead.

Son, Jesus—the Son of the living God—modeled leadership by washing the feet of His followers. That is the foundation of godly leadership. Humility. Service. Integrity. Never assume you deserve special treatment because of your position.

Guard your heart. Stay small in your own eyes. And let your leadership always look like Jesus.

I love you, son. I hope you always know it. —Dad

Leadership, Authority, and Kingdom Influence

CHAPTER NINETY-TWO
Don't Let Your Gift Become Your God

Son,

God has gifted you in so many incredible ways. I see the talent, the strength, the potential He's placed in you. But I want to caution you about something important: *always remember where those gifts came from.*

When a person is gifted, the temptation is to start putting faith in the *gift* instead of the Gift *Giver.* And the moment that happens, the very thing God intended to bless you becomes an idol that limits you.

I once asked a friend whose own gift eventually destroyed him what he would tell his younger self. He said, *"The second you start believing your own hype, you're already on your way out."*

He was right. Believing your own hype... Trusting in your own strength... Thinking you can do it without God (or placing the *major* on you and the *minor* on God)... Ignoring the warnings of the Holy Spirit... Putting yourself above others...

These are the traps that take down gifted people every day.

And son, I learned this lesson the hardest possible way.

On the day an attempt was made on my life, the Holy Spirit told me three separate times, *"Go back to your office."* And three times I told God, *"Even if they try to attack me, I'm strong enough to take them both."* I believed in my own strength. I believed in my own ability. What I didn't know was the one variable God already saw—and my pride nearly got me killed.

That same pattern plays out spiritually in the lives of countless gifted believers. What God intended as a strength becomes a weakness because they stopped drawing power from Him. Your gifts were never designed to operate independently from the One who gave them.

Son, the potential God has placed inside you is unstoppable *if* you stay aligned with Him—*if* you seek His kingdom first, *if* you walk in humility, *if* you acknowledge Him in everything you do.

Just remember this: Your greatest enemy won't likely be dressed like the devil—it will be dressed like the version of you who is deceived into trusting the *gift* more than the *Giver*.

Don't fall into that trap. Stay humble. Stay grateful. Stay surrendered. And God will make your path straight.

I love you, son. I hope you always know it. —Dad

Leadership, Authority, and Kingdom Influence

CHAPTER NINETY-THREE
Leadership Without Entitlement

Son,

Benjamin Disraeli once said, *"Next to knowing when to seize an opportunity, the most important thing to know in life is when to forgo an advantage."* [3] Abraham Lincoln put it this way: *"Nearly all men can stand adversity. But if you want to test a man's character, give him power."* [4] And Proverbs 27:21 (paraphrased) teaches, *"Fire tests silver and gold, but a man is tested by the praise he receives."*

Those aren't random thoughts—they all point to the same truth: nothing exposes a man's real character like the way he handles authority.

One of the biggest traps people fall into is believing they deserve special treatment because of their title or position. It destroys influence, erodes trust, and creates environments full of resentment. The moment someone thinks they're above others, they've already stepped out of God's design for leadership.

Whether someone is a parent, pastor, police officer, or politician—authority is given by God, and it must be handled with humility. Godly leadership has two primary responsibilities:

1. **To protect people.**

2. **And to empower people.**

When entitlement settles into a leader's heart, everything shifts. Their role becomes about *self* instead of *service*. Pride and entitlement start walking hand-in-hand, and suddenly they believe they deserve advantages, exemptions, or special treatment that others don't get. That's the opposite of Christlike leadership.

Son, entitlement always reveals itself in the small things—cutting corners, expecting privilege, assuming rules apply to everyone except you. But godly leadership does the opposite. It leads by example. It chooses integrity when nobody sees. It lives under the same expectations it asks of others.

Always remember: every person you meet is someone's child—and most importantly, they're God's child. If the Lord ever entrusts people to your care, treat them with honor. Don't ever assume your position makes you better or more deserving. God holds leaders to a higher standard, and He pays close attention to how they steward their influence.

Jesus had all of heaven at His disposal, and yet He knelt down and washed the feet of His followers. That is leadership! That is greatness! That is the model you are called to follow.

People will always matter more than process, position, or power. Remember that when you lead them.

I love you, son. I hope you always know it. —Dad

Mastering Your Mind and Inner World

CHAPTER NINETY-FOUR
Guard Your Imagination, Guard Your Life

Son,

Your imagination is one of the most powerful tools God has given you. Most people never realize this, but we often place our beliefs—not in reality—but in the *outcomes we imagine.* And whatever you consistently imagine, you eventually begin to extend faith toward.

That's why you have to be incredibly careful about the voices you allow to shape your thoughts. If you let media, fear-based narratives, or propaganda feed your imagination, your belief system will slowly start to form around the dangers, anxieties, and worst-case scenarios they present. Without realizing it, you start cooperating with the very outcomes they're trying to make you afraid of.

That is misplaced faith.

When Scripture tells us in Philippians 4:8 to think on things that are good, pure, noble, and virtuous, it isn't just poetic language—it's instruction for spiritual survival. Your imagination feeds your faith. The things you meditate on become the soil your belief system grows in.

When you spend time imagining negative or godless scenarios, you're extending faith in the wrong direction. But when you visualize God's promises, when you meditate on His Word, when you imagine the future He is calling you into—you're aligning your faith with Heaven. You're cooperating with God. The bible even says in John 15:19 that Jesus didn't do anything except what He *"sees"* the Father doing. I believe He *"saw"* with the imagination and mind of the Spirit.

Son, what you think about consistently will shape the person you become. Proverbs 23:7 says, *"As a man thinks in his heart, so is he."* That's not just philosophy—it's a spiritual law. Faith collapses possibilities into realities. Your thoughts are often the first stage of that process.

Even science is catching up to what Scripture has always taught. The world calls it the *"law of attraction,"* but I'm convinced it's simply faith operating the way God designed it to—vision becoming substance.

Every victory or defeat happens first in the mind. If you learn to master your meditations, you will learn to master your life.

So, guard your imagination. Fill it with God's truth, not the world's fear. Dream with Him, not with your anxieties. Your thoughts will either build your future or sabotage it—so choose them intentionally.

I love you, son. I hope you always know it. —Dad

Wisdom, Discernment, and Godly Decisions

CHAPTER NINETY-FIVE
Don't Let Foolish Voices Shape Your Life

Son,

Proverbs 13:2 (MSG) says, *"Become wise by walking with the wise; hang out with fools and watch your life fall to pieces."* That's not just a poetic warning—it's a reality you'll see play out over and over again.

The truth is, the world is full of fools who are absolutely convinced they're wise. Loud voices. Confident voices. Influential voices. But foolish still. And if you're not intentional, their noise can start to shape your perspective without you even realizing it.

So hear me: ***Do not allow foolishness to influence your life.*** You fight it proactively by refusing to entertain what you know is stupid, destructive, or contrary to God's Word. Don't give it an inch. When you feed roaches, they stay and multiply—foolish ideas work the same way. Don't feed them.

When political correctness or cultural trends contradict biblical truth—discard them. When the news tries to create fear, outrage, or confusion—discard it. When someone's fear-driven narrative is designed to profit off your panic—discard it. When popular ideologies sound smart but undermine God's design—discard them.

You always have a choice in which voices you allow to influence your thinking. The world will offer you endless opinions, but only God's Word offers life-giving truth. Be discerning. Choose wisdom over noise. Choose truth over trends. Choose conviction over convenience.

Son, be God's man—steady, grounded, and anchored in truth even when the world around you loses its mind.

I love you, son. I hope you always know it. —Dad

Leadership, Authority, and Kingdom Influence

CHAPTER NINETY-SIX
The Last Word Belongs to God

Son,

One of the things I've learned over the years is this: *God is so good at turning negative situations into something beautiful that people often assume He was the One who sent the negative circumstance in the first place.*

But that's not how God works.

The Bible says in Romans that God works *all things together for our good*. That doesn't mean everything that happens is good. It doesn't mean every circumstance is *"God's will."* And it certainly doesn't mean God sends pain just so He can fix it later.

What it *does* mean is this: **God refuses to let tragedy have the final word in your life.** He is faithful to redeem what the enemy meant for harm. He steps into broken moments and builds something new out of them—not because He caused the damage, but because He loves His children too much to leave them in the ruins.

Son, you won't always understand why certain things happen. Life will hand you moments that break your heart, confuse you, or make you question what God is doing. When those times come, remember what Jesus Himself said: *The enemy is the one who comes to steal, kill, and destroy.* Jesus came so that you could have life—and have it abundantly.

God is good. He is faithful. He is for you, even when circumstances look like they're against you. Trust His heart, even when you can't trace His hand. He has never lost the ability to redeem, restore, and rewrite the story.

I love you, son. I hope you always know it. —Dad

Healing Pain and Growing in Emotional Maturity

CHAPTER NINETY-SEVEN
Love Big Anyway

Son,

When I worked as a detective, I learned how to shut my emotions off like flipping a switch. It wasn't intentional at first—it was survival. After a while, I got so good at it that I went years without shedding a single tear. I could separate myself from anything painful. Redirect my thoughts. Disassociate. Go numb.

A few years ago, I flipped that switch again. Not because I wanted to forget, but because remembering hurt too much. A song, a hallway, a small detail in the room—anything could trigger a wave of memory, and I just wasn't ready for it. So I shut it down. Redirected. Moved on.

But last night was different. For the first time in years... I remembered, and it didn't hurt. I actually smiled.

I was listening to a song from my childhood and heard a chord progression I hadn't heard in forever—one that *he would've used when he played and sang*. And instead of pain, I felt warmth. So this morning on the way to work, I put on his music. I sang along. I remembered sitting in the studio while those songs were recorded. I remembered the laughter, the moments, the impact. I gave myself an hour just to *remember*.

Son, loving big is a double-edged sword. If you love deeply, you can also hurt deeply. The pain of loss can run deeper than you expect. But hear me—**love big anyway.** People are worth it. Relationships are worth it. Legacy is worth it.

I wouldn't be who I am today without his influence. And when I look back now, I don't feel the sting anymore. I miss him, but the feeling I felt last night and today was more being *thankful* for what that season gave me.

Would I change things if I could? Maybe. But truthfully, I don't know how I could've navigated it differently. Life doesn't always give us perfect options. Sometimes it just gives us a moment, and we do the best we can with the integrity we have.

So here's my challenge to you: *When you face painful, complicated, emotionally charged moments in life, slow down. Talk to God. Listen for His peace. And then make the decision you believe is right—even if it's hard.* Because at the end of the day, integrity is what lets you look in the mirror without regret.

Son, love big. Live with integrity. And when it hurts, trust that God can heal the places you can't fix on your own.

I love you, son. I hope you always know it. —Dad

Healing Pain and Growing in Emotional Maturity

CHAPTER NINETY-EIGHT
Dis-Appointment

Son,

When your experience doesn't meet your expectation, disappointment is often the result.

Think about that word *disappointment* for a moment:

- Dis – not, the opposite of

- Appointment – assigning a job, role, or position

To feel *dis-appointed* is to feel removed from the place you believed you were called to stand.

One of the most fascinating people in Scripture to me is Daniel. Babylon went to war with Israel, defeated them, and carried people into captivity or killed them. King Nebuchadnezzar chose Daniel—one of Israel's wisest and part of the royal family—to serve in his court as a slave.

As was customary, Daniel was likely castrated and made a eunuch. His identity was stripped. His name was changed from Daniel ("God is my judge") to Belteshazzar ("Bel protect his life"), honoring a pagan god. He was appointed among the king's *magicians* because of his prophetic gift—his calling renamed, reframed, and redefined by a pagan king.

Nebuchadnezzar took Daniel's family, his title, his legacy, his dignity, his identity, and seemingly even his calling. From the outside, it looked like Daniel had been completely DIS-appointed.

But Scripture records no protest from Daniel. He doesn't argue. He doesn't correct the king. He doesn't stand up to announce, *"I'm a prophet, not a magician,"* or *"I serve the one true God!"* He simply remains faithful to God in private and waits until the king calls upon him.

And even when Nebuchadnezzar asks for the interpretation of a dream that foretells judgment, Daniel doesn't gloat. He doesn't lash out.

He doesn't say, *"You're finally getting what you deserve."* Instead, he says, *"O king, I wish this dream were about your enemies…"*

Son, that astounds me. If I were in Daniel's shoes, I would've been waiting for the chance to repay the king for everything he took. But Daniel understood something deeper: *When God is the one who appoints you, no man can dis-appoint you.*
Not captivity.
Not injustice.
Not loss.
Not the opinions of others.
Not even circumstances that look like defeat.

You must know who appointed you, who you belong to, and what God has called you to do. And then—just like Daniel—you remain faithful wherever your feet tread. Because the gifts and callings of God are without repentance (Romans 11:29). What God places on your life, no one can remove.

People may rename you. Life may reroute you. Circumstances may strip away what you thought your future would look like. But they cannot un-appoint what God has appointed.

The same God who appointed Daniel has appointed you.

I love you, son. I hope you always know it. —Dad

Healing Pain and Growing in Emotional Maturity

CHAPTER NINETY-NINE
When It's All True

Son,

As I've gotten older, I've lived with the tension of knowing what happens behind closed doors. I've studied and heard *behind-the-scenes* stories from those who were there of men and women who were used powerfully by God in public, while at the very same time their private lives were a checklist of what *not* to do as Christian leaders. And it has often made me ask the question:

"What if it's all true?"

What if God really does choose to use broken, imperfect people to impact a broken, imperfect world... and every part of the story is true? What if the good you saw—the miracles, the sermons, the impact—was genuinely God? And what if the failures and flaws you heard about were true as well?

Does the bad cancel the good God did through them? Should it?

In the cancel-culture world we live in, people elevate leaders to a level of idolatry, and then when those leaders don't live up to that idolatry, we want to erase them completely. But son, people today aren't much different than people in Bible days. God's leaders back then were not superhuman. They were just humans in need of a Savior—just like us. I believe that's part of why Scripture includes both their victories *and* their failures. There's a lesson in the balance.

Today, when we tell the stories of modern leaders, we feel the need to briefly mention their successes and then rush straight to a disclaimer about their mistakes—almost as if we're afraid someone will think we're defending their failures if we acknowledge the good.

But why can't we do both? Why can't we honor the good while recognizing their humanity? Why can't we be grateful for their impact while having compassion for their collapse? Why can't we thank God for His grace, realizing that without His mercy, any of us could end up in the same place?

I ask you, *"What if it's all true?"* because Scripture shows us that God is capable of using deeply flawed people for His glory. He took a murderer named Paul and made him the author of two-thirds of the New Testament. He took Rahab—a prostitute—and made her part of the lineage of Jesus. He took the wisest man who ever lived, Solomon, and allowed his writings to become part of Scripture even though much of Ecclesiastes reflects the thinking of a man who had drifted far from God.

Maybe the whole story—the successes and the failures—speaks more truth than the carefully edited version we prefer to repeat. Maybe the point is that God is faithful even when people aren't. Maybe the lesson is to learn with grace, not judgment.

Son, don't be quick to erase people. Learn from the whole picture. Honor what God did. Have compassion for where they fell. And remember—every one of us stands by grace alone.

I love you, son. I hope you always know it. —Dad

Healing Pain and Growing in Emotional Maturity

CHAPTER ONE HUNDRED
The Lens You Choose

Son,

It takes no effort at all to look at life through the lens of what's missing. It's funny how we'll pray for God to open a door, meet a need, or fix a problem—and then the moment He does, we complain about it. We forget how far He's already brought us. We forget we're no longer where we used to be.

There's nothing wrong with wanting to move forward. Scripture says, *"Without vision, people perish."* Vision matters. Goals matter. Growth matters. But what I'm talking about isn't your vision for tomorrow—it's the lens you use to process today.

You can be dissatisfied and thankful at the same time. You can acknowledge what's uncomfortable without losing sight of what's good.

You can be dissatisfied that you didn't get enough sleep... and thankful for a warm, comfortable bed.

You can be dissatisfied sitting in rush-hour traffic in the rain... and thankful you're not biking twenty miles to work.

You can be dissatisfied that it's freezing outside... and thankful your heater works.

You can be dissatisfied paying $4.50 for gas... and thankful you have a car, a job, and the means to provide for your family.

You can even be dissatisfied that your reality doesn't yet look like your dream... and thankful that you serve a faithful God.

The problem is most people get stuck living in the parking lot of *"I'm dissatisfied."* And if you stay parked there, you'll never merge onto the highway that thankfulness opens up.

Yes, there should always be a healthy tension that pushes you to grow. But the trap that comes with dissatisfaction is focusing more on what is *not* instead of what *is*. When that happens, your vision gets clouded. Your dreams shrink. Your perspective becomes small. You end up framing your entire life by what's missing rather than by what's possible.

Son, what you focus on becomes the soil your future grows in. Focus on the negative, and negativity multiplies. Focus on God's goodness, and your faith begins to ignite with new possibility.

Call it reaping and sowing, call it the law of attraction, call it whatever you want—the principle is the same: gratitude creates the climate where vision grows and breakthrough takes root.

I'm not asking you to deny reality. I'm asking you to choose the lens that propels you forward in faith—not the one that traps you in limitation. Don't let dissatisfaction become the ceiling over your life. Let thankfulness be the soil where faith for your future thrives.

I love you, son. I hope you always know it. —Dad

Mastering Your Mind and Inner World

CHAPTER ONE HUNDRED ONE
The Purina Cantina - Don't Become Cat Food

Son,

Years ago, after some of our family immigrated from Vietnam to Detroit, Michigan, I took one of your cousins out into a field to fly a kite. We were standing in a freshly mowed area next to tall weeds when, trying to scare me, he suddenly yelled, "Aaron!!! TIGER!!!"

I fell down laughing and later explained to him that the only way that would be possible is if one had escaped from the zoo. But for him, growing up where he did, that was an absolutely real and reasonable threat.

As I thought about it later, I realized something important. I had never grown up in an environment where I had to consider the possibility of a 600-pound predator silently stalking me through tall grass. But he had. His awareness wasn't fear—it was survival.

Scripture tells us that our enemy prowls around like a lion, seeking whom he may devour. Big cats hunt covertly. Their prey is often completely unaware it's being stalked until it's too late. The Bible paints a clear picture: whether we recognize it or not, we live in a world where there is a very real spiritual enemy intent on stealing, killing, and destroying. (John 10:10)

Yet many believers don't take that threat seriously—and I believe the consequences can be severe.

So hear me, son: take your enemy seriously—and take yourself seriously.

Jesus has given us authority over *all* the works of the enemy. As a man, and as a child of God, you are not meant to be passive—you are meant to be a protector. You stand between the enemy and a world that is often unaware it's under attack.

That's why one of the most important things you can do in your life is to feed your spirit daily.

A warrior doesn't enter battle hungry, unarmed, or distracted. He keeps his sword sharp. He stays alert. He strengthens himself so that when the fight comes, he's ready.

Life gets busy. Distractions multiply. It's easy to go all day without feeding your spirit—just like skipping meals—until suddenly you're weak, unfocused, and blindsided.

Don't let that happen.

You don't have to live in fear—but you *do* need to live prepared.
Stay fed.
Stay alert.
And be ready when the fight finds you.

I love you, son. I hope you always know it. —Dad

Deepening Faith and Intimacy with God

CHAPTER ONE HUNDRED TWO
The Kingdom Has Arrived

Son,

Lately, when I walk into a new environment, I'll say out loud—sometimes even shout it, *"The Kingdom has arrived!"* This morning, as I pulled into the parking garage at work, I rolled down my window & declared it again: *"The Kingdom has arrived!"*

A few hours later, I found myself only a few spaces away from my car when a woman suddenly began screaming. Her daughter was in the front seat, having a full grand mal seizure. I went straight to the passenger side, opened the door, reached inside, & declared, *"In the name of Jesus!"*

Something shifted immediately—not with the daughter, but with the mother. The moment I said the name of Jesus, it was as if clarity came over her. It was like she suddenly remembered who she was. She jumped into the driver's seat, reached across her daughter, laid her hands on her, & in a thick African accent began to pray with authority:

"In the name of Jesus, I take authority over this & command it to stop!"

She spoke the promises of God over her daughter—boldly, fiercely, like a woman who had rediscovered her spiritual identity. And slowly, her daughter came back. The seizure stopped.

Sometimes, son, we just need to be reminded of who we are.

It's easy to forget in the darkness what we knew in the light—especially when something hits us out of nowhere. But there is power in the name of Jesus. His name pulls the compass of our heart back to true north. His Word says that by His stripes we were healed. His Word says that no weapon formed against us will prosper. His Word says we have authority over all the works of the enemy—because the same Spirit that raised Christ from the dead lives inside of us.

I was ready to step in and bring the Kingdom of God into that situation on behalf of that woman & her daughter—but that day, I think my assignment was different. My role was to remind that African mama of the authority she already carried in Jesus. And once she remembered…she handled it beautifully.

Son, you carry the Kingdom of God everywhere your feet tread. Use that authority to push back darkness, to heal, to restore, & to remind others—especially those who have forgotten—who their Jesus is.

I love you, son. I hope you always know it. —Dad

Healing Pain and Growing in Emotional Maturity

CHAPTER ONE HUNDRED THREE
Choose Compassion

Son,

When I was around five years old, I was exposed to sexuality by a neighborhood friend who, looking back, I'm convinced had been molested himself.

Throughout my adolescence, grown men made inappropriate advances toward me. Once, while I was skateboarding, a man walked up in front of all my friends and told me he wanted to have sex with me. I was mortified. Later, when I worked as a waiter in restaurants, gay men would frequently hit on me, and I remember asking myself, *"What is it about me that makes them think I'm interested?"* Over time, the discomfort and confusion turned into anger, and eventually into hatred. I didn't understand my own emotions, and I didn't understand theirs—so hatred felt like the easiest response.

Then, in Bible college, I met Shawn.

We sat next to each other in English class and quickly became close friends. He was about ten years older and always offered gentle, thoughtful counsel. I would talk to him about your mother, about God, about the hardships I was facing. And often—without knowing who he was—I would vent my frustration about the gay men who hit on me at work... and how much I hated them for it.

He never corrected me. Never defended himself. Never pushed back. He just listened with kindness.

A few months later, I returned home for a short season. When I came back to campus, I asked a group of friends where Shawn was.

"Aaron... Shawn's dead. You didn't know? He had AIDS. He got radically saved last year and moved here to spend whatever time he had left serving God."

I was devastated.

Suddenly every conversation replayed in my mind—all the times I carelessly expressed hatred toward people *"like him..."* and he never flinched. He never made it about himself. He never stopped being my friend. He never let my ignorance change his love for God or for me.

Son, Shawn changed me. Not by arguing. Not by announcing his pain. Not by correcting me. **His compassion exposed how wrong my perspective had been… and his love softened a place in me that hatred had hardened.**

I should have been a friend to him, but instead he chose—in his final year of life—to be a friend to me.

Don't let bitterness, fear, or painful experiences turn your heart against people God loves so deeply. You will never know the full story behind someone's struggle. But I can tell you this with certainty: The kind of love that Shawn showed me has the power to transform even the hardest heart. It transformed mine.

Choose compassion, Son. You'll never regret it.

I love you, son. I hope you always know it. —Dad

Deepening Faith and Intimacy with God

CHAPTER ONE HUNDRED FOUR
When Grief Whispers, Speak the Word

Son,

Grief is a dangerous fight. It has the power to overwhelm, distort reality, and whisper lies that contradict everything God has spoken over your life. And yet, I want you to understand this clearly: *it is okay to grieve. It's necessary. It's human. Even Jesus wept.*

But in every stage of grief, you must anchor yourself to the Word of God. Feelings shift. Thoughts wander. Pain speaks loudly. But God's Word remains steady, trustworthy, and true.

Grief often moves in stages:

1. **Shock and Denial**

2. **Pain and Guilt**

3. **Anger and Bargaining**

4. **Depression, Reflection, and Loneliness**

5. **The Upward Turn**

6. **Reconstruction and Working Through**

7. **Acceptance and Hope**

And in each stage, Scripture speaks directly to the battle:

1. Shock and Denial

"Fear not, for I am with you; be not dismayed, for I am your God. I will strengthen you… I will help you… I will uphold you…" —Isaiah 41:10, NKJV

When your world feels shattered, remember: **you are not alone.**

2. Pain and Guilt

*"Gaze upon Him, join your life with His, and joy will come. Your faces will

glisten with glory. You'll never wear that shame-face again." —Psalm 34:5, TPT

God heals shame—not with lectures, but with love.

3. Anger and Bargaining

"Honor Me by trusting in Me in your day of trouble. Cry aloud to Me, and I will be there to rescue you."—Psalm 50:15 (TPT)

God is not intimidated by your anger; He invites your honesty.

4. Depression, Reflection, and Loneliness

"Be strong and courageous… for the Lord your God goes with you. He will not leave you or forsake you." —Deuteronomy 31:6, ESV

"And behold, I am with you always, to the end of the age." —Matthew 28:20, NKJV

Even when you feel alone, **you are never abandoned.**

5. The Upward Turn

"Trust in the Lord with all your heart… In all your ways acknowledge Him, and He will direct your paths." —Proverbs 3:5–6, AMPC

Healing begins when you let God lead again.

6. Reconstruction and Working Through

"He who dwells in the secret place of the Most High shall remain stable and fixed under the shadow of the Almighty… I will say of the Lord, He is my refuge and my fortress…" —Psalm 91:1–2, AMPC

In your rebuilding, God becomes your stability.

7. Acceptance and Hope

"For I know the plans I have for you… to give you hope and a future." —Jeremiah 29:11, NIV

"Those who hope in the Lord will renew their strength…" —Isaiah 40:3 (NKJV)

When hope returns, strength rises with it.

Son, I share these scriptures because grief will try to isolate you. It will whisper lies— *"You can't go on… You're alone… Your story is over…"* But the Word of God confronts every one of those lies with truth.

When grief whispers, you answer back with, *"Thus saith the Lord."*

Don't let the only voice you hear be the one in your head. Take captive every thought. Speak the Word out loud. Remind your soul of what is true.

When darkness tries to settle in, remember what God taught you in the light. His Word will always be a lamp to your feet and a light to your path.

You will be tempted to back away from God and try to navigate the pain alone. Don't do it. RUN TO HIM. He will meet you in your weakness with strength, in your sorrow with comfort, and in your grief with hope.

The enemy does not get the final word over the territory God assigned to you. Not today. Not ever.

I love you, son. I hope you always know it. —Dad

Your Identity in the Father's Heart

CHAPTER ONE HUNDRED FIVE
As He Is, So Are You

Son,

There's a scripture I've always loved—one packed with truth about who you really are. 1 John 4:17 (NKJV) says: *"Love has been perfected among us in this: that we may have boldness in the day of judgment; because as He is, so are we in this world."*

Son, in life there will be moments when you walk through hardship, disappointment, failure, or unexpected detours. Those seasons can shake you. They can make you question who you are, who God says you are, or who you once believed you could become. That's why identity must be anchored in something deeper than circumstance. It has to be rooted in the Word of God.

When everything feels uncertain, when you don't feel strong or capable or worthy, you return to what God said—and remember this: **"As Jesus is, so are YOU in this world."** Not *"will be someday."* Not *"after you fix everything."* Right now. In this world.

Christ already paid the price for every failure and every attack, and God promises to work *all things together for your good. (Romans 8:28)*

As you grew up, I taught you that *"can't"* is a four-letter word we don't use in our house. You could say *you didn't know how yet*, or that *you needed help*, but you were never allowed to declare inability over yourself. Why? Because Scripture says:

-You can do ALL things through Christ. (Philippians 4:13)
-You have the Spirit of wisdom. (Ephesians 1:17)
-You can call on God and He will answer and show you mighty things you do not know. (Jeremiah 33:3)

As God's son, you carry *His* nature. You are a joint heir with Christ. You reflect your Father because His Spirit lives within you.

1 John 3:1 says, *"We ARE children of God."* Not *trying* to become children. Not *hoping* someday to be worthy. We *are*.

So, we don't strive to imitate Christ from the outside—we express Christ from within.

Because…

As He is holy, we pursue holiness.
As He is light, we walk in light.
As He is love, we love boldly and sacrificially.
As He forgives, we forgive.
As He ministers, we minister.
As He fights for us, we fight the good fight of faith—because faith works through love.

And Son…

You *can* get up.
You *can* forgive—yourself or others.
You *can* begin again.
You *can* overcome.
You *can* push through.
You *can* win.
You *can* walk in strength and victory…

Because you are not just *my* son—you are **God's** son.

Don't ever let the enemy convince you otherwise.

I love you, son. I hope you always know it. —Dad

Building Legacy and Finishing Strong

CHAPTER ONE HUNDRED SIX
Breaking the Cycle, Building a Legacy

Son,

Just because things have *"always been a certain way"* does **not** mean you are bound to continue the cycle. A single generation can flip an entire family line by choosing differently—choosing better.

I mean no dishonor in what I'm about to say, but I think it's fair to acknowledge that my grandfather—your great-grandfather on my dad's side—understood far more about crime and survival than about Jesus and Godliness. He carried deep childhood wounds and trauma, and although he loved his family deeply and was always kind and loving to me to me, many of the stories from his life reveal a man shaped more by hardship than by hope.

My dad once told me that when he was young and they moved into a new neighborhood, his father handed him a pipe and told him to *go find the biggest kid and beat him up… and not come home until he did.* That was the *"street survival"* mentality he was raised with—fight first, protect yourself, trust no one, stay hard.

Until I was about eight years old, your grandfather—my dad—began raising me with some of those same survival instincts. But then something changed. One day he came to me, sat me down, and apologized. He told me that his father hadn't raised him with a godly perspective, and he was choosing a different path. From that moment forward, everything shifted. He began pouring the things of God into me, teaching me Scripture, wisdom, character, and helping me become the man I am today.

He made a decision—a generational decision—to do things God's way.
And the ripple of that one choice is now flowing through me to you.

And today, as I write these letters, I'm carrying that legacy forward into your generation… and prayerfully into the ones that will follow you.

Here's the point, son: **It is never too late to change direction and do things God's way.**

There are things I modeled well for you, and there are things—some of which I've addressed in these letters—that I could have done better. And I believe with all my heart that you will take the good, learn from the imperfect, and choose to be an even stronger, wiser, more Godly example for your children than I was for you.

People say, *"A wise man learns from his mistakes."* But the truth is… anybody can learn from their own mistakes. It takes a *truly wise* man to learn from the mistakes and instruction of others.

Be that man. Seek God for direction. Ask Him to shape you into the best, most godly man you can possibly be. And walk in the wisdom of His ways.

I love you, son. I hope you always know it. —Dad

Building Godly Character and Integrity

CHAPTER ONE HUNDRED SEVEN
Small Choices, Strong Character

Son,

There's a popular idea called the *Shopping Cart Theory*. It suggests that a simple act—returning your shopping cart to the designated stall instead of leaving it for someone else—reveals something about a person's character. The thought is this: *people who do what's right even when no one is watching demonstrate good character and self-governance, while those who leave the cart for someone else to deal with show a lack of responsibility.*

Now, is this a flawless litmus test for character? No. But there *is* something valuable hidden in the principle: *a mature man takes responsibility for his actions, his contributions, and his impact—without waiting for someone else to do what he should do.* As a man, you own your mistakes and fix what you broke. That's what integrity requires.

I've watched this *"shopping cart mentality"* show up in bigger areas of life. It looks like blame shifting, refusing accountability, or excusing poor decisions by pointing to the failures of others. But son, that is the mentality of a slave, not a free man.

What do I mean by that?

A slave lives under the control of another. In the spiritual sense, people who lack integrity are often still enslaved to sin—shaped by bad examples and trapped in cycles of victimhood, powerlessness, and irresponsibility. They repeat patterns they never challenged, and justify choices they shouldn't have made.

But Scripture says, *"He whom the Son sets free is free indeed."* (John 8:36)

When you belong to Jesus, you are no longer a slave—you are a son. You carry a new name. You represent a new Kingdom. And with that identity comes responsibility.

As sons of God, we don't shrug and say, *"Someone else will take care of it."* We don't cut corners. We don't hide our failures. We don't justify poor behavior by comparing ourselves to others. We take responsibility because everything we do is ultimately *"unto the Lord."* We honor Him in the unseen moments—in the small decisions, the quiet sacrifices, and the mundane choices that no one else may ever notice.

The man who doesn't *"return his metaphorical shopping carts"* in life reveals a heart still centered on self. But the man with the heart of Jesus—the man set free—acts differently. He thinks differently. He carries himself differently. He lives as one who knows who his Father is and represents Him with honor.

Your actions reveal your nature. Make sure what you display reflects your Heavenly Father well.

I love you, son. I hope you always know it. —Dad

Discipline, Consistency, and Spiritual Growth

CHAPTER ONE HUNDRED EIGHT
What You Learn in the Climb

Son,

There's an old saying: *"It's an uphill climb."* It means that reaching the top of the mountain is often a grind—but you never get the mountaintop perspective without first walking through the valley and pushing your way up the slope.

So often, on our way to the metaphorical *"top,"* we resent the pain of the climb. But here is the truth few people understand: ***what you learn during the climb is what sustains you at the top.*** There are lessons in life that only pressure, resistance, and even heartache can teach you. Sometimes the pain feels like it's going to break you—but if you refuse to quit, that same pain will shape you, strengthen you, and prepare you.

In my own life, I can tell you confidently that I have been shaped just as much by what I *survived* as by what I've been *blessed* with. In hindsight, there are things I would never want to walk through again... yet I can honestly say those very things helped form the man I am today. What the enemy meant to destroy me, God used to build me—because **God never wastes pain.**

I'm wiser, stronger, more compassionate, and a better leader, husband, and father because of what I learned when I put my faith in God and He walked me through seasons meant for my destruction. He is faithful, and He truly does make all things new.

Now, this doesn't mean we should sabotage our lives through foolish choices. As Paul said, *"Should we continue in sin so that grace may abound?"* Of course not. But it *does* mean that when you find yourself in seasons of difficulty—darkness, exhaustion, pain, confusion—you can still rejoice. Why? Because even when the enemy attacks, God refuses to let tragedy have the final word. He turns the very thing meant to break you into the launching pad for your destiny.

Jesus put it this way: *"In this world you will have trouble. But take heart— I have overcome the world."*

And son, when the Overcomer lives inside you,
His authority becomes your authority.
His power becomes your power.
His victory becomes your victory.

Whatever you're facing—*it will pass.* God is faithful. Stay the course.

I love you, son. I hope you always know it. —Dad

Deepening Faith and Intimacy with God

CHAPTER ONE HUNDRED NINE
You Carry Heaven with You

Son,

Many times, in these letters, I have reminded you of this Romans 8:11 truth: *the same Spirit who raised Christ from the dead lives in you.* I've often said it this way—because that Spirit lives in you, *you carry heaven into every place where you encounter hell in the earth.*

Recently, I've been reflecting on what Scripture calls *the fruit of the Spirit.* Galatians 5:22–23 (AMPC) tells us: *"But the fruit of the [Holy] Spirit [the work which His presence within accomplishes] is love, joy (gladness), peace, patience (an even temper, forbearance), kindness, goodness (benevolence), faithfulness, gentleness (meekness, humility), self-control (self-restraint, continence). Against such things there is no law [that can bring a charge]."*

When you walk into any environment, you don't just carry the *dunamis*—the explosive, authoritative power of the Holy Spirit to confront the works of the enemy—you also carry the fruit of the Spirit to transform atmospheres and shift hearts.

You carry love that heals.
Joy that strengthens weary souls.
Peace that quiets chaos.
Patience that steadies the overwhelmed.
Kindness that leads others toward repentance.
Goodness that reveals God's character.
Faithfulness that builds trust where trust has been broken.
Gentleness that disarms hostility.
And self-control that subdues anger and restores order.

This means something, son.

You don't walk into rooms accidentally. You don't encounter broken people randomly. And you don't carry God's Spirit casually.

When you choose to live aware of who you are and who God is in you, you become a **living demonstration of the Kingdom**—not just in word, but in power and presence. Darkness doesn't retreat because you are loud; it retreats because you are submitted, yielded, and filled with His Spirit.

So walk deliberately. Love boldly. Stand firmly. And never forget that when you show up, God shows up with you.

I love you, son. I hope you always know it. —Dad

Discipline, Consistency, and Spiritual Growth

CHAPTER ONE HUNDRED TEN
Salvation Is Free—Blessing Is Cultivated

Son,

I was reading a passage of Scripture this past week, and an important detail stood out to me. Hebrews 11:6 tells us that *without faith it is impossible to please God,* **because** anyone who comes to Him **must believe** that He exists and that He rewards those who diligently seek Him.

That verse is significant, because many people assume God will automatically bless them at the same level as others simply because they are *Christians*. But that's not what Scripture actually teaches.

It is true that God's love and our salvation are unconditional. Nothing can separate us from His love, and His promises are "yes and amen" to His covenant people. However, while God's **love** is unconditional, His **blessings** are often conditional.

The Word tells us in Galatians 6:7 that *God is not mocked—whatever a man sows, **that** he will also reap.* Hebrews 11 reminds us that if we want to please God, *we must believe not only that He is, but that He rewards those who **diligently seek Him.***

When you combine the principle of sowing and reaping with this truth, it becomes clear that love alone is not the only factor connected to blessing. Many people look at the lives of others and feel as though God is playing favorites, because they see different levels of favor or provision. What they don't always see are the seeds that were sown long before the harvest appeared.

God's love for you is always secure—but abundance is not something you're entitled to without investment. Seeds of sacrifice. Seeds of generosity. Seeds of time. Seeds of obedience. Seeds of love. Seeds of diligence. You cannot be careless in your relationship with God and expect the fruit that comes from faithfulness and pursuit.

Salvation is free and you cannot earn it. But blessing is often the fruit of obedience, diligence, and seeking God with intention.

Dad's Letters

I love you, son. I hope you always know it. —Dad

Discipline, Consistency, and Spiritual Growth

CHAPTER ONE HUNDRED ELEVEN
The Power of Thankfulness

Son,

As I was driving into work today, I was struck with a sobering realization: *there are people in the world right now praying for the life I have.*

Their health is failing. Their families are falling apart. They are financially devastated. Some don't know God or have any hope for their future.

There are people wishing for just one more sunrise. One more conversation. One more opportunity to pursue their calling. One more chance to give a gift. One more moment to tell someone they love them.

As human beings, we're often deceived into seeing the cup half empty—focusing more on what isn't than on what is. This morning, I sensed God gently correcting my perspective and reminding me to be thankful for the blessings He has already placed in my life.

So here's the lesson I want to pass on to you: **be intentionally thankful.**

The person who looks for reasons to complain will always find them. But the person who looks for reasons to be thankful will find those too.

While I would never want you to settle for less than what God has promised you, I do want to encourage you to live with gratitude—even as an expression of your faith. Even in difficult seasons, there is always something you can thank God for.

Pitiful or powerful? That choice is yours. Complainers live pitiful lives. Thankful people walk in strength.

And never forget this: *with God, not only are all things possible, but we have a living hope—a faith-filled expectation—that He is always working things together for our good.*

He loves you. He is working on your behalf. Thank Him for what is—and for what is coming—because with God, you have the promise of a great future.

I love you, son. I hope you always know it. —Dad

Building Godly Character and Integrity

CHAPTER ONE HUNDRED TWELVE
The Power That Shapes You

Son,

The Word of God will change your life. Many believe David wrote Psalm 119:11 when he said, *"I have hidden Your Word in my heart, that I might not sin against You."* I believe he understood something most people miss: *the Word strengthens us to become who God created us to be and to stand against everything the enemy wants us to fall for.*

A few years ago, the Institute of Biblical Research conducted a major study on Bible engagement. What they discovered shocked even the researchers. People who read their Bible **once a week** showed almost **no measurable impact** in their spiritual lives. Those who read **two or three times a week** experienced only a small, inconsistent effect.

But once a person reads the Bible **four or more times per week**, the data shifts dramatically.

Scripture calls God's Word *"a lamp unto our feet and a light unto our path."* This study simply confirmed what God has been telling us all along: *when you seek first the Kingom of God and prioritize His way of doing and being, everything else in life begins to align.*

Here is what the research found—when someone engages the Bible four or more days a week, the odds of falling into certain temptations drop significantly: [5]

- Drinking to excess ↓ 62%
- Viewing pornography ↓ 59%
- Sexual sin ↓ 59%
- Gambling ↓ 45%
- Lashing out in anger ↓ 31%
- Gossip ↓ 28%

- Lying ↓ 28%
- Neglecting family ↓ 26%
- Overeating or mishandling food ↓ 20%
- Mishandling money ↓ 20%
- Bitterness ↓ 40%
- Destructive thoughts ↓ 32%
- Hiding struggles ↓ 32%
- Difficulty forgiving others ↓ 31%
- Discouragement ↓ 31%
- Loneliness ↓ 30%
- Difficulty forgiving oneself ↓ 26%
- Unkind thoughts ↓ 18%
- Fear and anxiety ↓ 14%

And the positive effects were just as powerful:

- Scripture memorization ↑ 407%
- Sharing their faith ↑ 228%
- Discipling others ↑ 231%
- Giving generously ↑ 416%

Across eight years and over 100,000 people surveyed, one truth remained the strongest and most consistent predictor of spiritual growth: **Engaging Scripture four or more times a week.**

Son, this is why I keep telling you to build your life on God's Word. Not because it earns you points with God, but because it strengthens your heart, renews your mind, and aligns your life with the identity God gave you.

If you want clarity, read the Word. If you want strength, read the Word. If you want freedom, stability, wisdom, and courage—read the Word.

Everything God promises becomes more real, more powerful, more readily available, and more active in your life when His Word becomes a regular part of your rhythm.

Make it a priority. Make it a habit. Make it your foundation.

You will never regret it.

I love you, son. I hope you always know it. —Dad

Building Godly Character and Integrity

CHAPTER ONE HUNDRED THIRTEEN
Becoming the Man God Made You to Be

Son,

There have been seasons in my life where I didn't feel like a *"good man."* People have said it to me a lot lately—your mom said it again this morning as I walked out the door—but that hasn't always been my internal reality. I've battled depression. I've fought through seasons of questioning my worth. I've carried the weight of failure, and I've paid dearly for some of my mistakes.

Son… I haven't made a *lot* of mistakes, but the ones I made were very costly. One of them delayed my development for years and cost me over a million dollars in lost wages. Mistakes can do that—they can take what seems like a moment to make, but years to recover from.

But here's what I want you to hear: **Those failures didn't define me—they refined me.**

In this season of my life, I want something different than I ever wanted before. I want to be the best man I can possibly be with the time I have left. The best father I can be to you. The best husband I can be to your mom. The best son I can be to my parents. The best leader and pastor God allows me to be. And most importantly, the best representative of Jesus I can be on this side of eternity.

For most of my life, my ambitions were about *me*. On the outside, few people would have ever seen it—but on the inside, I knew the truth. My drive, my goals, the things I pursued… they were fueled by selfish ambition, insecurity, and a desire to prove myself.

But something shifted in me these last few years. God has developed in me what I can only describe as a *father's heart*. A father's heart doesn't strive to be known—it desires to give.

A *father* wants to pour strength into others. A *father* wants his life to lift someone else's. A *father* wants to leave a legacy, not for his own name, but for those coming behind him.

And son, in this season, God has changed my desires. I no longer care if people know my name; I want them to know *His.*

Recently, I've watched God open blind eyes. I've watched Him heal chronic pain. I've watched Him set people free from burdens they carried for years. And do you know what I felt?

Not pride. Not ambition. Not the old desire to be impressive.

I felt a longing for people to know the God who healed them. I want to be the kind of man whose life points people toward Jesus—not away from Him. I want to challenge people to pursue *more* of God, not be the reason they avoid Him.

Son, you will make mistakes in your life—I pray none of them cost you what some of mine cost me. But even if they do, hear me clearly: *God never wastes pain! If you yield it to Him, He will use even the worst moments to shape you into the man He designed you to be.*

Let *Him* refine your heart early. Let *Him* shape your ambitions now. Let *Him* teach you how to live as a man whose purpose is bigger than himself.

That is the kind of man who changes the world. That is the kind of man who reflects his Father. That is the kind of man I see in you.

I love you, son. I hope you always know it.—Dad

Your Identity in the Father's Heart

CHAPTER ONE HUNDRED FOURTEEN
The Power of "Thank You, Daddy"

Son,

You were not even two years old when you taught me one of the greatest lessons I've ever learned about the heart of a father—and, ultimately, about the heart of God.

You had just discovered a new phrase: *"I want this."* We were walking through a children's aisle one night when you spotted a box with two plastic motorcycles inside. The box was almost too big for your little arms to carry, but you grabbed it anyway. You waddled toward me, straining under the weight, your back arched and your voice determined as you lifted it as high as you could and said, *"I want this."*

Son... the cuteness factor of that moment was off the charts.

I smiled, took the box from your struggling hands, and said, *"Okay, Daddy will buy this for you."* Walking to the car, you were practically vibrating with excitement. Honestly, I think I was just as excited to watch you enjoy the gift as you were to receive it. I opened the box right there so you wouldn't have to wait until we got home.

You grabbed the little motorcycles—*"Blue mo-cyco! Red mo-cyco!"*—and made the most enthusiastic engine sounds I've ever heard when you said, *"vroom vroom!"* Your joy made my joy overflow.

But the moment I'll never forget happened halfway home.

The car grew quiet. The radio was barely audible. And from the darkness of the back seat, in this tiny, tender voice, I heard you say for the very first time: ***"Thank you, Daddy."***

Son... that moment melted me. Something in me shifted as your father. I turned around and said softly, *"You're welcome, son... your daddy loves you."* And inside, I was already trying to think of what else I could bless you with. Your gratitude moved my heart. It stirred a desire in me to do even more for you—not because you earned it, but because thankfulness opens doors that nothing else can.

Since then, even as a toddler, you learned that *"Thank you, Daddy"* carried weight. Sometimes you'd say it because you genuinely felt grateful. Sometimes because you wanted a little attention. Sometimes because you needed a hug. But you instinctively discovered a principle that many grown men never understand: **Gratitude moves the heart of a father.**

And son… if it moves *my* heart, imagine what it does to the heart of *God*.

That night in the car, I began understanding aspects of God as *Father* that I had never grasped before. We often approach Him with our wants, our needs, our heaviness, our desires—and He listens. He loves. He provides. But there is something uniquely powerful about coming to Him with a thankful heart.

Not because God needs our gratitude… But because **gratitude aligns our heart with His goodness.**

It breaks entitlement.
It silences fear.
It repositions our perspective.
It unlocks favor—not manipulative favor, but relational favor.
The kind that flows naturally from love.

Son, you're an adult now. Your world is changing. Responsibilities are increasing. Life will stretch you, challenge you, and require strength you're still growing into. But never forget this lesson you taught *me* at two years old: ***Thankfulness will carry you farther than talent, intelligence, charisma, or strength ever will.***

Be the man who says, *"Thank You, Father,"* even before the blessing fully manifests. Be the man who lives in awareness of what God has already done. Be the man whose gratitude opens his heart to receive even more of what God longs to pour out.

Because in that still, calm voice—the same voice that whispered in my spirit that night—you will hear Him say: *"You're welcome, son… Your Father loves you."*

I love you, son. I hope you always know it. —Dad

Healing Pain and Growing in Emotional Maturity

CHAPTER ONE HUNDRED FIFTEEN
Guard Your Peace with Fierce Intention

Son,

A couple of years ago, one of my closest friends—a retired Navy SEAL and one of the toughest men I've ever known—called me while he was visiting Nashville. *"Hey Davis, come pick me up..."* he said. You know the type of man he is: the kind whose *smile* in a dangerous situation is somehow more intimidating than most men's glare.

We sat alone in my Camaro while I talked through some things I had been struggling with. And let me tell you... when you're opening up to a man who has survived things you can't even imagine, your own problems feel embarrassingly small. But he didn't judge me. He didn't minimize it. He just listened.

And at the end of our conversation, he said something I will never forget: *"Aaron, I don't give ANYTHING permission to steal my peace."*

I can't tell you much else about that conversation, but *those words* echoed in my mind for weeks. When the pressure increased, I could hear his voice again: *I don't give anything permission to steal my peace.* And every time, the same realization hit me square in the chest—I had a choice.

Son, that's the part most people forget. You may not always get to choose your circumstances... But you *always* get to choose your response.

You decide where your mind goes. You decide what you meditate on. You decide who or what you give power to influence your state of being.

And with that choice comes responsibility—responsibility for how you carry yourself through the day, how you respond to adversity, and how you guard the things God told you to steward.

Jesus said, *"My peace I give to you."* (John 14:27) But He didn't say the world wouldn't try to take it.

So here's the question I ask myself often, and I want you to start asking it too: ***"What am I giving permission to today?"***

Are you empowering fear? Anger? Worry? Offense? Someone else's dysfunction? Or are you empowering peace, joy, and the presence of God?

I can tell you one thing, son—I refuse to live as a victim. I refuse to hand my peace to people who didn't give it to me in the first place. And I refuse to surrender what God entrusted to me just because the day gets hard.

Guard your peace fiercely. It's one of the most valuable treasures you will ever possess.

I love you, son. I hope you always know it. —Dad

Leadership, Authority, and Kingdom Influence

CHAPTER ONE HUNDRED SIXTEEN
The Power of Unity

Son,

There's an old African proverb that says, *"If you want to go fast, go alone. If you want to go far, go together."* The older I get, the more I realize how true that really is. Dreams—real dreams, God-sized dreams—are rarely accomplished without partnership.

Think about Pharaoh and Joseph. Both had a dream. Both had a vision. But neither could fulfill that dream without the other. God brought them together because unity was required for the assignment to be accomplished.

Partnership is simply another word for unity. And unity creates a kind of strength and momentum that you will never find on your own.

Let me tie in a little science for you. There are two primary ways to produce energy with atoms: **nuclear fission** and **nuclear fusion**.

- **Fission** is when an atom is divided. It produces energy… but only to a point.

- **Fusion** is when atoms combine. And according to scientific understanding, fusion multiplies the power released—seven times more than fission.

Division produces something, but unity produces *exponential* power comparatively.

Son, the same principle is true in life. If you try to do everything alone, you might move quickly at first—but you won't go very far. God designed us to accomplish great things *together*. Some of the dreams God puts in your heart will require strategic partnerships with people inside your current circle. Others will require partnering with someone completely outside your normal sphere—someone whose vision doesn't compete with yours but actually complements it.

Don't overlook the people God sends into your life. Don't dismiss the ones whose strengths fill your gaps. And don't be afraid to link arms with someone whose passion moves in the same direction as your calling.

Most world-changing dreams are too big for one person. And that's by design.

Look for unity. Look for partnership. Look for the people God brings alongside you—not to take the world *from* you, but to help take the world *with* you.

You were never meant to do this life alone, so don't try.

I love you, son. I hope you always know it. —Dad

Building Legacy and Finishing Strong

CHAPTER ONE HUNDRED SEVENTEEN
What Money Can't Buy

Son,

Last week, while talking with someone, a thought came to me that hit deeper than I expected. It came during one of those quiet moments of inner reflection—when you slow down long enough to ask yourself what truly matters in life and what all the money in the world could never buy.

I thought about you... and I realized something that settled so firmly in my heart that it stopped me in my tracks: ***If someone offered me every dollar on the planet in exchange for you, I wouldn't even consider it. Not for a second.***

It made me think about how many people spend their lives grinding for the dollar—chasing wealth, chasing fame, chasing recognition, chasing the *"next thing"* that promises fulfillment but never actually delivers. And they pay for it with the most valuable things they have: time, presence, connection, and relationship.

Son, if you are worth more to me than every dollar on earth, then why would I ever allow the pursuit of money to cost me the time I have with you? Why would I place a job, or a passion, or even a ministry above the relationship God trusted me to steward as your father?

The truth is—I wouldn't. And I won't. That is a line I've drawn in the sand that cannot be bought.

Yes, God expects me to provide for you and to take care of my responsibilities as a man. That is part of walking in integrity and stewardship. But there must always be balance, because everything we pursue has a *cost*—and only a fool pays more than something is worth.

The world may call a man *"rich"* if he has money, influence, or success... but what does that matter if he loses the very people his heart was created to love?

So, here's the real question: **Who is richer?** The man with all the money in the world? Or the man who holds what no amount of money could ever buy?

Son, I am the richest man I know—not because of what I own, but because of who I get to love, raise, and walk beside.

Never forget where true wealth is found. Treasure the people God entrusts to you. Money can be replaced. Time cannot.

I love you, son. I hope you always know it. —Dad

Discipline, Consistency, and Spiritual Growth

CHAPTER ONE HUNDRED EIGHTEEN
The Quitter's Harvest

Son,

Today I had a conversation about a young man who used to be part of our church. He was frustrated—angry, even—because when he made some bad decisions and walked away, he didn't feel supported by the friends he expected to stand with him. Instead of taking responsibility, he quit… and then blamed God for the fallout. He compared his life to those who were thriving and grew bitter that his own story didn't match theirs.

Sadly, as a pastor, I've seen this more times than I can count. People who find it easier to *quit early* and *assign blame* rather than fight through difficulty to see victory. They overlook a simple truth: *if every deed is a seed, then today's experience is often the harvest of what was planted yesterday.* Sometimes by us; sometimes by others whose decisions overlap our lives. Good or bad, seeds grow.

In my own life, most of my harvests—both the painful and the beautiful—have been directly tied to what *I* planted. That's why I'm always bewildered when people throw in the towel too soon, then get angry at God for the *"quitter's harvest"* that follows.

They compare their wilted field to the one who stayed faithful through the drought… …the one who kept planting when it was dry, …the one who toiled when no one noticed, …the one who carried water for miles to keep the seed alive, …the one who protected what he sowed until the season shifted …and the harvest finally matured.

You cannot blame God for what *you refused to keep cultivating* when it felt like more work than you wanted to give.

Premature quitting negates a mature harvest. And like it or not, the reward of quitting is always the same: **you don't reap the harvest of the field you walked away from.**

Let me pause here and make an important distinction: *Quitting prematurely is not the same as letting go when God says it's time to move on.*

There are seasons when releasing one thing is the very act of obedience required to embrace the next. Wisdom knows the difference.

But quitting early? Throwing in the towel before the fight is finished? Walking away before God says the round is over?

That is not transition—that is forfeiture.

Son, if God plants a seed in you… fight for it. If He shows you a future… cultivate it. If He entrusts you with a calling… protect it until the season is right.

Don't envy the harvest of a man who simply refused to quit. Do the work. Stay faithful. And trust God with the outcome.

I love you, son. I hope you always know it. —Dad

Deepening Faith and Intimacy with God

CHAPTER ONE HUNDRED NINETEEN
When Fear Loses Its Grip

Son,

What would you do if you were *ten times bolder*? If anything comes to mind when you read that question, then something—some fear, some hesitation—is influencing how deeply you pursue your God-given destiny.

When this question came to me while I was driving this morning, my first response was, *"Nothing."* And honestly, that answer revealed to me just how far I've come. There was a time when my list would've been long—things I avoided, things I hesitated to attempt, things that intimidated me so much they dictated my direction.

But over the years, that list has shrunk. And it didn't happen by accident. It happened by consistently facing the things that once terrified me.

Son, courage doesn't exist without fear. Courage is choosing to move forward *even while fear is present.*

It's not that I don't *feel* fear anymore—of course I do. I've just become more committed to walking straight into whatever scares me until fear loses its grip.

I remember a time when standing in front of a live camera absolutely tormented me. I would rehearse every word over and over, pacing before going on, terrified that I would mess up again. The anxiety was overwhelming... But I did it anyway. Afraid.

And somewhere along the way—fear broke. Not all at once, but gradually, as I refused to bow to it.

People often ask, *"Pastor Aaron, I've been doing it for six weeks and I still feel afraid... what should I do?"*

My answer? **Do it seven.** And if you're still afraid? **Do it eight.** Then nine. Then ten. Do it until fear dies—or you die trying. But do not let fear win.

Every dad knows that when a child falls off a bike and skins his knee, he *must* get back on if he will ever learn to ride. If he's allowed to stay off the bike because he's afraid of falling again, he learns a crippling lesson—that fear gets the final say. And that lesson, if unchallenged, will limit his progress for the rest of his life.

This principle applies to everything.

When fear is allowed to win, the spoils of its victory are far greater than they appear in the moment. Fear doesn't just steal opportunities—it steals confidence, dreams, identity, purpose, and destiny.

So, Son... Take back what fear has stolen. Face what intimidates you. Challenge what tries to silence you. And step boldly into everything God has placed in your heart.

You can do all things through Christ who gives you strength.

I love you, son. I hope you always know it. —Dad

Discipline, Consistency, and Spiritual Growth

CHAPTER ONE HUNDRED TWENTY
Well-Fertilized Growth

Son,

Many people live with the mentality that *"everything happens for a reason,"* as if every hardship is part of God's predetermined cosmic script. I don't fully agree with that. But I *do* believe this: *when the Bible says God works all things together for our good, it means* **He assigns purpose to what was intended to destroy us.**

You know some of my story, but not all of it. Attempted murder... months of physical rehabilitation... PTSD... depression... anxiety... financial devastation... betrayal... being taken advantage of... feeling forgotten... feeling abandoned... dishonored... misrepresented... lied to... cheated... stolen from... unfairly attacked... years spent trying to recalibrate...

And that's just the adult years. Add the emotional confusion of my childhood, and son... I could write a book. (Smirk.)

I joke that I earned a PhD from *Manure Occurreth University*—but here is the truth I learned in those dark classrooms: *In His faithfulness, God never left me alone—not once.*

There were seasons where the pain made no sense. Seasons where I felt completely blindsided. Seasons where I wondered how any of it could possibly be redeemed. But over time I realized something that changed my life and I've said it in several of these letters: **God never wastes pain.**

Sometimes the pain comes from our own choices. Sometimes it comes from the choices of others. But when we yield it to Him, God has a way of transforming the very resistance that was meant to crush us into the very thing that strengthens us.

Son, I am stronger than most people I know because I've had to push through more adversity than most people I know. I've had to learn how to walk through the dark with no map—and because of that, I can now help others find their way through it too. The very places meant to break me became the training grounds that built me.

Would I ever want to relive any of that *"manure...?"* Absolutely not! But my growth has been well-fertilized.

And I believe with everything in me that **all things work together for our good** because God refuses to let tragedy be the final word in our lives. Not then. Not now. Not ever.

So if you encounter seasons in your life where *manure occurreth,* hang on, Son. This season will pass. It *will* get better. He is faithful to finish what He started in you.

I love you, son. I hope you always know it. —Dad

Building Legacy and Finishing Strong

CHAPTER ONE HUNDRED TWENTY-ONE
The ROI of a Life Well Invested

Son,

When I use my bank account as the measuring tape for my success, it's easy to question my worth. It hasn't always seemed like the years of investment—my life, my time, my energy—have produced the return I expected. But when I place money on the scale beside the lives that have been transformed… the people who are still here because I showed up… the world-changers I've been entrusted to help shape in different seasons of their journey… there isn't a number that could ever outweigh that value for me.

Sometimes you just have to put things in perspective. The *cost* pales in comparison to the *return* when you realize that compensation doesn't always reflect value.

As a leader, I've walked with people through some of the darkest seasons of their lives, and I know beyond any doubt that if I hadn't been there, some of them would be in a very different place today. In the last month alone, God has allowed me to experience several *"full circle"* moments—moments where I was able to see people I had poured into years ago now living full, healthy, thriving lives.

Today, a metro police officer stepped out of his car, walked straight to me, and hugged me tighter than anyone has in a long time—big smile on his face. He's a married man now, with three children, serving his community and thriving in his purpose. As he talked about his wife and each of his kids, I saw a light in his eyes. He was happy. He was fulfilled.

And as I remembered the broken young man he used to be, and the long, painful season I walked him through, the thought hit me: **"This is what it's all about… It's never a bad investment when you invest in people."**

I'm thankful God chose me to be one of the investors. A remarkable ROI, for sure.

Son, don't lose sight of what God values most. As you invest your life, your time, your strength, and your heart—remember: *God's greatest treasure is people.* And investing in people is always worth it.

I love you, son. I hope you always know it. —Dad

Healing Pain and Growing in Emotional Maturity

CHAPTER ONE HUNDRED TWENTY-TWO
Defined by God, Not by Wounds

Son,

One of the loudest lies being pushed in our world today is the idea that *everyone is a victim*. Culture wants people offended, fragile, helpless, and defined by their wounds instead of their worth. But you, Son—you are a child of God. And **a child of God is never a victim.**

The enemy knows that if he can convince you that you're powerless, you'll start acting powerless. That's the agenda behind the deception. But Scripture doesn't call you a *victim*. It calls you an *overcomer*. A *conqueror. The head and not the tail. Above only and not beneath.* You are defined by God—not by culture, not by circumstances, and not by whatever battles you've walked through.

Hear me clearly: *You can be a victim or a victor, but you cannot be both.*

When you believe the lie, you empower the liar. And the enemy would love nothing more than to keep you living small, thinking small, and expecting defeat. But Jesus didn't die for you to live defeated. He died to make you free—spiritually, mentally, emotionally, and in every battle you face.

You are not what happened to you. You are not what people said about you. You are not the labels society tries to put on you. You are who God says you are.

And the Bible says you can do all things through Christ who strengthens you. Not some things—all things. That means every challenge you face can be overcome, every setback can be redeemed, every attack can be defeated, and every place the enemy tried to break you can become a place God builds you.

As a believer, you have both the right and the responsibility to reject any mindset that contradicts what God says about you. Never allow society, circumstance, or pain to lower your identity beneath what Heaven has declared. Stand tall. Walk boldly. Live as the victor you were created to be.

Victim or victor? Pitiful or powerful? Son, you have to choose. And I know which one you were made for.

I love you, son. I hope you always know it. —Dad

Building Legacy and Finishing Strong

CHAPTER ONE HUNDRED TWENTY-THREE
Legacy Doesn't Replace Relationship

Son,

Over the years, I've lost count of how many people have told me they were Christians because their grandfather was a minister, or because they were baptized as a child, or because they went to church with their family growing up. In their minds, they have an *association* with God through the actions of others—but very often, they've never had a personal encounter or relationship with Him themselves.

It's as if they believe they can ride someone else's faith into a relationship with God. But son, it doesn't work that way.

God has given every one of us free will and a personal invitation to know Him. A relationship with God is not inherited, transferred, or forced. No one can cultivate it for you, and no one else's obedience can substitute for your own. We don't enter heaven on the coattails of our parents' faith or our grandparents' devotion. Scripture is clear: *"Everyone who calls on the name of the Lord shall be saved"*—but each person must respond for themselves.

We see this principle clearly in God's covenant with King David. God promised to bless David's lineage **if** his sons and grandsons sought and obeyed Him as David did. And God was faithful to His word. When they pursued God, they experienced covenant blessing. When they turned to idolatry, they suffered loss. When they repented and returned to Him, God restored what had been broken. The covenant promises were always available—but the experience of them required personal obedience and relationship.

Each of us is given that same opportunity through Christ. We all have direct access to God and the covenant blessings that come with being His sons. But that relationship can only be entered individually. *You* must confess with your mouth that Jesus is Lord. *You* must believe in your heart. *You* must seek Him for yourself if you are going to find Him.

As your father, there are things I can do—pray for you, stand in the gap during difficult seasons, and offer guidance. But there are other aspects of your walk with God and the direction of your life that only you can take responsibility for.

Years ago, when I was facing a painful season, my dad said something to me I've never forgotten: *"Son, if I could take this pain for you, I would. But you're a man now. This is your family—and I can't fight this one for you."*

That's the reality of becoming a man. There comes a moment when you are responsible to take the lead for your life and your family. I can't do that for you. These letters were written to help you see clearly, to think rightly, and to walk wisely—but your faith, your obedience, and your relationship with God are yours to walk out.

One day, when this life is over and you stand before the Father, He won't say, *"Your dad was faithful—come on in."* He'll say, *"Well done, My good and faithful son. Welcome home."* And it will be **your life** He is commending.

Seek Him with all your heart, son. It will be worth it.

I love you, son. I hope you always know it. —Dad

Healing Pain and Growing in Emotional Maturity

CHAPTER ONE HUNDRED TWENTY-FOUR
Your Lens Is Your Battlefield

Son,

There is a common misnomer that once you become a Christian and God makes *all things new* in your life, everything becomes an easy, downhill coast from there. But while it is true that God strengthens you for battles you could never have fought in your own power, do not be disillusioned—there is a very real war for your soul and for establishing the Kingdom of God in the earth.

God would not give you weapons if He did not expect you to engage in warfare.

A significant aspect of spiritual warfare is understanding how you see your battles. At a foundational level, Satan is after your lens—because if he can distort your lens, he can influence your actions. Your perspective shapes how you perceive reality, and how you perceive reality shapes how you respond. This is why it is essential that you allow God's Word to shape the lens through which you frame every battle.

Satan seldom touches the reality you're living—he targets the lens you're living *through*. He doesn't dismantle your calling—he distorts your confidence in it. He doesn't sabotage your relationships—he warps your interpretation of them.

Scripture instructs us to *"enter His gates with thanksgiving and His courts with praise." (Psalm 100:4 KJV)* In seasons of warfare, choosing thanksgiving and praise is not emotional convenience—it is a spiritual strategy. These are sacrificial decisions to keep seeing God for who His Word promises Him to be, in spite of what you are facing. God never promised that you wouldn't fight battles; He promised that He would never leave you or forsake you. (Hebrews 13:5)

David saw God as the One who prepared a table before him in the presence of his enemies. When you choose to see God as *the One who empowers, loves, surrounds, strengthens, and promises victory to you*—your agreement becomes an extension of your faith. And faith is what moves the mountains in front of you.

When you see God through the eyes of faith as *your strong tower*, the fruit of His Spirit becomes your inheritance. Joy becomes your weapon. Peace becomes your portion. Thanksgiving becomes your battle cry.

Thanksgiving is agreement with God's goodness in spite of the circumstances. Complaining is agreement with the enemy's narrative.

One is rooted in faith; the other in unbelief. When you **complain** about your circumstances, you place your **agreement** in what the enemy desires for you—and in doing so, **you empower the very thing you are complaining about**. Whether you realize it or not, you partner with the wrong voice.

The Word tells us that *where two agree touching anything, it shall be done (Matthew 18:20)*, and that *when you declare a thing, it shall be established (Job 22:28)*. Seen through that lens, complaining becomes a prophetic utterance—speaking life into what you should be resisting. But when you approach battles with **thanksgiving and praise**, your gratitude contradicts the enemy's lies and aligns you with the courts of heaven.

So, Son… If everything you said came to pass in your life, how intentional would you be with your words? Would you bless or curse? Speak life or death? Empower fear or empower faith?

I caution you: take every thought captive, shape your lens in alignment with God's Word, watch your words, and wield praise and thanksgiving as intentional weapons of spiritual warfare.

I love you, son. I hope you always know it. —Dad

Healing Pain and Growing in Emotional Maturity
CHAPTER ONE HUNDRED TWENTY-FIVE
One Morning at a Time

Son,

In Ezekiel 46, God instructs His people to *prepare an offering for Him every morning*. At first glance it may seem like a small detail, but what I want to share with you is deeply important. While we no longer prepare physical sacrifices in the ways they did, our lives are now meant to honor God as living sacrifices.

In Ezekiel, there was a rhythm of devotion—an intentional daily act flowing from a desire to do what pleased the Lord. Psalm 63 echoes this: *"Early in the morning will I rise up and seek You,"* revealing David's heart to honor God with the first fruits of his time.

Isaiah 50 adds another layer: *"Morning by morning He awakens me... to listen."*

Scripture paints a consistent picture: God values intentional daily devotion, and so did the men who walked closely with Him.

Faithfulness to God is built one morning at a time. That relationship grows through your intentionality to prioritize Him in your conversation with Him and in the reading of the Word. His Word promises that He never leaves or forsakes us, and that He is both a Father and a Friend who loves consistently and completely. But here's the truth: *even though He never leaves you, without intentional time in His presence, you may find yourself feeling distant from Him.*

Proximity is not the same as intimacy. You can be in the same room with someone and still be far from them in your heart.

Relationships—human and divine—are cultivated through time, conversation, and intentional pursuit. This is why I'm encouraging you to always make space for God in your mornings, in your thoughts, and in your days. Your relationship with Him will be the most important relationship you ever develop.

It's usually not sin that first creates distance between us and God—more often, it's distance from God that opens the door for sin. (Read that line again.)

Be aware. Be intentional. Build your life with God one morning at a time.

I love you, son. I hope you always know it. —Dad

Healing Pain and Growing in Emotional Maturity

CHAPTER ONE HUNDRED TWENTY-SIX
Be Slow to Judge What You Don't Yet Understand

Son,

Years ago—long before he became the guitar player for one of the most famous country stars alive today—*"Johnny"* was just a new Christian attending my church. He was a *what you see is what you get* kind of guy, and we got along great. One day he approached me and said, *"I think all this God-and-healing stuff is bullcrap, but I want to know what you think."*

After we talked, he said something that stuck with me: *"I don't know how to process all of that, but I trust you...and I'm going to stay open to it."*

Not long after that, his wife—who had been told she could *never* have children—was healed. And in that same meeting, he was healed from a lifelong injury that had caused him constant difficulty. By choosing to stay open to what he didn't fully understand, he experienced what he once believed was impossible.

Son, be careful about being too critical of things you do not yet understand.

The Bible absolutely teaches us to judge righteously, but I can tell you with certainty that *the you today* and *the you twenty years from now* will not see everything the same way. Growth, wisdom, and experience change how you understand God.

Mark Twain is paraphrased as saying, *"It's not what you don't know that gets you into trouble—it's what you know for sure that just ain't so."*

There is real danger in thinking too highly of your own perspective. When your confidence becomes arrogance, you shut the door to correction, revelation, and blessing. The Bible warns us not to judge, and I believe much of that instruction is rooted in protecting us from our own blind spots.

I've watched many people judge something simply because they didn't understand it—and in doing so, they alienated themselves from receiving the very thing God may have wanted to give them through that which they judged.

Years ago, I was in a church service where a man at my feet was having what looked to me like a *very unusual encounter with God*. I whispered under my breath, frustrated, *"God, why does this kind of stuff always happen right in front of me?!"*

I wasn't expecting Him to reply…but He did.

He said, **"Aaron, I meet people right where they are—and that is where he expected to meet Me today."**

In other words: *"I'm his Father. You are not. And this is not yours to judge."* My only response was, *"Yes Sir."*

Here's what a lifetime of walking with God has taught me: **What you judge, you disqualify yourself from receiving from.**

Jesus said, *"These signs will follow those who believe."* **Belief** is the prerequisite. Signs never follow those who refuse to believe. (Read that line again.)

Honor begets honor. Dishonor begets dishonor. You reap what you sow. And you cannot receive from what you mock, criticize, or dishonor.

As a pastor, I've learned to be very slow to say, *"God always"* or *"God never,"* because He rarely fits inside the limitations of my own understanding. Unless Scripture states something definitively, I've learned to say, *"In my experience, God often…"* or *"In my experience, God rarely…"*—because He is bigger than my boxes.

So here is my caution to you: **When you are critical of what you don't understand, you close the door to what God may have wanted to use to bless you.**

Those who don't believe God heals…never seek Him for healing. Those who don't believe God provides…never seek Him for provision. Those who don't believe God saves…never call upon Him for salvation.

And many people alienate themselves from what God longed to do for them—because they dishonored it with their words before they ever gave God a chance.

Stay humble. Stay teachable. Stay open. And let God be bigger than your understanding.

I love you, son. I hope you always know it. —Dad

Healing Pain and Growing in Emotional Maturity

CHAPTER ONE HUNDRED TWENTY-SEVEN
When You Fall, Come Home Quickly

Son,

When God blesses your life—when He speaks to you through His Word, when He sends someone with a *word* of encouragement or instruction, when He opens a door of opportunity or gives you fresh vision—the Bible tells us that the enemy comes *immediately* to try to uproot that seed. (Mark 4:15)

And in a similar way, when you make a mistake... when you choose something you're ashamed of... when you do something you know God wouldn't approve of... or even when you fail publicly and feel exposed—the enemy is right there again, trying to whisper a different lie: *"You're disqualified."*

Son, hear me clearly: *No matter what, I will always love you—and so will God.*

No one is ever truly *disqualified* in the Kingdom of God. Yes—sometimes our decisions require recalibration. Yes—sometimes our choices alter routes and delay destinations. And yes—the rebuilding process can take time when God restores what the enemy tried to destroy in us.

But this remains unshakably true: *God is faithful to complete the work He began in you*—if you will humble yourself before Him and allow Him to lift you up.

Just because you *screwed up* does not mean you are permanently *a screw-up*. Your failures do not define you. Your mistakes do not label you. God defines you—and nothing else.

You're not disqualified, but restoration requires something of you: *Repentance*—which simply means changing your mind and agreement with sin. *Submission*—bringing your heart back under God's leadership. *Surrender*—allowing Him to restore you as the loving Father He is.

The enemy will try to convince you that you don't deserve

restoration… and honestly, from a purely human standpoint, he might even be right. But that's the beauty of the Gospel: In Christ, we don't get what we deserve—He took what we deserved, so we could receive what *He* deserves.

You don't earn restoration. You receive it.

So, if you make a mistake—come back quickly. Don't run. Don't hide. Don't let shame delay your healing. The longer you run from the God who restores, the longer it takes to recover what was lost.

I love you, son. I hope you always know it. —Dad

Mastering Your Mind and Inner World

CHAPTER ONE HUNDRED TWENTY-EIGHT
Don't Take the Bait

Son,

I've seen far too many men's lives destroyed by the simple deception of momentary sin. You must always remember: **the purpose of the distraction is always destruction.**

There is a fish called a *stargazer*. To look at it, it just appears evil—beady eyes, sharp teeth, a big fat body that looks like Jabba the Hutt with fangs. Any discerning prey would instinctively stay far away from it. But the stargazer is as smart as it is ugly.

It buries itself beneath the sand until only its eyes and mouth are barely visible. Then it takes a small appendage inside its mouth—something that looks just like a worm—and wiggles it above the sand as bait. When a hungry fish swims near to take what looks like an easy meal, the stargazer explodes upward, sucking the prey into its jaws with a powerful vacuum force *while simultaneously shocking it with electricity* from organs behind its eyes.

Once the curious prey swims toward the bait, it's as good as dead.

The Bible describes Satan in a similar way, saying he roams the earth *"like a roaring lion seeking whom he may devour."* (1 Peter 5:8) Deception is always the bait. Pride, lust, greed, selfishness, anger, shame, unbelief, disobedience—if the stargazer can get you to move toward the bait, the intent is always your destruction.

And here's the thing, son: **the bait never looks like danger.** It always looks appealing. It always looks harmless. It always looks like a small compromise you think you can manage.

But it will destroy your life. It is never as harmless as it appears.

If you can learn early what the bait looks like—if you will use wisdom, discernment, and the Word of God—you can save yourself, your family, and your legacy from tremendous pain.

Don't take the bait. See the temptation for what it is, and deliberately choose God's way every time.

I love you, son. I hope you always know it. —Dad

Deepening Faith and Intimacy with God

CHAPTER ONE HUNDRED TWENTY-NINE
Dream With God

Son,
When I was a young man, I remember staring up at the stars one night, frustrated and feeling defeated by the experiences life had handed me. In tears—and admittedly a little dramatic at that age—I said to God, *"I have dreams that are as vast as the stars…"*

If I had been God in that moment, I probably would have laughed at me. But He didn't. Instead, He revealed Himself in a way I had never considered when He gently responded, *"I know, Aaron. I put them there."*

That moment became the beginning of my understanding that it is not only okay to dream with God—it's essential. Without a dream or vision, we walk without a compass.

In Scripture, God gave Joseph a dream when he was still just a boy. That dream sustained him through betrayal, slavery, false accusation, prison, disappointment, and being forgotten. But Joseph held on—and because he stewarded his calling with faith, the dream God gave him eventually became the path that led him into his destiny.

Reaching that dream wasn't easy. But Joseph didn't quit.

Son, you were created in the image of God. Greatness is woven into your DNA. God says you are the head and not the tail, above only and not beneath. His Word promises that you are more than a conqueror through Christ who empowers you.

Your heavenly Father is the King of the universe. You are a joint-heir with Christ. The Spirit of the Living God—the same Spirit who raised Jesus from the dead—lives inside you.

As a child of the Most-High God, you carry the authority of the One who said:

- "Greater works shall you do…"

- "Only believe…"

- "Do not doubt…"
- "Speak to the mountain…"

Jesus never questioned who He was. And you don't have to either.

I want to encourage you—don't ever let the enemy convince you otherwise. Just like he tried with Jesus, he will try with you. He will attempt to shake your identity, your confidence, and your calling. But if you will simply choose to see yourself the way God sees you… if you will dare to dream with Him… if you will embrace His vision for your life…

The Bible promises that nothing will be impossible for those who believe.

Dream boldly, son. Dream faithfully. Dream with God. Those dreams are there because He put them there.

I love you, son. I hope you always know it. —Dad

Building Godly Character and Integrity

CHAPTER ONE HUNDRED THIRTY
You Are Not What You Feel — You Are What You Decide

Son,

It is so easy to let your emotions dictate your entire state of being. I understand it—when you're walking through seasons of pressure or attack, the emotions attached to those struggles can feel overwhelming. Depression, anger, frustration, anxiety, worry, disappointment, and fear all demand attention, and if you don't confront them directly, they can shape outcomes you never wanted.

Over the years, I've heard many people say things like, *"That's just who I am,"* as a justification for whatever negative emotion they've chosen to project onto the world around them. *"I'm just an angry person. I'm just jealous. I just worry a lot."* What they're really saying is that they've surrendered their responsibility of personal growth. They've convinced themselves that transformation isn't possible, when in truth, **what you tolerate you authorize to exist**.

I once confronted a man who physically abused his wife. His excuse was, *"I can't help it—she just makes me so mad."* I asked him if he had children. He said yes—a little girl. I asked him, *"If your daughter were sitting on my lap and I said I would shoot her if you lost your temper... could you control yourself then?"* He lowered his head and admitted he could. My response was simple: *"Then it's not that you can't control yourself... it's that you don't want to."*

Son, you are not what you *feel*. You are what you *decide*.

You can meditate on negative thoughts and feed negative emotions, or you can take every thought captive, just like Scripture tells us to. You can choose to allow feelings to run your life, or you can choose to align your mind, emotions, and actions with who God says you are.

At the end of the day, your outcomes are shaped by your choices—your willingness to plant the right seeds and water them consistently.

But here's the hope I want you to hold onto:

You *can* do all things through Christ who strengthens you. You *can* rise above emotional impulses. You *can* choose discipline over excuses, peace over anger, faith over fear, and purpose over pain.

And when you choose God's way over your own, you won't just survive those difficult seasons—you will grow through them, becoming stronger, wiser, and more aligned with the man God designed you to be.

You're not stuck. You're not powerless. And you're never alone in the fight.

I love you, son. I hope you always know it. —Dad

Your Identity in the Father's Heart

CHAPTER ONE HUNDRED THIRTY-ONE
Identity and the Enemy's Favorite Lie

Son,

I want you to pause and really consider something: *Why do you think the enemy, when he tempted Jesus at the end of His forty-day fast, attacked Him specifically in the area of identity?* The very first words out of Satan's mouth were, *"If you are the Son of God..."* Every temptation started with that same challenge. His strategy wasn't just about bread, glory, or power—it was about getting Jesus to question *who He was.*

And Jesus responded the same way every time: **by declaring the Word of God.**

This is why I have emphasized over and over in these letters that the Bible is God's Word, and it *is* **the Truth**. You cannot win battles you fight in your mind, emotions, or environment if you are not anchored to truth. And the truth is not based on what you feel, not based on circumstances, and not based on your past. Truth is what God says—and everything else either aligns with it or opposes it.

We live out what we believe about ourselves. That's why identity matters so much. If the enemy can get you to doubt who God says you are, he can influence how you think, how you act, and how you show up in the world. A person who doubts their worth will struggle to add worth to others. A person who doubts their calling will walk timidly even when God has created them to lead with confidence.

But once you know and believe who God says you are, everything changes. The enemy loses his leverage. Confidence rises. Peace returns. Strength awakens. Purpose clarifies. You stop living small. You stop apologizing for the gifts God placed inside you. You step into rooms carrying the awareness that the same Spirit that raised Christ from the dead now lives in you—and because of that, you bring something into that space that the world desperately needs.

Truth produces freedom. Jesus said, *"I am the way, the truth, and the life."* That same Jesus lives in you. His Spirit empowers you to bring answers where there are problems, peace where there is chaos, and direction where there is confusion.

Like Joseph, whether your circumstances look like a prison or a palace, you still carry God's answer. God doesn't send you into places to blend in—He sends you to influence, to uplift, to lead, to add value.

Son, never forget who you are, and never let the enemy rewrite what God has already spoken over your life.

I love you, son. I hope you always know it. —Dad

Discipline, Consistency, and Spiritual Growth

CHAPTER ONE HUNDRED THIRTY-TWO
Living in the Tension Between Calling and Becoming

Son,

Before you were born, I wrote a poem titled, *"Who Am I Really?"* I was wrestling through a season where the war between who God called me to be and who I felt I had become felt almost unbearable. Here's what I wrote:

Who am I really?
There's conflict inside of me
With so much I want to be
And so much I want to see
But so much that cannot be
There's two sides that make me, me
And both sides won't let me be
At war most constantly
Tearing apart internally
How am I to find victory
When for trees the forest cannot be seen
A general with no army to lead
A vocalist with no song to sing
A visionary with only shattered dreams
A musician with only broken strings
Trying to grasp what's just out of reach
Wanting to understand what no one can teach
Striving to share with no words to speak
And the answer to one question I seek…
…after all, who am I, really?

The reason I'm including this in your letters is because I want you to know—without question—that **there will be seasons when you must live in the tension between what isn't yet and what you know God has spoken about your future.**

That tension is not failure. It's not punishment. Many times, that tension is **training** for the next season God is preparing you to step into.

Just like increasing a bench press, you never start with the weight you hope to lift. Depending on how lofty the goal, three things determine whether you'll reach it:

Discipline. Resistance. And time.

You have to show up daily—through soreness, through the tearing and rebuilding of muscle, and through the repetition of pressing lighter weight long before you can shoulder heavier weight.

Spiritual growth works the same way.

You show up.
You push the *"lighter weight."*
You stay consistent when you don't feel strong.
You keep leaning into God when everything in you wants to quit.

Over time, the discipline + resistance + consistency produce strength you didn't know you had. Then one day, you lift what once would have crushed you.

Spiritual resistance is painful. Showing up daily, especially when you feel overwhelmed or discouraged, is difficult. But that season of discipline is what prepares you for the breakthroughs God has already planned for you.

This is why Galatians 6:9 tells us, **"Do not lose heart in doing what you know to do, for in due season you WILL reap—if you do not quit."** (Galatians 6:9)

You *are* promised the victory. God *will* make your path straight. You *are* more than a conqueror through Christ who gives you strength.

Hang in there, Son. This season will pass—and you'll be stronger because of it.

I love you, son. I hope you always know it. —Dad

Your Identity in the Father's Heart

CHAPTER ONE HUNDRED THIRTY-THREE
You Are Enough — Because God Says You Are

Son,

Every man I've ever spoken with about whether he's *"done enough"* or *"been enough"* eventually admits he feels like he's missed it in that category. Many years ago, a high school friend commented on one of my posts and said something along the lines of, *"Of all of us from the neighborhood, you're the one who made it."* He saw me as a success by his standard. But what he didn't know were the countless times I've looked in the mirror and felt like a failure was staring back at me.

I will say this to you over and over because I never want you to forget it: *When you believe the lie, you empower the liar.* The Bible tells us that one of Satan's primary identities is *"the accuser of the righteous."* It also tells us he is the father of lies and that there is *no* truth in him. This is why it is absolutely essential that God's Word—not your feelings, not your shame, not your critics—sets the standard for truth in your life. Scripture says that when you *know* the truth, the truth will set you free.

But if you don't know the truth—if you haven't resolved ahead of time that what God says *is* the truth—you can be certain the accuser will whisper lies in your ear:

"You're not enough."
"You'll never be enough."
"You're a failure."
"You won't amount to anything."
"You're defined by your losses."
"You've let everyone down."

And if you don't already know what God has said about you, those accusations may sound believable.

Here is what you must hold onto: God does not treat you the way you think your mistakes deserve. God is not holding your sin against you—Satan is. God's Word says He removes your sin so far from you that He doesn't even remember it. In His love, God declares:

"You are enough."
"There is nothing wrong with you."
"My Son has cleansed you."
"I accept you."
"You are forgiven."
"You are My child."
"You are worthy of My love."
"I make all things new in your life."
"And I love you."

Son, do not let the lies of the accuser define you or set the standard for what you believe. If what you are hearing does not line up with God's Word, it is a lie—period.

Let God's voice shape your identity... not the voice of your enemy.

I love you, son. I hope you always know it. – Dad

Discipline, Consistency, and Spiritual Growth

CHAPTER ONE HUNDRED THIRTY-FOUR
Nothing Means Nothing

Son,

Over the years I've met so many people who genuinely believe that God could never love them. For years, when I would talk with your great-grandfather, he would tell me he had done so many things he regretted—things he wasn't proud of—and he simply couldn't fathom how God could love or forgive him. It wasn't that he lacked a heart for God, nor that he didn't desire a relationship with Him. He just didn't believe he was *worthy* of God's love or acceptance.

This is why it is so important that we allow God's Word—not our emotions, not our experiences, and certainly not our shame—to define what is true. If we try to rationalize the things of God with only our natural minds, we will almost always land on an incorrect conclusion.

As we've talked about many times in these letters, one of Jesus' primary purposes was to *"reveal the Father."* That was necessary because people—especially the religious ones—had painted God as harsh, punitive, distant, and unloving. But Jesus modeled something entirely different. He told His followers, *"If you want to know what my Father is like, look at Me. I am the exact representation of the Father."*

Jesus revealed a God who is a loving Father—one who desires good things for His children. We know this today because Scripture makes it unmistakably clear.

In the same way, there are many other biblical truths we have to embrace **by faith,** even when our emotions struggle to grasp them. On one hand, Scripture teaches us what sin is, how salvation works, the authority we have as believers, the power of faith, and so much more. We accept these realities because the Bible is our ultimate standard of truth.

I'll be the first to admit: it doesn't always make sense to the natural mind *how* or *why* confessing that Jesus is Lord and believing God raised Him from the dead secures our salvation. But we know it is true because God's Word says it is true.

Likewise, I understand how someone like your great-grandfather could struggle to believe God loved him in spite of his failures. Many people feel that way. But the Bible speaks plainly in Romans 8: ***NOTHING can separate us from the love of God.*** I want you to read that chapter after this letter and let it sink deeply into your heart.

Because when God says *"nothing,"* He means **NOTHING**.

Not your past.
Not your failures.
Not your rebellion.
Not your sin.
Not your darkest moment.
Not your weakest day.
Not your confusion.
Not your questions.

Nothing means *nothing*.

And even if your emotions can't fully comprehend *why* God feels that way about you, your lack of comprehension doesn't change truth. God's Word is true whether or not you can make sense of it in the moment.

He loves you—because He *chooses* to love you. Not because you earned it, and not because you are perfect… but because He is.

I love you, son. I hope you always know it. – Dad

Building Godly Character and Integrity

CHAPTER ONE HUNDRED THIRTY-FIVE
The Seeds You Sow Shape the Life You Live

Son,

The Bible is very clear that generosity—in your time, talent, and treasure—is incredibly important to God. I separate those three categories intentionally, because generosity is not measured only in dollars. Time, talent, and treasure are *all* forms of currency you can sow into people, and each one advances the Kingdom of God in unique ways.

I know many business leaders who work a ridiculous amount of hours. They may not always have extra time or physical energy to give, but through their financial generosity they fund the ministry that flows through the lives of others. When they succeed in business and sow their finances into God's work, they are fulfilling their own ministry lane. The same is true for those who volunteer their time or who serve God with their gifts and abilities. All of it matters, and all of it is seed.

I begin this letter with that distinction because when we talk about generosity—or about the laws of sowing and reaping—we are not looking exclusively through the lens of money.

The Bible says in Galatians 6:7, *"Do not be deceived: God is not mocked. For whatever a man sows, that he will also reap."* Second Corinthians 9:6 tells us that *"the stingy sower reaps a meager harvest, but the generous sower reaps abundantly."* And Malachi 3:10 gives us the only place in Scripture where God says, *"Test Me in this,"* inviting us to sow generously and watch Him pour out blessings too great to contain.

Son, it is undeniable—biblically and practically—that God values and blesses those who are generous with their time, talents, and treasure. Scripture also makes it clear that when we withhold seed, we negate harvest. It makes sense: every one of us has the ability to plant something meaningful into the world, but if we refuse to put seed in the ground, it would be irrational to expect a harvest. Yet many people do exactly that. They see others experiencing blessing—friendships, opportunities, favor, resources—and feel overlooked, never recognizing that those individuals are likely reaping the fruit of seeds they faithfully planted in previous seasons.

The lesson is this: **God is not mocked. Whatever you sow, that is exactly what you will reap.** If you sow kindness, you'll reap kindness. If you sow faithfulness, you'll reap faithfulness. If you sow loyalty, you'll reap loyalty. If you sow blessing, you'll reap blessing. But if you sow selfishness, impatience, strife, or bitterness, you cannot expect to harvest God-honoring fruit. Seeds always produce after their own kind.

It's not punishment. It's not God withholding from you. It's simply the law of seedtime and harvest doing exactly what God established it to do. Don't plant weeds in the same garden where you're hoping to grow fruit—because weeds always choke out the harvest.

I love you, son. I hope you always know it. —Dad

Your Identity in the Father's Heart

CHAPTER ONE HUNDRED THIRTY-SIX
Understanding Grace The Right Way

Son,

Because of the contradictions between what was preached and what was modeled, I had a difficult time understanding God's grace for many years. Every pastor I ever heard—including myself—taught that we are saved by grace through faith, and that this salvation is *a gift* we could never earn by being good enough or working hard enough.

That message sounded great during the one or two Sundays a year when *"grace"* was the theme. But the other fifty weeks of the year? The sermons revolved around sin, hell, fear, and an altar call begging people to repent of anything they might have done that week that could send them to hell if they died on their way home. It was unbalanced. It was inconsistent. And it was theologically contradictory to the very *grace* we claimed to believe.

While sin absolutely separated us from God *before* we were saved, what was preached felt less like a transformation from death to life and more like a hamster wheel—saved one moment, *"spiritually dead"* the next time you had a less than Godly thought. Scripture teaches that salvation is **not by works**, yet the message delivered was that condemnation *was* by works.

But here's the truth the Bible declares plainly: *"There is now NO condemnation for those who are in Christ Jesus."* That means when you mess up, you are not thrust back into spiritual death—you are positioned under grace, covered, upheld, and loved in spite of your failures.

On the opposite extreme, I've also heard the argument: *"God doesn't care if you sin because grace covers it."* That is every bit as inaccurate. Grace doesn't give you permission to sin; **grace gives you power NOT to sin.** As long as you're trying to be *"good enough,"* you're still trying to earn what only God can freely give. But when you finally realize that your best could never be enough **without** the grace of God, something shifts. You rest in the security that your salvation is rooted in *His* power, not your performance. That's when sin loses its power over you.

God hates sin because it hurts *you*, not because it hurts Him. Grace is His gift so that you wouldn't spend your life striving to earn something impossible, but instead live empowered by His Spirit beyond the reach of sin's control. (Read that line again)

If understanding grace is ever a subject you struggle to understand, I strongly encourage you to read a book titled, *GraceWorks* by Tony Sutherland. It is one of only a few books that have truly transformed my life. Tony is a trusted friend, and everyone I've ever recommended that book to has been deeply impacted.

Striving without ever arriving was never God's intention. Grace gives what you could never achieve and covers what you could never fix. It is His gift—completely undeserved, yet fully yours.

I love you, son. I hope you always know it. —Dad

Your Identity in the Father's Heart
CHAPTER ONE HUNDRED THIRTY-SEVEN
God's Kid First

Son,

When you were about two years old, your mother and I were wrestling with some decisions that would have required us to place you in daycare. I did *not* like the idea of strangers having such a significant role in raising my son. Frustrated, I called my pastor and explained everything.

I'll never forget his response: *"Aaron, he's God's kid first…"*

Looking back, I can admit that my hesitation and anxiety in that moment came more from fear than from faith. I was overwhelmed by all the *what-ifs* of an environment I couldn't control. Pastor Danny's reminder was simple but profound—God entrusted you to me, but you belonged to Him long before you were mine.

Over the years, I have had to return to that truth again and again. When I worried about finances… you were God's kid first. When I questioned whether I was doing a good job as your dad… you were God's kid first. When you made choices I didn't agree with… you were God's kid first.

And while I had a responsibility to steward your life, to guide you, and to do my best as your earthly father, I also had to trust that when I reached the limits of my humanity, He never reached the limits of His divinity. He is a far better Father than I could ever hope to be.

Here's the parallel—this isn't just a parenting lesson for your future children. It's also a truth about the dreams, callings, and passions God places inside you.

You can trust Him with your future because you are His kid first. You can dream big because He planted those dreams. You can believe beyond your circumstances because He is a good Father who gives good gifts. You can trust His promises because as His child, you are entitled to them.

Many times in my life, when I didn't know what to do naturally, I had to fall back on trust—trust that *the Father* who gave me the assignment would also guide me through it.

I want you to know, son: you can trust Him that same way.

I love you, son. I hope you always know it. —Dad

Mastering Your Mind and Inner World

CHAPTER ONE HUNDRED THIRTY-EIGHT
What Do You See?

Son,

Proverbs 29 tells us that *without vision, people perish*. It's simple but profound: without guiding purpose or direction, people lose their way and eventually suffer for it. This is why Scripture also tells us that God's Word is a *lamp to our feet and a light to our path (Psalm 119:105)*. In times of difficulty—storms, darkness, confusion—the Word brings insight, clarity, and power when vision would otherwise be limited or even impossible.

Before you were born, I went on an extended fast—no meats, no sweets—for several months. In that season, I was seeking God for direction. Near the end of that fast, I was looking at myself in the mirror when I heard that still, small voice ask, **"Aaron, what do you see?"**

I knew God was drawing me into a conversation, but I didn't understand the question. And Son, let me tell you something early: if God ever asks you a question, it's never because He doesn't know the answer—it's because He's inviting you deeper.

Confused, I answered, *"I see nothing..."* Immediately He replied, *"Then you will hear nothing."*

I knew instantly I had answered incorrectly.

A bit shaken, I looked again—more intentionally—and heard the same question: **"Aaron, what do you see?"** Not wanting to miss it a second time, I spoke what little I understood: *"I see Aaron Davis, the son of Larry Davis, the son of Lawrence Davis..."*

It wasn't profound, but it was honest—and God honored it.

In a moment, the presence of God overwhelmed me as He opened my eyes in a vision to things I had not deeply considered: my calling not just as a pastor, but as an ambassador of His Kingdom... the weight of the assignment... the legacy tied to my obedience... and the generational impact—on others, on eternity, on you.

For years afterward, in seasons of darkness, discouragement, and intense storms, I have returned to that vision. It became an anchor when everything else seemed to shake.

Son, Scripture is filled with declarations about *who you are, who God is*, and *what He intends to accomplish in and through you*. But if you don't learn to **see yourself** in the mirror of His Word, you may wrongly assume His promises are for someone else.

They aren't. They're for you. And when you begin to see yourself through His eyes, He will reveal Himself to the world through your life.

I love you, son. I hope you always know it. —Dad

Deepening Faith and Intimacy with God

CHAPTER ONE HUNDRED THIRTY-NINE
Faith Works When You Work It

What does it profit, my brethren, if someone says he has faith but does not have works? Can faith save him? If a brother or sister is naked and destitute of daily food, and one of you says to them, "Depart in peace, be warmed and filled," but you do not give them the things which are needed for the body, what does it profit? Thus also faith by itself, if it does not have works, is dead.
James 2:14-17 (NKJV)

Son,

If faith without works is dead, then when you face a situation that challenges your faith, you must first ask: *"What do I need to believe to succeed?"*

Before anything else, you must resolve in your heart that God's Word—not your emotions, not your circumstances, not your fears—sets the standard for your belief system. God is God, and you are not. So when situations arise that provoke thoughts contradicting what God has said or promised, the first step is to reground your mind in His Word, even when everything around you is trying to preach a different message.

Next, ask yourself, *"What do I need to do or say to come into agreement with what God has spoken?"* This is where the *"works"* of faith come in. When doubt and unbelief are screaming through your circumstances, you must intentionally speak the Word of God over what you're facing.

Scripture puts enormous weight on the power of your words:

- *Life and death are in the power of the tongue.* (Proverbs 18:21 KJV)
- The tongue is like a *rudder*, steering your life in the direction of your words. (James 3:1-11)
- Blessing and cursing should not flow from the same mouth. (James 3:10)
- When you *speak to a mountain* and do not doubt, it will move. (Mark 11:23, Matthew 21:21)
- You can *declare a thing*, and it shall be established. (Job 22:28)

Even salvation itself is rooted in this truth: *"Confess with your mouth, believe in your heart, and you shall be saved."* (Romans 10:9-10) Your verbal agreement with God matters.

Faith without action is nothing more than an idea. Jesus often activated a person's faith by putting them into motion—"Rise and walk," "Stretch out your hand," "Go wash in the pool of Siloam." Faith works when you work it.

Son, **what you tolerate, you authorize to exist.** In other words, you get what you tolerate. But what you *bind* on earth will be bound in heaven, and what you *loose* on earth will be loosed in heaven (Matthew 18:18). That means your cooperation matters.

The same Spirit that raised Christ from the dead lives in you (Romans 8:11). That covenant identity comes with real authority and real power. Don't take lightly what scripture instructs clearly. Don't let anyone—especially modern *"teachers of the law"*—talk you into a powerless, passive Christianity that denies what Scripture clearly teaches.

Stand firm. Speak truth. Act in faith.

I love you, son. I hope you always know it. —Dad

Building Legacy and Finishing Strong

CHAPTER ONE HUNDRED FORTY
Be the Husband Who Loves Like Christ

Son,

When I was younger, I was a bit of a jerk.

Like so many young men, I thought I knew everything. I was selfish, arrogant, and absolutely convinced of my own *"rightness."*

Shortly after your mother and I got married, your grandfather—her dad—asked me to go for a walk with him. Obviously, he had noticed some of these traits in me, and he was trying to offer some needed balance. He said, *"You know, with these Raymond* (her maiden name) *women, sometimes you just have to say you're sorry—even when you know you weren't wrong."*

That landed like a lead balloon with my 20-year-old self. From my perspective, apologizing when I wasn't wrong meant losing self-respect, and I was convinced your mother wouldn't respect me either if I didn't stand my ground when I *knew* I was right. So I said, *"Yeah, that ain't ever gonna happen."*

He calmly replied, *"If I had that attitude, I would have been divorced a long time ago..."* And I—brilliant in my youthful arrogance—said, *"If that's the cost, so be it."*

And just like that, the conversation was over. Like I said… arrogant, know-it-all jerk.

To this day, I don't completely agree with the absolute *literal* application of his advice, but I now deeply understand the *spirit* of what he was saying.

Ephesians 5 says it this way: **"Husbands, love your wives as Christ loved the church and gave Himself up for her."**

The church can be imperfect. The church can be wrong. The relationship can get messy. But Christ loved her so much that He laid down His life for her—humbling Himself, sacrificing Himself, and doing whatever was necessary to help her become everything she was created to be.

From that perspective of love, apologizing in moments of conflict isn't about admitting to something you didn't do. It's about being willing to *lay down yourself* in order to create an environment where your wife can flourish.

Be that kind of husband, Son. Love your wife so deeply, so sacrificially, so intentionally, that your leadership helps her become everything God created her to be.

I love you, son. I hope you always know it. —Dad

Building Legacy and Finishing Strong

CHAPTER ONE HUNDRED FORTY-ONE
The Power of Relationship: The Weight of Choosing a Wife

Son,

Next to your relationship with God, the most important decision you will ever make is choosing the woman who will become your wife—the person you will walk with for the rest of your life.

When I was a young man, someone told me, *"Don't marry someone you can live with; marry someone you can't live without."* It may sound simple, but the heart of that statement is true. Marriage isn't just about compatibility—it's about covenant. It's about who you choose to build a life with, grow with, fight through storms with, and stand beside when life doesn't go according to plan.

Every marriage has highs and lows, seasons of ease and seasons of challenge. Culture will tell you to *"just follow your heart,"* but Jeremiah 17:9 reminds us that the heart can be deceitful—driven by emotions, impulses, and temporary desires. Proverbs 3:5-6 instructs you to *"trust in the Lord with all our heart and do NOT lean on your own understanding..."* This is why you need more than feelings. You need discernment. You need wisdom. You need God's voice in the center of your relationship decisions.

Your wife will be the one person who can make you feel more supported—or more discouraged—than anyone else on earth. Your mother and I have been together for over 30 years, and I can tell you with all sincerity that her faith in me—especially in moments when I didn't believe in myself—has been one of the greatest strengths in my life. Her prayers, her encouragement, her loyalty, and her willingness to stand beside me in hard seasons held me up more times than I can count. I don't know how I would have made it without her.

Ephesians 5 instructs us to love our wives like Christ loves the Church—with tender devotion, selflessness, sacrifice, and leadership. We are called to care for her as we care for our own body, to protect her, support her, and treat her with honor.

But son, many people enter marriage today thinking about what they can *get* rather than what they can *give*. They hold an unspoken exit strategy—*divorce if things stop feeling easy*. I've watched many people walk through that pain, and the breaking of a family can be worse than death.

Remember this: *she may be your wife, but she is God's daughter first*. As a father, if anyone ever mistreated my daughter, it wouldn't go well for them. And in the same way, if you will keep in mind that your wife belongs to God long before she belongs to you, it will help you carry that relationship with reverence and responsibility.

Not everyone is compatible. Looks fade. Charm diminishes. And someone who is beautiful on the outside can become painfully unattractive if their character, integrity, and spiritual maturity don't align with God's standard for your life.

So involve God in the entire process—before marriage and after. Don't compromise your standards for love, honor, or integrity when choosing the woman you will build a family with. If the Holy Spirit leads you, this will become one of the most fulfilling decisions of your entire life. But if you let emotions lead the way, the consequences can be devastating.

I love you, son. I hope you always know it. —Dad

Building Legacy and Finishing Strong

CHAPTER ONE HUNDRED FORTY-TWO
The Power of Relationship: Kids

Son,

Before your mother and I got married, I told her that if she ever wanted children, she shouldn't marry me—because I didn't want kids. Now, almost 30 years later, I can tell you without hesitation: *I was an idiot!* I had no idea what I didn't know. Being a father has been one of the greatest joys of my entire life.

Watching you grow... learning beside you... laughing with you... helping you process, mature, and navigate life—not just raising a child but training a man—has been one of the most meaningful experiences God has ever entrusted to me.

I realize not everyone has had a father as involved or intentional as I've been with you. That's why these letters matter and I've published them as a book and not just a collection for you. They give perspective, guidance, and a voice many young men never otherwise receive.

But son, hear me clearly: *I haven't done everything right.* There are moments I look back on with deep regret—moments when I dropped the ball and made decisions I wish I could undo. And when I examine those times honestly, every single regret came from failing to govern my emotions—specifically anger—and placing you in a situation where your sense of worth or your sense of safety probably felt compromised.

If I could go back and fix anything as a father, it would be this: I would be far more intentional to never let you feel angry *because* of me, or fearful *of* me.

Ephesians 6:4 instructs fathers not to provoke their children to anger, but to raise them with discipline and instruction from the Lord. I have never regretted disciplining you. I have never regretted instructing you. Those were a father's responsibilities. What I regret is the times I did it through frustration instead of through patience—moments when you feared the tone of my voice more than the consequences of your actions.

Scripture tells us that children are a gift from the Lord (Psalm 127:3), and that is undeniably true. Children will bring you tremendous joy… and at times, tremendous frustration. But your job as a father will always remain the same: *to train your children in the way they should go so that when they are older, they don't depart from what you've taught them.* (Proverbs 22:6)

You are the adult. Lead by example. Seek God for direction. Govern your emotions. And when you fail—and you will at times—be quick to own it and even quicker to apologize. That humility will teach your children as much as any discipline ever will.

I love you, son. I hope you always know it. —Dad

Building Legacy and Finishing Strong

CHAPTER ONE HUNDRED FORTY-THREE
The Power of Relationship: Kids - Part 2
Train Up a Child

Train up a child in the way he should go [and in keeping with his individual gift or bent], and when he is old he will not depart from it.
Proverbs 22:6 (AMPC)

Son,

Since you were a little boy, I often told your teachers, our family, pastors—anyone who would listen— *"I'm not raising a child; I'm training a man."* I've always tried to look beyond who you were in the moment and see who you were becoming. Proverbs 22:6 says to train up a child in the way **they** should go, and I took that seriously, even when it went against popular opinion or my own internal caution.

I remember sitting at dinner with our pastor when you were around twelve. He looked across the table and said to me, *"I thought you were messing up with how you were raising him... but I see now, you were right and I was wrong."* That moment meant more than he realized.

What most people never knew is that I prayed for wisdom regarding how I raised you from the time you were a baby. I never wanted to raise you to become who *I* wished I had been—I wanted to help you become who **you** were created to be, the man God dreamed over your life long before I held you in my arms.

One moment stands out clearly. When you were fifteen, you told me you wanted your motorcycle license. My immediate response was, *"No. Wait until you're eighteen and can decide on your own."* But as I walked away, I heard the still, small voice of the Holy Spirit whisper: *"When he turns eighteen, he will do exactly what you did—buy a bike he can't handle and learn the hard way. Or you can spend the next three years when you can set every parameter and permission for his riding, imparting into him the thirty years of knowledge you've gained... and train him for what he'll do with or without your help."*

That was a scary proposition. I didn't like the idea of you riding on the road. If it had been any other kid, the answer would've stayed *"no."* But for you, I knew the *right* thing wasn't the *safe* thing—it was the *intentional* thing.

There were times I said, *"no"* to something small because I felt a check in my spirit. And other times, I said, *"yes"* to something *risky* because I sensed God leading me to. Parenting you wasn't about fear; it was about obedience.

Ultimately, son, this is how you must live your life. Ask God what to do. Listen for the leading of the Holy Spirit—especially when you have a family of your own. Don't make decisions carelessly or fearfully. Include God in your process. Step out in faith when He directs you. And trust that He will guide your steps every time.

I love you, son. I hope you always know it. —Dad

Building Legacy and Finishing Strong

CHAPTER ONE HUNDRED FORTY-FOUR
The Power of Relationship: Friends

Son,

There's a saying you'll hear from leadership teachers around the world: *"The difference between who you are today and who you'll be in five years is found in the books you read and the people you surround yourself with."* It may sound cliché, but I'm convinced it's true.

One thing I've learned is that God does not anoint *lone wolves*. He advances His Kingdom through relationship and partnership. A mentor once told me, *"When God wants to promote you, He sends a relationship. When the enemy wants to distract you, he sends a relationship."* And that's why who you allow close to you in your inner circle matters so much.

The Bible tells us to love everyone—even our enemies—but that doesn't mean everyone deserves access to your inner world. Some people need to be loved from a distance. When the wrong person gets too close, their proximity increases their influence, and the wrong influence can steer your life in the wrong direction.

Son, God has a plan for your life. Protect what He is doing in and through you.

Proverbs 4:23 says, *"Above all else, guard your heart, for out of it flows the wellspring of life."* Your heart is the source of your calling, your decisions, and your relationships. Guarding it isn't *fear*—it's *wisdom*.

You can't live paranoid about every person's intentions, but you can stay sensitive to the Holy Spirit. Pay attention when peace is missing. Pay attention when something feels off. Pay attention when God gives you that *inner check*.

Pray for *"iron sharpening iron"* relationships—friends who push you closer to God and align with your destiny. And pray against the distractions the enemy will try to use to pull you off course.

When God confirms a relationship, invest in it. Be present. Be intentional. But when something doesn't align with who God is shaping you to be, create distance with the same intentionality.

Finally, realize this: most relationships are seasonal. Very few last a lifetime. Be the friend, brother, or leader you're meant to be in each season—and when that season ends, give yourself and others the grace to move into the next chapter God has prepared.

I love you, son. I hope you always know it. —Dad

Mastering Your Mind and Inner World

CHAPTER ONE HUNDRED FORTY-FIVE
Speak Life

Son,

The Bible says that life and death are in the power of the tongue (Proverbs 18:21). That isn't poetic language—it's a spiritual law. Your words carry weight. They shape environments, influence how people see themselves, strengthen faith, or destroy hope. That's why I've always told you: *speak life.* Use your words to build people up, and to strengthen yourself. Never let careless or destructive words slip out of your mouth, because even if they seem small or insignificant, they are anything but.

I often compare this truth to firearm safety. Anyone who handles a weapon understands the rules: *always keep the barrel pointed downrange, never point it at anything you don't intend to destroy, and don't touch the trigger until you're ready to fire.* These principles are drilled into shooters because when a weapon is mishandled, the consequences can be instant and irreversible.

Words are no different. In the hands of someone immature or undisciplined, words can wound deeply. They can kill confidence, damage relationships, or plant lies that stay with a person for years. But in the hands of someone trained—someone intentional—words become tools of healing, strength, encouragement, and truth. In the hands of a marksman, a firearm is precise. In the hands of a wise man, words carry precision and purpose.

Scripture says that blessing and cursing should not come from the same mouth. And Son, you cannot release the life of God and the poison of the enemy at the same time. One will always drown out the other. That's why discipline in your speech matters.

I've taught you from a young age that your words carry power. They shape atmospheres. They influence how your friends feel about themselves. They create an internal reality inside your own heart. They tear down lies. They reveal truth. They express love. They bring peace. And if you're not careful, they can do the exact opposite—hurting the people you care about and limiting the future God designed for you.

Choose your words with intention. Speak life over yourself. Speak life over your future. Speak life over the people God places in your world.

Because your words don't just describe your reality—they help create it.

I love you, son. I hope you always know it. —Dad

Your Identity in the Father's Heart

CHAPTER ONE HUNDRED FORTY-SIX
Part 1 - Jesus Came to Show You the Father

Son,

There's something that happens inside a man when he becomes a father. Suddenly, you understand things about God that you never saw clearly before. You start to see His heart in a different way—His patience, His love, His desire to protect and guide. Being your dad has taught me more about the Father-nature of God than any sermon ever could.

But not everyone has had that kind of example. Many people struggle to relate to God as Father because their fathers were absent, abusive, distracted, or simply broken. And honestly, this misunderstanding isn't new. Even in Jesus' day, people had distorted ideas about who God really was. Religion had painted Him as distant, angry, strict, and hard to please.

That's why Jesus came—*to reveal the Father.*

The Bible tells us Jesus came for three reasons: **to reveal the Father** (Matthew 11:27)**, to destroy the works of the enemy** (1 John 3:8)**, and to save what was lost** (Luke 19:10). And Son, everything Jesus taught, every miracle He performed, every conversation He had was meant to show us what the Father is truly like.

In John 14, Philip said, *"Lord, show us the Father."* And Jesus responded, *"If you've seen Me, you've seen the Father."* That one verse settles it—Jesus is the perfect picture of God. So, you have every right to question anything someone teaches about God that doesn't look like Jesus.

So what did Jesus reveal about the Father?

He revealed a Father who loves His children (John 3:16). A Father who doesn't want to condemn you but rescue you (John 3:17). A Father who stays close, even in your hardest moments (Matthew 28:20). A Father who provides (Philippians 4:19), protects (Luke 10:19), and teaches truth that sets you free (John 8:31–32). A Father who forgives (1

John 1:9), celebrates His kids (Luke 15), and has grace when you mess up (Ephesians 2:8–9). A Father who wants you to live abundantly (John 10:10) and even do greater things in your life than Jesus did in His (John 14:12). A Father willing to lay down His life to save you (John 19). A Father who made you His heir, carrying His name and His inheritance (Romans 8:15–17).

One of my favorite moments in Scripture is the woman caught in adultery in John 8. Every religious voice said she was guilty and deserved death. But Jesus—God in the flesh—knelt down beside her and said, *"Neither do I condemn you."* He didn't see a sinner. He saw a daughter.

Son, even if you didn't have the perfect example of a father on earth, you still have the perfect example of a Father in heaven—because Jesus showed you exactly who He is.

And I want you to always remember this: You were made to carry the same love, the same compassion, the same power, the same Spirit, and the same Kingdom that Jesus carried everywhere He went. The same Spirit lives in you! No matter where you go or what you do, He is always with you, and you are called to further what He began.

I love you, son. I hope you always know it. —Dad

Your Identity in the Father's Heart

CHAPTER ONE HUNDRED FORTY-SEVEN
Part 2 That Which Was Lost

Son,

In the previous chapter, I shared how the Bible reveals that Jesus came with three divine assignments:

1. **To reveal *the Father***
2. **To destroy all the works of the enemy**
3. **To save/restore that which was lost**

We spent time discussing the first—to reveal the Father—and what that means for how you see God. In this letter, I want to walk you into the next two: how Jesus destroyed the works of the enemy, and how He restored everything mankind surrendered in the beginning.

There's something God built into you that many people never discover: you were created to walk in authority. Not arrogance, not pride—*authority*. The kind of authority a son carries because his Father gave it to him.

Most people live their whole lives feeling tossed around by circumstances, temptation, fear, or the lies of the enemy. **They think they're powerless.** They think they're victims. They think the devil is stronger than they are. But that's not what God says, and it's not what Jesus saved and restored to you.

When God created mankind, He placed us on this earth with purpose and gave us dominion. He didn't send Satan to some distant corner of the universe—He sent him here, because from the very beginning, God intended that His children would rule over the enemy, not run from him.

But when Adam sinned, he handed over the authority that God had given him. That's what was *lost* —*authority*. And Son, that's what Jesus came to restore.

Jesus didn't just save *people*—He saved **that which was lost** (Luke

19:10 & Matthew 18:11): direct relationship with God, authority, freedom, peace, healing, and the ability to carry the culture of heaven into the earth. Everything sin caused—bondage, chaos, death, fear, confusion—Jesus crushed at the cross. Scripture says He was wounded for our sin, bruised for our iniquities, punished so we could have peace, and beaten so we could be healed (Isaiah 53:5). Salvation is not just a ticket to heaven; **it's heaven empowering your life right now.**

But here's what you need to understand:

Authority only works if you believe you have it.

Most people live defeated because they hesitate. They wonder if they're allowed to fight back. They don't know what belongs to them. They wait for God to do something He already empowered them to do.

But Son, *you* don't have to live like that.

Jesus Himself said: *"I have given you authority… over all the power of the enemy, and nothing will harm you."* (Luke 10:19)

Not some power—**all** the power.

You don't have to be a pastor or a spiritual giant to walk in victory. When the enemy lies, you can command him to shut up. When fear tries to creep in, you can tell it to go. When temptation whispers, you can stand your ground and resist—and Scripture promises the devil will flee from you.

He is not over your head. He is under your feet.

And Son, that's where he belongs.

Walk like a man who knows who his *Father* is. Carry yourself as one who has authority, because you do. Don't surrender your ground. Don't give the enemy permission to stay in places he was defeated. When you speak with faith, heaven backs you.

Remember: You were created to rule, not to be ruled over.

I love you, son. I hope you always know it. —Dad

Your Identity in the Father's Heart

CHAPTER ONE HUNDRED FORTY-EIGHT
You Are Who God Says You Are

Son,

One of the biggest battles you'll face in life isn't against people, circumstances, or even the enemy—**it's the battle of who you believe you are.** The world will try to label you. Your mistakes will try to define you. And the enemy will whisper lies every chance he gets, hoping you'll agree with them.

But you cannot build your identity on what you see in the mirror or what you feel in a weak moment. You must build it on what God says about you.

Yes, you'll make mistakes. Yes, you'll have days where you don't feel worthy. But grace changed everything. Grace has a name—and His name is Jesus. The moment you gave your life to Him, the old version of you died. Your sin was covered. Your spirit came alive. You became a completely new creation.

So, when you wonder, *"Who am I really?"* hear me clearly:

You are who God says you are.
You are forgiven.
You are accepted.
You are made righteous—not because you earned it, but because Jesus paid for it.
You are more than a conqueror.
You are loved without conditions.
You are called according to His purpose.
You are no longer defined by what you've done, but by what He has done for you.

Son, so many believers struggle because they still feel like they have to earn God's approval. But *you didn't become righteous by "doing righteousness" any more than Jesus became sin by "doing sin."* He took on your sin so you could take on His righteousness. It's a gift—not a wage.

People who live with constant guilt, shame, and feelings of

unworthiness often do so because they genuinely want to please God—but they don't yet understand the freedom grace gives. *Grace doesn't make you want to sin; it empowers you to finally walk free from it.* When you know who you are in Christ, your actions begin to align with that identity almost effortlessly. I believe this is why Jesus said, *"If you love Me, you will keep My commandments."* (John 14:15) Proximity to Him provides freedom from what would otherwise control you.

But when you live in fear, condemnation, or self-loathing, you reject what God says about you and live beneath the life He intended. You behave like someone God never said you were.

Those who know they are loved by God carry themselves differently. They respond differently. Their confidence isn't arrogance—it's the confidence of a child who knows he is loved even in his weakness. Scripture says, *"Those who know their God will be strong and do great exploits."* (Daniel 11:32) The strength doesn't come from *perfection*—it comes from *identity*.

Son, the way you see yourself matters. The Bible says, *"As a man thinks in his heart, so is he."* (Proverbs 23:7) If you believe a lie, you will live like it's true. If you believe God's truth, you will rise into everything He created you to be.

Imagine having a million dollars in the bank but starving because you didn't know it was yours. That's how many people live—rich in Christ, but spiritually starving because they never embraced who they truly are.

You are who God says you are. Now the only question is whether you will believe it.

I love you, son. I hope you always know it. —Dad

Building Legacy and Finishing Strong

CHAPTER ONE HUNDRED FORTY-NINE
Courage to Kill What Your Father Tolerated

Son,

What you do in this life matters. Every choice you make will place before you opportunities for victory or defeat, for intentionality or compromise. None of us walk through life without enemies to face. Some battles are new, and some have been passed down through generations.

My grandfather battled rage. My father battled rage. And before you were ever born, I made a decision: *that particular giant would not be passed down to you.* What you tolerate, you authorize to exist and I fought it—hard—because I refused to let it become your default inheritance. And looking at you now, I can see the difference. You are more centered, more steady, and far less emotionally driven than I was at your age. I believe that's partly because I confronted that giant instead of leaving it at your doorstep.

In 1 Kings 2, just before his death, King David commissions Solomon—his son and the next king—to serve God passionately. But then something shifts. David begins listing unfinished business... situations he should have dealt with himself but didn't. And because he left those issues unresolved, **Solomon inherited battles that belonged to his father.**

Son, you will have your own giants to slay—but you shouldn't have to slay mine. I have done my best to confront the giants in my life so they would not become your burden. Now I'm commissioning you to do the same. Do not take your role in God's Kingdom lightly. Don't allow sin or compromise to slip into your life, your marriage, or your home. What you tolerate or fail to deal with will become the unfinished business your children and grandchildren are forced to confront.

Be intentional. Be the godly example your family needs. Be the priest of your home. Let your walk with God become the standard by which your children measure their own spiritual strength. Always remember: *you carry the Kingdom of God into every place you see hell in the earth.* Part of your calling is to kill giants—and then raise the next generation of giant slayers.

Let your legacy say, *"He taught us how to fight."* But son… never leave your unfinished business for your children to clean up. That is an unfair burden and a failure in leadership.

I love you, son. I hope you always know it. —Dad

Building Legacy and Finishing Strong
CHAPTER ONE HUNDRED FIFTY
Your 100 Year Dot

Son,

The older you get, the more you realize how true the saying is: *"Life is short."* It feels like yesterday you were born, and now you're stepping into manhood. Thirty years have passed since I married your mother—it feels like ten. And in another thirty, I'll be in my eighties. Time moves faster than you expect, and the older you become, the more you realize, **time is a thief.**

In the last decade, I've watched many loved ones step into eternity. Losing people is painful, but Scripture becomes clearer with age: *"We don't mourn as those who have no hope."* (1 Thessalonians 4:13) When I was twenty, the thought of living 60–80 more years seemed huge—and the idea of waiting that long to see someone again felt unbearable. But at fifty, I see differently: even eighty years is nothing compared to eternity.

Several years ago, my friend—an Army Ranger—lost his eighteen-year-old son in a tragic accident. I can't fathom the depth of his grief. The week after, we sat together at a coffee shop. Though he was a warrior, I could tell he was deep in despair.

I pulled a pen from my pocket, took his hand, and drew a tiny dot on his wrist—about the size of a ladybug. Confused, he stared at it. I said, *"Right now, living the rest of your life without your son feels impossible. But imagine that dot represents a full 100-year human life. From your limited perspective, 100 years feels enormous. But life doesn't end after one dot. When we leave this world, we step out of time and into eternity."*

Then I drew more dots along his arm. *"Each dot is another hundred years. And another. And another. These dots don't even begin to touch eternity. While you may not get to finish this 100-year 'dot' with your son, you will have endless hundreds of years with him in the presence of God."*

"This is why believers don't mourn like those without hope," I told him. *"Death is temporary. Eternal life is limitless."*

Months later, he met with me again. He lifted his sleeve and showed me a new tattoo—a single dot on his wrist. He told me that perspective saved his life that day and gave him hope for the future.

Son, live for Jesus every day. Make every day count for the Kingdom. Don't let the enemy steal your time through sin, distraction, or compromise. God places tremendous value on this single 100-year dot of your earthly life—so honor it. Enjoy it. Steward it well. But hold it loosely.

Because your eternity doesn't end with this dot… it begins there.

I love you, son. I hope you always know it. —Dad

Building Legacy and Finishing Strong

ONE HUNDRED FIFTY-ONE
A Father's Instruction

PROVERBS 4 (TPT)

A Father's Instruction

1Listen to my correction, my sons, for I speak to you as your father. Let discernment enter your heart and you will grow wise with the understanding I impart. 2My revelation-truth is a gift to you, so remain faithful to my instruction. 3For I, too, was once the delight of my father and cherished by my mother—their beloved child. 4Then my father taught me, saying, "Never forget my words. If you do everything that I teach you, you will reign in life." 5So make wisdom your quest—search for the revelation of life's meaning. Don't let what I say go in one ear and out the other. 6Stick with wisdom and she will stick to you, protecting you throughout your days. She will rescue all those who passionately listen to her voice. 7Wisdom is the most valuable commodity—so buy it! Revelation-knowledge is what you need—so invest in it! 8Wisdom will exalt you when you exalt her truth. She will lead you to honor and favor when you live your life by her insights. 9You will be adorned with beauty and grace, and wisdom's glory will wrap itself around you, making you victorious in the race.

Two Pathways

10My son, if you will take the time to stop and listen to me and embrace what I say, you will live a long and happy life full of understanding in every way. 11I have taken you by the hand in wisdom's ways, pointing you to the path of integrity. 12Your progress will have no limits when you come along with me, and you will never stumble as you walk along the way. 13So receive my correction no matter how hard it is to swallow, for wisdom will snap you back into place—her words will be invigorating life to you. 14Do not detour into darkness or even set foot on that path. 15Stay away from it; don't even go there! 16For troublemakers are restless if they are not involved in evil. They are not satisfied until they have brought someone harm. 17They feed on darkness and drink until they're drunk on the wine of wickedness. 18But the lovers of God walk on the highway of light, and their way shines brighter and brighter until the perfect day. 19But the wicked walk in thick darkness, like those who travel in fog, and yet don't have a clue why they keep stumbling!

Healing Words

20Listen carefully, my dear child, to everything that I teach you, and pay attention to all that I have to say. 21Fill your thoughts with my words until they penetrate deep into your spirit. 22Then, as you unwrap my words, they will impart true life and radiant health into the very core of your being. 23So above all, guard the affections of your heart, for they affect all that you are. Pay attention to the welfare of your innermost being, for from there flows the wellspring of life. 24Avoid dishonest speech and pretentious words. Be free from using perverse words no matter what!

Watch Where You're Going

25Set your gaze on the path before you. With fixed purpose, looking straight ahead, ignore life's distractions. 26Watch where you're going! Stick to the path of truth, and the road will be safe and smooth before you. 27Don't allow yourself to be sidetracked for even a moment or take the detour that leads to darkness.

Son,

As we come to the end of these letters, I want to bring you back to where it all began—to the instruction that has shaped everything I've shared with you. Read these words again now in light of all we've walked through together, and consider how each lesson was meant to be lived, not just learned.

In Proverbs 4, Solomon—renowned for his wisdom—writes a "father's instruction" to his sons. In that passage, he references the teachings handed down from his own father, King David. When I read this section in *The Passion Translation*, I'm moved by the heart of a loving father who genuinely desires good things for his children. Solomon wanted his sons to succeed. He had seen the blessings that came from his father's pursuit of God's heart and instruction, and he had also witnessed the failures of his father who loved the Lord deeply yet sometimes lost his way in his own humanity, pride, lust, and power.

Yet despite receiving profound godly instruction—and despite watching his father, David's life unfold with both triumphs and painful lessons—Solomon did not follow the Lord with the same humility. And because he neglected the instruction he had been given, he, his legacy, and the nation of Israel ultimately suffered for it.

Solomon's life, leadership, and most importantly, legacy could have been radically different had he been intentional with what he was taught. **Wisdom without implementation is worthless.** But wisdom that is embraced and lived out? The results are limitless. That is why I've written these letters—so that you don't merely *receive* wisdom, but so you learn how to practically *apply* it.

I've written this book as a reference and a roadmap—something to equip you, your legacy, and anyone who reads these letters long after we are gone. My hope is that you will learn early in life the principles that took me a lifetime to understand and implement.

Son, much of this will sound familiar, because it is the same teaching, encouragement, and correction I've poured into you your whole life. For others reading this—many who may have never had the steady voice of a spiritual father speaking wisdom and truth into them—you've been invited into this family as a spiritual son of legacy. When you read these pages, I hope you could hear the voice of a loving father speaking directly to you. The fact that you have read them all means that you have not treated these letters as if they were written for someone else, but taken them personally, applied them intentionally, and understood that I wrote them with *you* in mind.

Beneath *my* voice, I hope you were able to hear the voice of your heavenly Father—the One who gives wisdom, who loves you fiercely, and who wants you to know His heart so deeply that your life, your identity, and your future are shaped by His truth.

Finally, I hope that as you came to the closing line of each chapter—*"I love you, son. I hope you always know it."*— You heard it not only from me as a spiritual father, but also from the God who loves you more than you will ever fully comprehend.

I'm eager to hear the victories that will come from what you learned in these letters. I look forward to celebrating your accomplishments. And I cherish the knowledge that I will rejoice with your legacy—my legacy—from the grandstands of glory, as the wisdom imparted in these pages continues echoing into eternity.

I love you, son… and for my spiritual sons reading this—I love you too. I hope you always know it. — Dad

Building Legacy and Finishing Strong

CHAPTER ONE HUNDRED FIFTY-TWO
Last Letter:
Lead Well — Your Legacy Begins Now

Son,

This is the final letter in this set. I began writing this collection four years ago, and now here we are—at the end of this season. On one hand, I feel a deep sense of fulfillment. On the other, I grieve, because completing this series means something precious is concluding as you step into this next season of your life. But endings and beginnings often walk hand in hand, and as I've been shaping these last instructions to you, the Lord has simultaneously been leading me through 1 & 2 Kings and 1 & 2 Chronicles—studying the great victories and heartbreaking failures of the covenant leaders of God's people.

Bondage creates mentalities that take strong leadership to break. Israel lived 400 years under pagan masters who imposed systems, beliefs, and practices completely contradictory to the ways of God. Those years forged mental strongholds and spiritual dysfunction that rippled through generations. It took God-appointed leaders—men who chose obedience over convenience—to break those strongholds and turn the hearts of the people back to Him.

But as you read about Israel's kings, you watch idolatry slip back in again and again. Solomon, son of David—the wisest man who ever lived—married wives from pagan nations against the clear instruction of the Lord. And as I've reiterated so many times throughout these letters, *what you tolerate, you authorize to exist.* His compromise opened the door for generations of divided kingdoms, fractured families, wars between tribes, and spiritual chaos.

Yet every time a king humbled himself, tore down the idols, rebuilt the altars, restored honor to God's Word, and led the people back to Him—God restored the covenant blessings. The key was this: *it took a leader willing to confront what was out of alignment with God's will and bring his people back into right relationship with the Lord.* It was a leader who permitted the dysfunction, and it was a leader who corrected it.

Son, I don't know the full extent of the leadership mantle God will place on your life. Maybe you will simply lead your family with strength and conviction. Maybe you'll lead teams, businesses, ministries, or communities. Maybe you'll influence hundreds. Maybe thousands. Maybe nations. But whatever capacity God entrusts to you, lead well.

Whether your season is the prison or the palace, understand this: ***you shape the culture, the direction, and the legacy of those assigned to your care.*** You can model the ways of God—or you can lead others into generational chaos. You hold the power to steer the ship and safeguard every soul aboard. That is a sacred honor. And that is a tremendous responsibility.

Do not take it lightly.
Do not take a day off from your calling.
Do not forsake your responsibility when the season feels heavy.

Lead your family in the ways of the Lord. Tear down the idols and ungodly patterns inherited from previous generations. Empower those you lead with wisdom, truth, and courage. Be the man who establishes a legacy of Godliness that continues long after the name on your tombstone has faded.

Fix what is broken.
Right what is wrong.
Fight for justice.
Walk with uncompromising integrity.
Do not bow to defeat.
When you fall, get back up.
Never quit.

Follow God with unwavering faith. Slay the giants that mock the greatness of the God who lives within you. Take back everything the enemy has stolen. And impart into others the wisdom, faith, and strength to do the same.

Go be the man God created you to be.

I'm so proud of you. I believe in you. Being your dad is one of the greatest gifts God ever gave me! You will do great things, and I am excited to see the impact and legacy your life will leave. I'll always be cheering you on—from this side of eternity or the in the grandstands on the other side.

I love you, son. I hope you always know it. —Dad

Aaron D. Davis

A Guide for Group Study

For those who may wish to use this collection of *Dad's Letters* in a small group or men's group setting, I've provided an optional framework at the end of this book. The letters have been thoughtfully organized under ten thematic headings to help guide discussion and reflection in a more structured environment. While the book itself was written to be read devotionally and conversationally, this suggested layout is designed to support a themed based group study, with each section building intentionally on the one before it.

1. Your Identity in the Father's Heart

"For he chose us in him before the creation of the world to be holy and blameless in his sight. In love he predestined us for adoption to sonship through Jesus Christ, in accordance with his pleasure and will."
Ephesians 1:4–5 (NIV)

- Chapter One: God's Not Mad at You — Part 1
- Chapter Two: God's Not Mad at You — Part 2
- Chapter Three: God's Not Mad at You — Part 3
- Chapter Nine: God Doesn't Abuse His Kids
- Chapter Ten: I Trust You Daddy
- Chapter Twenty-Six: The Lie Of Sin Consciousness
- Chapter Twenty-Eight: Grace Is Stronger Than Your Shame
- Chapter Thirty-Five: The Father Who Dreams Over You
- Chapter Eighty-Six: You Are Enough
- Chapter Eighty-Seven: You Don't Know God
- Chapter One Hundred Five: As He Is, So Are You
- Chapter One Hundred Fourteen: The Power of "Thank You, Daddy"
- Chapter One Hundred Thirty-Six: Understanding Grace The Right Way
- Chapter One Hundred Thirty-One: Identity and the Enemy's Favorite Lie
- Chapter One Hundred Thirty-Three: You Are Enough—Because God Says You Are
- Chapter One Hundred Thirty-Seven: God's Kid First
- Chapter One Hundred Forty-Six: Part 1 - Jesus Came to Show You the

Father
- Chapter One Hundred Forty-Seven: Part 2 That Which Was Lost
- Chapter One Hundred Forty-Eight: You Are Who God Says You Are

2. Deepening Faith and Intimacy with God

> "And without faith it is impossible to please God, because anyone who comes to him must believe that he exists and that he rewards those who earnestly seek him."
> *Hebrews 11:6 (NIV)*

- Introduction: A Father's Instruction
- Chapter Six: Don't Quit: Faith Beyond Disappointment
- Chapter Seven: Faith Begins Where the Will of God Is Known
- Chapter Seventeen: Anchored in the Truth of God's Word
- Chapter Eighteen: When Your Experience Doesn't Meet Your Expectation
- Chapter Nineteen: When Your Experience Doesn't Meet Your Expectation Part 2
- Chapter Thirty: The God Who Fights Beside You
- Chapter Thirty-Two: The Power of a Surrendered Will
- Chapter Forty-Seven: God of the Watch
- Chapter Forty-Eight: God of the Watch — Part 2
- Chapter Forty-Nine: God Is Still Good
- Chapter Sixty-One: Choose His Way First
- Chapter Sixty-Two: Listen for His Voice
- Chapter Sixty-Three: Praise Is A Weapon
- Chapter Sixty-Four: Keep Praying Anyway
- Chapter Sixty-Five: God's Will, Your Part
- Chapter Sixty-Six: Live, Move, And Have Your Being In Him
- Chapter Seventy-Eight: The Reward of Putting God First
- Chapter Seventy-Nine: Discerning God's Voice
- Chapter One Hundred Two: The Kingdom Has Arrived
- Chapter One Hundred Four: When Grief Whispers, Speak the Word
- Chapter One Hundred Nine: You Carry Heaven with You
- Chapter One Hundred Nineteen: When Fear Loses Its Grip
- Chapter One Hundred Twenty-Nine: Dream With God
- Chapter One Hundred Thirty-Nine: Faith Works When You Work It

3. Building Godly Character and Integrity

> "Whoever walks in integrity walks securely, but whoever takes crooked paths will be found out."
> *Proverbs 10:9 (NIV)*

- Chapter Four: Your Word Is Your Oath
- Chapter Eight: Forge Your Own Path
- Chapter Thirteen: The Gold That Really Matters
- Chapter Twenty-Seven: Don't Be That Guy
- Chapter Twenty-Nine: Don't Assume—Be Intentional
- Chapter Thirty-Seven: Excellence is your Standard
- Chapter Forty-Three: Listen For the Lesson
- Chapter Fifty-Six: It's So Much Harder to Keep Your Mouth Shut Than It Is to Fight
- Chapter Fifty-Nine: Be A Man of Integrity
- Chapter Sixty: Stewarding Your Talent
- Chapter Sixty-Seven: Do It Well
- Chapter Sixty-Eight: Guard Your Heart Without Hardening It
- Chapter Seventy: Don't Do It—Even If They Deserve It
- Chapter Seventy-Two: Forgiveness is a Choice
- Chapter Seventy-Six: The Detail of Obedience
- Chapter Eighty-Eight: Better Than Fear
- Chapter Eighty-Nine: Humility Will Take You Further Than Pride Ever Will
- Chapter One Hundred Seven: Small Choices, Strong Character
- Chapter One Hundred Twelve: The Power That Shapes You
- Chapter One Hundred Thirteen: Becoming the Man God Made You to Be
- Chapter One Hundred Thirty: You Are Not What You Feel — You Are What You Decide
- Chapter One Hundred Thirty-Five: The Seeds You Sow Shape the Life You Live

4. Healing, Pain, and Growing in Emotional Maturity

"The Lord is close to the brokenhearted and saves those who are crushed in spirit."
Psalm 34:18 (NIV)

- Chapter Five: You Are Not Defined by Your Past
- Chapter Eleven: You Are Worth the Fight
- Chapter Twelve: Don't Let Fear Lead You - The Rockwall
- Chapter Twenty: "But Did You Die?" — The Perspective That Keeps You Going
- Chapter Thirty-One: Don't Live Your Labels
- Chapter Thirty-Four: The Heart of a Warrior
- Chapter Fifty-Seven: Don't Let Pain Set the Ceiling of Your Faith
- Chapter Ninety-Seven: Love Big Anyway
- Chapter Ninety-Eight: Dis-Appointment
- Chapter Ninety-Nine: When It's All True
- Chapter One Hundred: The Lens You Choose

- Chapter One Hundred Three: Choose Compassion
- Chapter One Hundred Fifteen: Guard Your Peace with Fierce Intention
- Chapter One Hundred Twenty-Two: Defined by God, Not by Wounds
- Chapter One Hundred Twenty-Four: Your Lens Is Your Battlefield
- Chapter One Hundred Twenty-Five: One Morning At A Time
- Chapter One Hundred Twenty-Six: Be Slow to Judge What You Don't Yet Understand
- Chapter One Hundred Twenty-Seven: When You Fall, Come Home Quickly

5. Discipline, Consistency, and Spiritual Growth

"No discipline seems pleasant at the time, but painful. Later on, however, it produces a harvest of righteousness and peace for those who have been trained by it."
Hebrews 12:11 (NIV)

- Chapter Fourteen: Guard Your Thoughts, Guard Your Future
- Chapter Fifteen: Don't Draw Back - Draw In
- Chapter Thirty-Three: Go Deep, Son
- Chapter Forty: The Wisdom Of Right Now
- Chapter Fifty-Three: See Beyond What You See
- Chapter Fifty-Eight: Make Decisions in Faith, Not Fear
- Chapter Seventy-Five: Garbage In Garbage Out
- Chapter Eighty-One: Lead with Strength, Not Fear
- Chapter Ninety-One: Guard Your Heart from Entitlement
- Chapter One Hundred Eight: What You Learn in the Climb
- Chapter One Hundred Ten: Salvation Is Free—Blessing Is Cultivated
- Chapter One Hundred Eleven: The Power of Thankfulness
- Chapter One Hundred Eighteen: The Quitter's Harvest
- Chapter One Hundred Twenty: Well-Fertilized Growth
- Chapter One Hundred Thirty-Two: Living in the Tension Between Calling and Becoming
- Chapter One Hundred Thirty-Four: Nothing Means Nothing

6. Leadership, Authority, and Kingdom Influence

"Be shepherds of God's flock that is under your care, watching over them—not because you must, but because you are willing, as God wants you to be; not pursuing dishonest gain, but eager to serve; not lording it over those entrusted to you, but being examples to the flock."
1 Peter 5:2–3 (NIV)

- Chapter Sixteen: Lead or Support—Know Your Moment
- Chapter Twenty-One: The Marks of a Leader of Leaders
- Chapter Twenty-Three: Title and Leader Are Not Synonymous
- Chapter Twenty-Four: Honor the Gift, Honor the Giver
- Chapter Twenty-Five: They're Looking For What You Already Have
- Chapter Thirty-Six: You're Just the Ass
- Chapter Thirty-Nine: People Before Process
- Chapter Forty-One: "Who" You Ask? They.
- Chapter Forty-Five: Famous To Me - Chapter Fifty-One: Include God in the Fight
- Chapter Fifty-Five: The Leadership That Washes Feet
- Chapter Sixty-Nine: The Power that Confirms the Message
- Chapter Seventy-One: The Elevation of Title Above Capacity
- Chapter Seventy-Three: Keep Your Eyes on the Right Battle
- Chapter Seventy-Four: Be Known for Love, Not Division
- Chapter Eighty: You Can't Lead the Unwilling
- Chapter Eighty-Two: Stay in Your God-Given Lane
- Chapter Eighty-Five: How You Fill Your Lane Matters
- Chapter Ninety: Call Out the King In Others
- Chapter Ninety-Two: Don't Let Your Gift Become Your God
- Chapter Ninety-Three: Leadership Without Entitlement
- Chapter Ninety-Six: The Last Word Belongs to God
- Chapter One Hundred Sixteen: The Power of Unity

7. MASTERING YOUR MIND AND INNER WORLD

"Do not conform to the pattern of this world, but be transformed by the renewing of your mind. Then you will be able to test and approve what God's will is—his good, pleasing and perfect will."
Romans 12:2 (NIV)

- Chapter Forty-Two: Choose to Sow Life
- Chapter Forty-Six: What's in Your Hand?
- Chapter Ninety-Four: Guard Your Imagination, Guard Your Life
- Chapter One Hundred One: The Purina Cantina - Don't Become Cat Food
- Chapter One Hundred Twenty-Eight: Don't Take the Bait
- Chapter One Hundred Thirty-Eight: What Do You See?
- Chapter One Hundred Forty-Five: Speak Life

8. Wisdom, Discernment, and Godly Decisions

"If any of you lacks wisdom, you should ask God, who gives generously to all without finding fault, and it will be given to you."
James 1:5 (NIV)

- Chapter Fifty: Choose Your Counsel Wisely
- Chapter Fifty-Two: Relationships Will Make or Break You
- Chapter Eighty-Three: Choose Thankfulness in Every Season
- Chapter Eighty-Four: Choose Grace Over Judgment
- Chapter Ninety-Five: Don't Let Foolish Voices Shape Your Life

9. Resisting Comparison and Cultural Pressures

"Am I now trying to win the approval of human beings, or of God? Or am I trying to please people? If I were still trying to please people, I would not be a servant of Christ."
Galatians 1:10 (NIV)

- Chapter Twenty-Two: Seeing Like God Sees – The Comparison Deception
- Chapter Fifty-Four: Don't Compare Your Way into Compromise

10. BUILDING LEGACY AND FINISHING STRONG

"I have fought the good fight, I have finished the race, I have kept the faith. Now there is in store for me the crown of righteousness, which the Lord, the righteous Judge, will award to me on that day—and not only to me, but also to all who have longed for his appearing."
2 Timothy 4:7–8 (NIV)

- Chapter Thirty-Eight: Intentional Fatherhood
- Chapter Forty-Four: Training Them to Live Without You
- Chapter Seventy-Seven: Legacy Lives Through You
- Chapter One Hundred Six: Breaking the Cycle, Building a Legacy
- Chapter One Hundred Seventeen: What Money Can't Buy
- Chapter One Hundred Twenty-One: The ROI of a Life Well Invested
- Chapter One Hundred Twenty-Three: Legacy Doesn't Replace Relationship
- Chapter One Hundred Forty: Be the Husband Who Loves Like Christ
- Chapter One Hundred Forty-One: The Power of Relationship: The Weight of Choosing a Wife
- Chapter One Hundred Forty-Two: The Power of Relationship: Kids
- Chapter One Hundred Forty-Three: The Power of Relationship: Kids- Part 2 Train Up a Child
- Chapter One Hundred Forty-Four: The Power of Relationship: Friends
- Chapter One Hundred Forty-Nine: Courage to Kill What Your Father

Tolerated
- Chapter One Hundred Fifty: Your 100 Year Dot
- Chapter One Hundred Fifty-One: A Father's Instruction
- Chapter One Hundred Fifty-Two: Last Letter: Lead Well — Your Legacy Begins Now

About the Author

Aaron D. Davis is a father, husband, pastor, speaker, and best-selling author whose life and work are rooted in a deep passion for faith, identity, and the power of a father's voice. With decades of experience walking with people through seasons of growth, struggle, and healing, Aaron writes not just as a teacher—but as a dad who understands the weight and responsibility of shaping the next generation.

A former Detective Sergeant and S.W.A.T. team officer, Aaron was medically retired after surviving an attempt on his life in the line of duty. That defining experience reshaped his understanding of what truly matters and reinforced his commitment to living—and leading—with purpose, humility, and intentional love. It also strengthened his resolve to speak life, wisdom, and encouragement into others, especially men who are searching for direction and belonging.

Aaron is the author of multiple best-selling books, including *Quantum Christianity: Believe Again – Discovering the Science of Scripture Uncovering the Mysteries of Faith*, *Limitless: You Can Experience the Freedom, Power and Potential You Were Created for*, and *PTCD: Post-Traumatic Church Disorder – Addressing the Elephant in the Sanctuary*. Through his writing, teaching, mentoring and coaching, he consistently blends biblical truth with real-world experience, offering practical wisdom that is honest, grounded, and hope-filled.

Dad's Letters was born from that same heart—a desire to pass on timeless truths, spoken with clarity and compassion, in the way a loving father would speak to his son. These letters reflect lessons learned not only through ministry and leadership, but through everyday moments of fatherhood, faith, and perseverance.

Aaron lives in Nashville, Tennessee, with his wife, Lisa, to whom he has been happily married for nearly 30 years. They are the proud parents of their son, Rocky. Above all else, Aaron hopes his words will remind readers that they are seen, known, loved by God—and never walking alone.

Other Books and Resources by Aaron D. Davis

To explore more books and audiobooks by Aaron D. Davis, visit his Author Central page at: amazon.com/author/tattoopreacher , his official website at TattooPreacher.com, or connect with him on social media where he's known as The Tattooed Preacher or @Tatoopreacher (X, LinkedIn, Instagram, Facebook, Youtube). You can also search "Tattoo Preacher" on YouTube to access his teaching series and a wide range of impactful video content.

Quantum Christianity: Believe Again

In *Quantum Christianity,* Aaron Davis explores the questions that often lead people away from faith—questions born from the gap between what we've been taught and what we've experienced. By uncovering the intersection between science and Scripture, he offers a deeper understanding of belief, challenging partial truths and revealing the surprising, hope-filled answers that await those who dare to ask, "There has to be more." (Available in paperback, hardcover and audiobook).

Limitless: You Can Experience the Freedom, Power, and Potential You Were Created For

In *Limitless,* Aaron Davis tackles the real struggles so many believers face—the frustration of battling the same sins, setbacks, and strongholds again and again. Through practical wisdom and biblical truth, he shows that you don't have to stay stuck in cycles of defeat. You were created for freedom, victory, and the limitless potential God designed for your life. (Available in adult, young adult, Spanish, and audiobook).

PTCD: Post-Traumatic Church Disorder – Addressing the Elephant in the Sanctuary.

Post-Traumatic Church Disorder (PTCD): Addressing the Elephant in the Sanctuary is a thoughtful and courageous exploration of the spiritual wounds many believers carry as a result of unhealthy church leadership. Drawing from decades of pastoral experience, real-life stories, and biblical truth, Aaron D. Davis gives voice to pain that has often gone unnamed while offering both compassion for the wounded and clarity for leaders. More than exposing a problem, *PTCD* invites readers into healing, accountability, and a healthier, Christ-centered vision of leadership—one rooted in restoration, humility, and renewed purpose.

Aaron D. Davis

Bibliography

[1] https://www.facebook.com/reel/943652133460942

[2] Mast, Dale L.. And David Perceived He Was King: IDENTITY - the Key to Your DESTINY (pp. 52-53). (Function). Kindle Edition. (Paraphrased Reference)

[3] https://www.brainyquote.com/quotes/benjamin_disraeli_133316#:~:text=Info,%2C%201804%20%2D%20April%2019%2C%201881

[4] https://quotationcelebration.wordpress.com/2018/06/01/nearly-all-men-can-stand-adversity-but-if-you-want-to-test-a-mans-character-give-him-power-abraham-lincoln-2/#:~:

[5] https://www.centerforbibleengagement.org/post/bible-engagement-a-key-to-spiritual-growth

www.ingramcontent.com/pod-product-compliance
Lightning Source LLC
Chambersburg PA
CBHW062057280426
43673CB00085B/455/J